DEMYSTIFYING ECONOMICS

The Student-Friendly Textbook

Allen W. Smith, Ph.D.
Professor Emeritus Eastern Illinois University

IRONWOOD PUBLICATIONS
Winter Haven, Florida

Library of Congress Control Number: 2011917804

ISBN 978-0-9770851-3-2

Printed in the United States of America

For my loving wife,

Joan Rugel Smith

Contents

1. Introduction to Economics   12
    Individual Choices   13
    Choices Facing Nations   18
    The Basic Economic Questions   23
    Basic Kinds of Economic Systems   24
    Microeconomics and Macroeconomics   26

2. The American Economy   30
    The Free-enterprise System   31
    The Amazing Invisible Hand   32
    The Importance of Competition   35
    The Price System   37
    Government Intervention   39
    Answering the Basic Questions   43
    Potential vs. Actual Performance
       of Economy   47

3. Gross Domestic Product   56
    The Concept of GDP   56
    Gross National Product   59
    Uses of GDP   60
    Determining the Level of GDP   62
    Equilibrium GDP   68
    Economic Growth   69

4. Unemployment   76
    Measuring Unemployment   77
    Types of Unemployment   80
    Underemployment   84
    Costs of Unemployment   85
    Methods of Controlling   86
       Unemployment

5. Inflation   95
    Measuring Inflation   96
    Types of Inflation   96
    Effects of Inflation   99
    The Unemployment-Inflation Tradeoff   102
    Methods of Controlling Inflation   104

6. Government Fiscal Policy   110
    Fiscal Policy in Theory   110
    Fiscal Policy in Practice   112
    Supply-side Economics   113
    Budget Deficits   115
    Clinton and a Return to Traditional
        Economic Policies   118
    Fiscal Policy Under George W. Bush   118
    The National Debt   119
    Balancing the Budget   122

7. Money and Banking   130
    What Is Money?   130
    Functions of Money   131
    Characteristics of Money   132
    Types of Money   133
    The Federal Reserve System   136
    Organization of the Federal
        Reserve System   137
    Functions of the Federal Reserve
        System   141
    How Banks Create Money   144
    Monetary Policy   148
    Monetarism   152

8. International Trade and Finance   159
    Why Countries Trade   160
    Barriers to Trade   165
    Arguments For and Against
    Trade Barriers   166
    International Finance   168

9. Business Organization and Market Structures 178
    Characteristics of Business Firms 178
    Forms of Business Organization 180
    The Importance of Competition 191
    Market Structures and Competition 192
    Government Efforts to Promote
        and Maintain Competition 202

10. Labor Economics and Labor Relations 210
    The History of American Unionism 210
    Collective Bargaining 218
    Wage Determination 226

11. The Laws of Supply and Demand 237
    Demand 237
    Supply 239
    Supply, Demand, and Markets 239
    Supply and Demand Determine Prices 240
    Supply and Demand Curves 244
    The Effects of Changes in
        Supply and Demand 250
    Government Interference with
        the Laws of Supply and Demand 255
    Elasticity of Supply and Demand 259

12. The Economics of the Firm 266
    Five Important Cost Concepts 266
    The Law of Diminishing Returns 270
    The Profit-Maximizing Level of Output 277
    Equating Marginal Cost and Marginal Revenue 281
    Profit Maximization Under Other
        Market Structures 282
13. Other Markets and Market Limitations 292
    Factors of Production 292
    Resource Markets 294
    Resource Demand is Derived Demand 296
    MRP, MRC and Profit Maximization 296

Land and the Concept of Economic Rent   297
Loanable Funds Market and Interest   300
Market Limitations   303

14. The Financial Meltdown and
    the Great Recession   313
    The Meltdown   313
    The Recession   321

Appendix: Measures of Economic
    Performance   332

Mini-Dictionary of Economic
    Terms and Concepts   339

Index   360

About the Author   368

Preface

This textbook is designed specifically for "pre-principles," introduction to economics courses. It covers most of the topics typically taught in a traditional principles course, but in a non-technical, reader-friendly format. It would be ideal for a general education course for non-economics majors.

Demystifying Economics is not intended to compete with the "one-size-fits-all' traditional, standard, 1,000-page principles textbooks, that can be used in most schools, from community colleges to the very top universities in the nation. It is specifically designed for students who may not have strong math backgrounds, or the aptitude for understanding the technical language used in most standard principles textbooks.

It is a "special needs" textbook, designed to give instructors an alternative to the standard principles textbook. Instructors who like to design their own principles course around a basic core text, that covers the basic essentials, will find this book to be a good core to build on. Students who master all of the content of this book will have a solid grasp of basic economics principles, allowing the instructor to enrich the course with his or her own supplemental materials.

The content of this book has been classroom tested over a period of many years in a variety of settings. Much of the material first appeared in the author's high school textbook, *Understanding Economics,* which was published by Random House in 1986. That, highly popular, book was used by more than 600 schools nationwide.

In 1996, Ironwood Publications first published Allen W. Smith's layman's guide to economics, entitled *Demystifying Economics: The Book That Makes Economics Accessible to Everyone.* Although that book was not intended to be a textbook, it made its way into many classrooms as a supplemental text. An expanded, second edition, of that book was published in 2000, and its popularity as a textbook increased. In 2008, Ironwood Publications released a third, further expanded, edition of *Demystifying Economics,* which became even more popular in the classroom. It was at that time that the author decided to begin writing a basic, easy-to-read, principles of economics textbook that could serve as an alternative to the 1,000-page, expensive major principles textbooks.

This new, student-friendly, textbook is in a class of its own. It is expected to be used as a basic text in some principles of economic classes, where instructors want more control over the content of the course, as well as in "pre-principles" courses. Also, MBA programs that enroll students who do not have a strong understanding of basic principles of economics, will find this book ideal for "refresher courses" in basic economics.

CHAPTER ONE

Introduction to Economics

Most people do not have a very clear or accurate understanding of what economics is about or how it affects them in their daily lives. Some believe it is a business subject, others think it is about money in general, and still others associate the word economics with personal finance. Actually, economics is about all these things and very much more. Economics is a science of such great importance that it is one of only six fields in which the coveted Nobel Prize is awarded for outstanding achievement each year.

Economics is the study of choice. Specifically, economics is *the study of how individuals and society choose to use limited resources in an effort to satisfy people's unlimited wants.* Both individuals and nations have limited resources. Individuals have only so much money and other assets, and only so much time. A nation has a limited number of factories and machines, working-age people, and natural resources. But, despite the existence of limited resources, people still have unlimited wants. We do not have nearly as much as we would like to have. Together, the problems of limited resources and unlimited wants form what is known as the problem of scarcity.

Individual Choices

Scarcity is the most basic of all economic problems. Since there are insufficient resources to enable individuals or nations to have everything they want, they must choose between alternatives when they would like to have both. When we choose between two alternatives, we incur a cost that economists refer to as *opportunity cost*. Opportunity cost is the highest valued benefit that must be sacrificed as the result of choosing an alternative.

For example, suppose you are considering buying a new television set, or taking a short vacation trip, among other things. However, you have only enough money for one of these choices. Therefore, you must decide which choice will give you the greatest satisfaction. Let's assume you consider the TV set and the vacation trip your two most attractive options of the various things on which you might spend your money. If you choose to buy the new TV set, the opportunity cost of your decision will be the potential vacation trip that you gave up. Similarly, if you choose the vacation trip, the opportunity cost will be the new TV set that you could have had.

Another example of opportunity cost is the cost of using your own money and labor to operate a business. Suppose you decided to invest $100,000 of your own money to start a new business, and you devote all your work time to that business. If you could have received a 10 percent return on your $100,000 by investing it in another way, the opportunity cost of using your money for the business is $10,000 per year. If you quit a job with a salary of $40,000 to work full-time in your own business, the opportunity cost of your labor is $40,000 per year. Thus the opportunity cost of your monetary investment plus the opportunity cost of your labor is $50,000 per year. In other words, you give up $50,000 of income in order to use your investment funds and your labor in your own business.

If during the first year of operation, your business shows an accounting profit of $54,000, your true economic profit is only $4,000 after deducting the $50,000 of opportunity cost for your investment and labor. You have earned $4,000.00 more by operating the business than you would have earned by continuing to work at your old job and invest your money elsewhere at a 10 percent rate of return. If your business does much better and shows an accounting profit of $150,000 for the year, then your true economic profit, after deducting the opportunity cost of your labor and investment, will be $100,000.

Every nation has a certain production potential at any given time. Various alternative combinations of output can be produced, given this potential. The alternatives can be illustrated by means of a production possibilities curve.

Assume Robinson Crusoe—the character in Daniel Defoe's novel who is shipwrecked on a deserted tropical island—has two sources of food available to him. They are breadfruit and fish. By experimenting over a period of time he finds that, if he devotes all of his allotted food-gathering time to collecting breadfruit, he can gather 40 breadfruit per day. On the other hand, if he devotes his entire day to fishing, he can catch 20 fish per day.

Table 1-1
Robinson Crusoe's Production Possibilities Schedule

Breadfruit Per Day	Fish Per Day
40	0
36	5
28	10
20	15
0	20

If Crusoe desires variety, he can have any of the combinations in Table1-1. Note that if Crusoe starts out devoting all his time to gathering breadfruit, he will not have any time left to catch fish. If he takes enough time to catch 5 fish, he will have enough time left to gather 36 breadfruit that day, and if he chooses to have 10 fish, he can have only 28 breadfruit. He could also have 15 fish and 20 breadfruit or 20 fish and no breadfruit.

Crusoe can choose any of the combinations in Table 1-1 as well as various additional combinations that fall between these points. However, he cannot have 40 breadfruit and 20 fish at the same time because that is beyond his production possibilities.

The data from Table 1-1 are plotted on a graph to make a production possibilities curve in Figure 1-1. Note that the quantity of breadfruit is measured on the vertical axis and the number of fish is measured on the horizontal axis. If Crusoe chooses the point at the very top of the vertical axis, he will have 40 breadfruit and zero fish. As he moves downward and to the right along the production possibilities curve, he obtains more and more fish but fewer and fewer breadfruit.

If Crusoe chooses the point all the way down the curve to the horizontal axis, he will have 20 fish and zero breadfruit. He can choose any point on the curve, but he cannot choose a point outside the curve. For example a combination of 30 breadfruit and 15 fish is not attainable because that point is outside the production possibilities curve, which is also called the production possibilities frontier. Crusoe could choose a point inside the curve, but by doing so he would fail to achieve his maximum production potential.

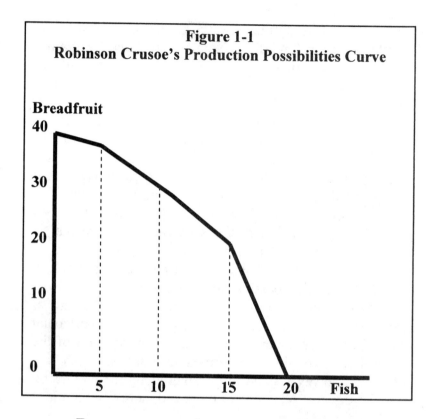

Figure 1-1
Robinson Crusoe's Production Possibilities Curve

Every economy has a production possibilities frontier, defining what it can produce with the resources available and the known methods of production. If it chooses to produce more of one item, then it must produce less of some other item in the present.

However, over time the production possibilities frontier moves outward as resources grow and production methods improve. For example, if Robinson Crusoe were to do without food for a long enough period to allow him to build a ladder and a fishnet, his production possibilities curve would move outward to the right. The ladder would enable him to climb up into the breadfruit trees and pick a lot more breadfruit per hour, and the fishnet would allow him to catch more fish during his allotted time for food-gathering each day.

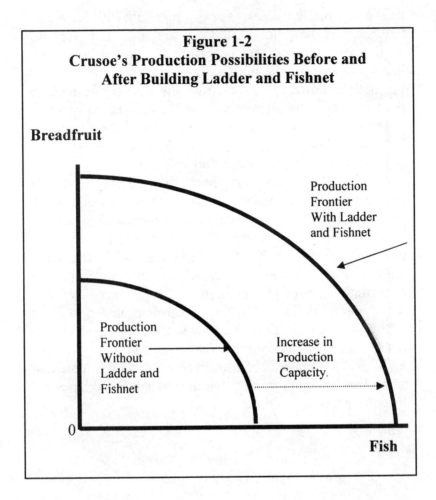

Figure 1-2
Crusoe's Production Possibilities Before and After Building Ladder and Fishnet

What is true for Robinson Crusoe is true for all countries. By spending less on consumer goods and more on factories and machines, a nation can increase its production possibilities, and thus increase its capacity to produce all goods and services. Investment in capital goods, such as factories and machines, is necessary for the economic growth of any nation.

Because of the problem of scarcity, we must choose how to get the most satisfaction from our limited money, time and other resources. For example, after we have met the basic needs of food, clothing, and shelter, if we still have some extra money to spend, we must decide what items will give us the most satisfaction. Once we narrow our options down to the best two alternatives, we make a final choice. The alternative that we give up in order to have the other one is the opportunity cost of the alternative that we choose. Similarly, we must make choices as to how we will use our limited time.

Although this may seem like almost a trivial exercise in decision-making, it is economics at work. And, of course, there are many very large decisions involving the use of your time and money. For example, if a young man or woman decides to attend college after graduating from high school, instead of taking a full-time job, the opportunity cost of attending college may involve thousands of dollars of potential earnings that he or she could have earned during the four years of college. On the other hand, the opportunity cost of not attending college may involve hundreds of thousands of dollars in potential additional lifetime earnings that the student could have had by getting a college degree.

Choices Facing the Nation

Just as individuals have to make choices in deciding how to use their scarce resources, the United States, like all other countries, must choose between alternatives when deciding how to use its scarce resources. We have a given quantity of natural resources, factories and machines, and labor with which to produce the nation's supply of goods and services. Thus, we can't possibly produce enough of everything to satisfy everyone's desires.

For example, total production is often divided into two categories—military production and domestic production. When the economy is operating at full capacity (all resources are being used), the only way we can have more military production is to produce fewer domestic goods and services. Likewise, the only way we can have more domestic production is to reduce military production. If we choose to produce more military goods, at a time when all resources are employed, the opportunity cost of doing so is the resulting decreased production of domestic goods and services. Similarly, the opportunity cost of increasing domestic production, at a time when the economy is operating at full capacity, is the inevitable decrease in military production.

As you already know, economics is the study of how individuals and society choose to use limited resources in an effort to satisfy people's unlimited wants. Satisfying such wants involves the production of economic goods and services. We will first define the terms "economic goods" and "economic services," and then turn our attention to the factors of production needed to produce them. As you will see shortly, deciding which goods and services to produce and how to produce them are two key decisions faced by every society.

Economic goods are things of value that you can see, touch, and show to others. They are things like bicycles, books, jewelry, and clothing. Economic goods also include such things as factories, stores, machines, and tools.

Economic services are intangible things that have value but often cannot be seen, touched, or shown to others. For example, suppose you go bowling on Saturday night. At the bowling alley, you pay for the rental of a pair of bowling shoes and a bowling ball and for the privilege of bowling several games. You enjoy the evening immensely and consider the outing worth the money you spent. However, in terms of tangible purchases, you have nothing to show for your money. This is an example of an economic service. Other examples of economic services are medical care, legal advice, movies, and national defense.

Factors of production, which are also called productive resources, are the basic resources needed for the production of economic goods and services. Economists traditionally have divided the factors of production into three basic categories: (1) natural resources; (2) capital goods; and (3) labor. In addition, many economists add a fourth factor of production, entrepreneurship, to the list.

Natural resources are things provided by nature. Land, air, water, forests, coal, iron ore, oil, and other minerals are examples of natural resources. Natural resources are the basic materials an economy has to work with. They are the starting point of all production, and they represent the most basic limitation on the productive capacity of an economy. In other words, no matter how much skilled labor and technological knowledge an economy has, it cannot create goods if it lacks natural resources.

Capital goods are human-made resources that are used for the production of other goods and services. Factories, machines, tools, railroads, trucks, and business buildings are all examples of capital goods. Without capital goods, natural resources would not be very useful. For example, timber is a natural resource. No matter how much timber a nation has, however, it is of little use unless capital goods are available to turn it into lumber, firewood, or other usable products. In this instance, possible capital goods might include a simple axe, a chain saw, or a giant sawmill.

It is important to distinguish between capital goods and consumer goods. Consumer goods—which are not a factor of production—are finished products sold to consumers for their own personal use. They include such things as food, clothing, TV sets, and computers. In contrast, *capital goods* are things that are used in the production of consumer goods and services as well as in the production of additional capital goods. A factory that manufactures TV sets is a capital good. Some things can be either consumer goods or capital goods, depending on how they are used. For example, an automobile purchased for personal use is a consumer good. However, automobiles purchased for use as taxis or for other business purposes are capital goods.

Labor, sometimes called human resources, is any form of human effort exerted in production. It includes all kinds of work. The work of a janitor, teacher, lawyer, engineer, and the governor of your state are all examples of labor. Labor is essential to production, since natural resources and capital goods are of no value unless they can be put to use.

The three factors of production described above—natural resources, capital goods, and labor—must be combined and organized before production can take place. This is where entrepreneurship, the fourth factor of production, enters the picture. Entrepreneurship may be defined as the function of combining and organizing natural resources, capital goods, and labor; assuming the risks of business failure; and providing the creativity and managerial skills necessary for production to take place. An entrepreneur is a person who carries out these tasks in the hope of making financial gains from the endeavor.

In order to better understand the important role of entrepreneurship, let us look at the fictitious small community of Rossville. For many years, the Rossville Tile Factory manufactured farm drainage tiles from the high-quality clay soil in the area. Most of the community's labor force was employed by that factory. However, new technology resulted in the development of plastic drainage tiles that could be sold for a lower price. This caused the company to begin reducing production and laying off workers until the owner of the Rossville Tile Factory finally decided to close the factory permanently. Thus, Rossville is a community with natural resources (high-quality clay), capital goods (the old tile factory), and labor, (the unemployed tile workers). The fourth factor of production—entrepreneurship—which had been supplied by the owner of the tile factory for many years, is now missing. As a result, the other resources—the clay, the tile factory, and the unemployed workers—are all idle.

Suppose that Sarah Sharpe, who has just inherited some money from her grandmother, is looking for a business opportunity. Sarah hears about the old tile factory, which is up for sale, and wonders if it might be used for the manufacturing of bricks. She knows that clay can be used for the production of bricks and has also found out that there are no brick factories nearby. Given the situation, Sarah thinks she can earn a profit by producing bricks in Rossville. She decides to convert the old tile factory into a brick factory, and soon the unemployed workers have new jobs. The entrepreneurship provided by Sarah has resulted in the combining of the other factors of production—the clay, the old tile factory, and the unemployed workers—to start a new production unit.

No town or nation has enough resources to produce everything its people want. Since any community or nation has only so many natural resources, working-age people, and factories and machines, it is possible to produce only so many automobiles, houses, appliances, weapons, and so forth. And there won't be nearly enough production to satisfy everyone's wants. Thus, difficult choices must be made in the effort to satisfy people's unlimited wants with limited resources.

The Basic Economic Questions:
What? How? For Whom

There are three basic economic questions that every nation of the world must consider when making these choices. They are (1) What goods and services shall be produced? (2) How shall they be produced? and (3) For whom shall they be produced?

The American economy is the primary focus of this book and, in Chapter 2, we will examine in detail how the American economy answers these questions. However, at this point, let's briefly look at how these questions affect all nations.

Every nation must have some method of deciding what combination of goods and services it should produce with its limited productive resources. For example, what portion of total production will be devoted to national defense needs, and what portion will be in the form of domestic items such as factories, schools, houses, automobiles, appliances, clothing, and so forth? As you already know, more military production means less domestic production, and more domestic production means less military production.

Once a nation has decided how many resources are going to be devoted to the production of domestic goods and services, it must decide what portion of domestic production will be in the form of capital goods (things such as factories, tools, and machines.), and what portion will be devoted to the production of consumer goods and services for current use. The greater the production of capital goods, the greater the future productive capacity of the economy. However, people will demand that a substantial portion of domestic production be in the form of consumer goods and services for current use. And, of course, there is the question of what kinds of consumer goods and services shall be produced?

After the question of what goods and services to produce is answered, it is necessary to decide how goods and services shall be produced. Will many workers, using simple tools, be used to produce goods and services? Or will highly sophisticated methods of production, involving complex machines and a much smaller number of workers, be used? The methods of production used by various nations will depend upon the number of workers and the level of technology they have.

Finally, there is the question of who gets the various items that are produced in any given nation. Since no nation can produce enough goods and services to satisfy everybody's wants, every nation must have some method of distributing the scarce goods and services to its people.

Basic Kinds of Economic Systems

Although every nation's economic system has some unique characteristics, there are basically three kinds of economic systems in the world. They are (1) traditional economies; (2) command economies; and (3) market economies. However, since there are no pure command economies or market economies, many economies are often referred to as mixed economies because they have some characteristics of both command and market economies. Let's briefly examine each of these.

Traditional Economies

Traditional economies are found primarily in the rural, non-industrial areas of the world. In these economies, which are often referred to as subsistence economies, there is no national economy. Instead, there are many small segmented economies, each centered around a family or tribal unit. In these economies, the family or tribal unit produces most of its own goods, and consumes what it produces. Thus, the basic questions of "what," "how," and "for whom," are answered directly by the people involved, with the answers usually based on tradition.

Command Economies

Before the downfall of their communist governments, the former Soviet Union, and the communist countries of Eastern Europe were command economies. Today, China is the best remaining example of a command economy. In command economies, the basic economic questions are usually answered by government officials. Command economies are often referred to as planned economies because the government engages in elaborate, detailed planning in an effort to produce and distribute goods and services according to the wishes of government leaders. Also, the government usually owns the means of production in command economies.

By their very nature command economies, such as the former Soviet Union and present-day Communist China, greatly restrict the freedom of the people. Since government leaders—not consumers—decide what will be produced, there are often critical shortages in these economies of items that the people very much want. Workers are not free to change jobs without government permission, and most people have difficulty finding adequate housing.

Market Economies

The United States, Canada, Japan, and many of the countries of Western Europe are market economies. A market economy is just the opposite of a command economy. In command economies, the basic economic questions are answered by the government. In market economies, individual households and businesses answer the basic economic questions through a system of freely operating markets. Furthermore, in market economies the means of production are usually privately owned. When we examine the American economy in the following chapter, we will take a detailed look at how a market economy operates.

Mixed Economies

In actual practice, there are no economies where the basic economic questions are answered totally either by government or by a system of freely operating markets. All major economies are mixed economies in the sense that both markets and government decisions play a role in answering the basic economic questions. In mixed economies, a distinction is usually made between the private sector and the public sector. There are enormous differences in the public-private sector mix of the major economies of the world. For example, in China most of the economic activity is in the public sector but, in the United States, most of the economic activity is in the private sector. Therefore, it is accurate to label China as a predominantly command economy, and the United States as a predominantly market economy.

Microeconomics and Macroeconomics

Before concluding this introductory chapter on the study of economics, we should point out that economists often divide the study of economics into two separate categories: macroeconomics and microeconomics. Macroeconomics is the study of the economy as a whole. It includes such topics as unemployment, inflation, and economic growth for the entire economy. Microeconomics, on the other hand, is the study of the individual parts of the economy.

Chapter Highlights

- Economics is the study of how individuals and society choose to use limited resources in an effort to satisfy people's unlimited wants.

- Together, the problems of limited resources and unlimited wants form what is known as the problem of scarcity, the most basic of all economic problems.

- Because of the problem of scarcity, individuals and nations must make difficult choices as to how best to use the scarce resources. They want to get the maximum satisfaction possible from their limited resources.

- Whenever individuals and nations choose between two alternative uses of a limited resource, there will be a cost involved which economists call opportunity cost. Opportunity cost refers to the next best alternative that is given up when a decision is made to use a resource in a particular way.

- There are three basic economic questions that every nation must answer. They are (1) What goods and services shall be produced? (2) How shall they be produced? and (3) For whom shall they be produced?

- Although every nation's economic system has some unique characteristics, there are basically three kinds of economic systems in the world. They are (1) traditional economies, (2) command economies, and (3) market economies. In actual practice, however, most of the major economies of the world are mixed economies in the sense that they have some characteristics of both command and market economies.

- In traditional economies, found primarily in the rural, non-industrial areas of the world, the basic economic questions are answered directly by the family or tribal unit with the answers usually based on tradition. In command economies, the basic economic questions are usually answered by government officials. In market economies, individual households and businesses answer the basic economic questions through a system of freely operating markets.

Important Terms
Match each of the following terms with the correct definition:

market economies	scarcity
command economies	economics
traditional economies	opportunity cost
mixed economies	capital goods

1. The study of how individuals and society choose to use limited resources in an effort to satisfy unlimited wants.
    economics

2. Economies found primarily in the rural, non-industrial areas of the world, in which the basic economic questions are answered directly by the people involved. *traditional*

3. The problem of limited resources and unlimited wants.
    scarcity

4. The next best alternative use of a resource that is given up in order to use the resource for a specific purpose.
    opportunity cost

5. Human-made productive resources, such as factories, tools, and machines, that are necessary for the production of economic goods and services. *capital goods*

6. Economies such as that of China.
    command

7. Economies found in the United States, Canada, Japan, and many of the countries of Western Europe, in which most of the economic questions are answered by a system of free markets.
    market

8. Economies that have characteristics of both command and market economies. *mixed*

Review Questions

1. Define economics. How does economics affect our lives?

2. Why is scarcity the most basic of all economic problems?

3. What is meant by the term "opportunity cost"? How does opportunity cost affect both individuals and nations?

4. What do we mean by the terms, "limited resources" and "unlimited wants"? How do they relate to the problem of scarcity?

5. What are the three basic economic questions that every nation must answer? What are some of the things that nations must consider when answering these questions?

6. What are the three basic kinds of economic systems? What are the characteristics of each?

Discussion Questions

1. Imagine a world without the problem of scarcity—a world where nobody had to work and people could have everything they wanted free of charge. Do you think you would enjoy living in such a world? Why or why not?

2. Try to think of several important decisions that you have made recently. What was the opportunity cost of each decision? Do you think the opportunity cost of any of your decisions was too high?

3. Why is it so important for Americans to develop a better understanding of economics?

CHAPTER TWO

The American Economy

The American economy, when operating properly, is one of the marvels of the world. It is a highly complex and abstract thing that almost defies description. Obviously, one cannot draw a picture, or take a photograph, of the economy. Yet, it is something very real.

Use your imagination for a moment in order to get some idea of what the economy is like. Imagine it as a gigantic mechanism, or device, which uses an enormous volume of inputs in the form of labor, natural resources, and tools and machines, to produce an incredibly large volume and variety of outputs in the form of finished goods and services, ranging from hamburgers and haircuts, to automobiles, houses, and space vehicles.

As incredible as this gigantic mechanism is, it is not perfect. It requires constant attention to keep it operating properly. It sometimes moves too fast, and at other times it moves too slowly. Thus, policy makers must frequently tap on the "brakes" or push down on the "accelerator pedal." This marvelous mechanism has no automatic pilot control on it. Thus, even when it reaches the point where it is operating at the maximum efficiency level, there is no guarantee that it will continue to operate in the proper manner for very long. Thus, it is necessary to constantly monitor the economy and take corrective actions when necessary. And it is absolutely crucial that those individuals who make decisions regarding adjustments to the economy have a sound understanding of how it works. Just as an inexperienced mechanic can do great damage to your automobile, economic policy makers who do not have a sound understanding of economics can do great damage to the economy. If the brakes are applied too hard, or the economy is accelerated too rapidly, it can take a long time for the economy to recover from the resulting damage.

The Free-enterprise System
The American economy goes by more than one name. It is often referred to as a "private-enterprise" or "free-enterprise" system. It is also known as an example of "capitalism" and as a "market economy." These terms are often used interchangeably and they mean almost the same thing. However, economists generally use the terms *capitalism* and *market economy* to refer to the American economy. Basically, capitalism is a form of economic organization in which businesses are privately owned and operated, and where freely operating markets coordinate most economic activity. It is because two of the most important characteristics of capitalism are private ownership of property and the freedom of opportunity to engage in business activities that the terms "private-enterprise" system and "free-enterprise" system are so often used to refer to the American economy.

The word, capitalism, emphasizes the private ownership aspect of the American economy, whereas the term, market economy, emphasizes the fact that a system of free markets makes most of the basic economic decisions. We will use the term market economy in most of our discussion because we are primarily interested in understanding how the basic economic questions are answered in the American economy.

Let's now look more closely at how the American

economy operates.

The Amazing Invisible Hand

If you live in a large city, you and millions of your fellow residents would be on the verge of starvation within a week or so if the tons and tons of food that must arrive in your city daily were to be delayed. Yet, you have probably never lost any sleep worrying about such a possibility. You probably feel confident that the food, as well as most other items you might wish to purchase, will almost always be in the stores waiting for you when you arrive. Like most other Americans, you probably just take it for granted that when you want to purchase something it will be available. You may not understand how the economic system works, but you are confident that it will provide you with most of the goods and services you need at precisely the time you need them. However, if you give the matter some thought, you will realize that the fact that the economy is able to deliver the proper amount of goods and services to people whenever and wherever they choose to buy them is a truly remarkable accomplishment. Who is responsible for the elaborate planning necessary to accomplish this task? The answer may surprise you.

Who Does the Planning?

Suppose you live in New York City and one day you suddenly have the urge to have banana pudding with fresh bananas and vanilla wafers as dessert for dinner. It's been a long time since you've had banana pudding, or purchased any of the ingredients necessary for making it. Yet, you can be almost certain that if you go to the nearest supermarket all the ingredients you need will be there waiting for you. The pudding mix and vanilla wafers may include sugar refined from sugar cane grown in Louisiana or Florida. The wafers will contain wheat flour produced from wheat that may have been grown in Kansas. And the milk you add to the pudding mix may have been produced on a dairy farm in upstate New York. Just think of all the people in all the various parts of the country who played a role in producing the products that will become a part of your dinner dessert.

But the most amazing part of all is the final ingredient, the fresh bananas. The highly perishable bananas had to be grown in a foreign country and shipped to your local supermarket at just the right time so they would be neither green nor overripe on the very day you decided you wanted them. How did all these people know to produce enough of these products, and how did your supermarket manager know to have the ingredients available when you arrived? They didn't know you were going to decide to have banana pudding on that particular day.

Who makes sure that New York City, and all the other cities and towns of the United States, have the proper amounts of each of the thousands of goods and services that the people need and want? Does the government of each city plan for the needs of its citizens? Or do the state and federal governments plan to have the right amounts of the various goods and services delivered to each geographic area at the proper times?

The answer to the above questions is that no government at any level determines either the production or the distribution of goods and services in the United States. If the government doesn't do the planning, then who does? As hard as it may be to believe, the answer to this question is, "Nobody." No individual, no business firm, and no government agency is responsible for seeing that all the economic needs of the people of New York City, or any other city or town, are met. Yet most of the needs are met. Goods and services are produced and distributed to the people in the correct amounts, at the proper times, and in the right locations.

The Invisible Hand Principle
        The production and distribution of economic goods and services in the United States is determined by the American economic system itself. Some economists say the economic system works like an "invisible hand" in determining what should be produced, how it should be produced, and for whom it should be produced. This invisible-hand principle was first identified by Adam Smith, a Scottish professor who published a monumental work entitled *The Wealth of Nations* in 1776, and who is generally considered to be the founder of economics.
        In this book Smith argued that, in a market economy, if individuals were allowed to pursue their own self-interests without interference by the government, they would be led, as if by an invisible hand, to achieve what is best for society. Although the American economy is very different from the type of economy that Adam Smith described in 1776, the principle of the invisible hand still applies to our economy in a modified way.
        With some exceptions, individual are generally motivated by economic forces. Most individuals tend to act in such a way as to obtain the greatest amount of satisfaction for the least amount of sacrifice or cost. Thus, businesses will attempt to maximize their profits, workers will seek higher wages and/or increased leisure time, and consumers will attempt to get the maximum pleasure from goods and services purchased at the lowest possible prices.
        In order to maximize profits, businesses must produce the goods and services that consumers wish to buy, and make them available to consumers at the correct times and in the right places. This partially explains why the ingredients for banana pudding are usually available in most supermarkets whenever individuals wish to buy them. Producers of these ingredients, and store managers, do not know which individuals are going to want these products

on any particular day, but they know that a certain number of people will probably want to purchase these items each day. If the producers and sellers want to maximize profits, they must have commodities available when and where consumers want them. By doing so, businesses are pursuing their own self-interests while at the same time providing for the interests of consumers. This is the "invisible-hand" principle at work.

The Importance of Competition

The American economy, today, is very different from the hypothetical market economy that Adam Smith described in *The Wealth of Nations* more than two hundred years ago. Smith described an economy with many small sellers engaged in such strong competition with one another that none were able to take advantage of consumers. Any efforts by a business to take advantage of its customers by raising prices arbitrarily high were doomed to failure because consumers would simply abandon the seller and buy the identical product from another seller at a lower price.

In Adam Smith's hypothetical economy, there were no giant corporations, no patent laws or other barriers to entry into an industry that would enable a company to gain exclusive rights to market a product, no labor unions, no government regulation, and no advertising or brand name products. In addition, Smith's economy was different in several other ways from today's American economy. Thus, Smith's contention that, if individuals were allowed to pursue their own self-interests, without interference by government, they would be led, as if by an invisible hand, to achieve what is best for society, does not apply to all areas of the American economy. Smith's hypothetical economy had built-in safeguards to prevent individuals and businesses from taking advantage of one another. The American economy does not always have such safeguards.

The key to successful operation of the invisible-hand principle is a high degree of competition. Many areas of our economy have a great deal of competition, whereas other areas have very limited competition. Take, for example, fast food restaurants. In most cities and towns, there are so many fast food restaurants that competition forces each restaurant to keep prices as low as possible and the quality of service as high as possible. If a restaurant fails to do these things, their customers will go to other restaurants, where prices are lower and service is better.

Thus, restaurants are pursuing their own self-interests when they try to keep prices competitive and quality high in order to attract as many customers as possible and thus maximize their profits. At the same time, consumers are pursuing their own self-interests when they patronize those restaurants that provide the highest quality for the least price. In this case, the invisible-hand principle is working. Both businesses and consumers are pursuing their own self-interests, and because there is a high degree of competition, their activities are leading to what is best for both.

Now let's look at an example where the invisible-hand principle does not work. Suppose a single drug company obtains a patent on a life-maintaining drug that is needed by millions of Americans in order to stay alive. If the single company has the exclusive right to sell the drug, it has no competition at all. Thus, it can charge an extraordinarily high price for the drug without losing customers because the customers must have the drug in order to live. Under such circumstances, the government might intervene and order the drug company to sell patent rights to one or more other drug companies in order to bring at least a little competition into this market.

There are many examples in the American economy in which competition is very limited, and thus sellers are in a position to take advantage of consumers in the form of high prices and low-quality service. In many small communities there is a single bank, single drug store, single movie theater, single grocery store, and so forth. On a national level, there are several industries where only a small number of companies control most of the nation's production, and thus are in a position to charge higher prices than would be the case if more competition existed.

In a later chapter we will take a more detailed look at the importance of competition in the American economy. We will look at things companies do in an effort to reduce competition, and what government does in an effort to increase competition. For the moment, though, suffice it to say that the invisible-hand principle applies in a modified way to some parts of our economy, but not to all parts.

The Price System

Although competition helps prevent individuals and businesses from taking advantage of one another when they pursue their own self-interests, even if we had adequate competition throughout the entire economy, it would not be sufficient to enable the economy to operate properly. An economy must also have a coordination and communication system through which the various sectors can interact with one another. The basic coordination and communication system of a market economy is the *price system.*

Through the price system, producers and consumers transmit valuable information to each other that helps keep the economy in balance. This information helps producers decide whether to increase or decrease production of various products. It also helps employees decide which careers to choose. Let's look at some examples.

Communicating Messages Between Buyers and Sellers

Suppose consumers decide they want more beef and less pork. How would they inform the beef and pork producers of their preferences? They would send a message through the price system by buying more beef and less pork. As more and more beef is bought, there will be a temporary shortage, causing a rise in the price of beef. As beef prices rise, beef producers will begin to increase their production of beef because, at the higher prices, beef production is more profitable.

At the same time that beef production is being increased, there will be a reduction in the production of pork. As consumers reduce their consumption of pork, there will be a temporary surplus, which will lead to lower pork prices. At the lower prices, pork production will become less profitable and thus less pork will be produced.

Communicating Messages Between Employers and Employees

In a market economy, employers and employees also send messages to each other through the price system. This communication helps to provide the proper allocation of workers among the various job categories.

Suppose, for example, that there is a surplus of accountants and a shortage of computer programmers. How will the price system restore balance to these two occupations? Competition among accountants for the scarce jobs in that field will cause a decline in the earnings of accountants. At the same time, the earnings of computer programmers will be increasing because potential employers will be competing with each other to hire the scarce computer programmers.

Since the earnings of accountants will be falling, and the earnings of computer programmers will be rising, young people planning a career in one of these two fields will be more likely to enter the higher paying field of computer programming. As more young people train to become computer programmers, and fewer train to become accountants, balance will be restored between these two occupations. Thus, the price system has communicated messages between employers and employees, and helped to correct the problems of shortages and surpluses.

Government Intervention

One of the most controversial aspects of the American economy is the question of how much government involvement in the economy is appropriate. Some people believe that the government should play a major role in the American economy while others believe government should play little or no role. Regardless of your view on this subject, I think you will agree that a certain amount of government involvement is necessary in any economy to ensure an orderly and equitable society. In the American economy, the government of the United States, a government of the people, by the people, and for the people, serves as rule maker and referee, protector, provider of collective goods and services, and sometimes as regulator of prices and the quality of services.

Making and Enforcing Rules

If you buy a new home, how can you be sure that someone will not later tell you that the house belongs to them instead of you, and attempt to evict you from the house? The answer to this question is that you will have a legal title or deed showing that you own the house, and anyone who tries to illegally take it from you can be arrested and sent to jail. This is just one example of the government serving as rule maker and enforcer of rules. There are many such examples. When a new car dealer sells you a car with a warranty, he or she must abide by that warranty because it is a legal contractual agreement. When you accept a job and sign a contract agreeing to work for a certain wage or salary, both you and your employer must abide by the terms of that contract. When you buy ten gallons of gasoline from a local gas station, the station owner cannot determine how much gasoline should be in a gallon. That has already been determined along with many other standards of measure.

Over time the government has established many rules, which it enforces. Can you imagine what it would be like to live in a society where there were no economic rules or nobody to enforce the rules that did exist? It would be much like a basketball game with no rules and no referees, except that the seriousness of the consequences would be much greater. In a sense, the government serves the same role in the economy that a referee serves in a sports event.

Protector

In the above examples, the government is protecting people from having their property illegally taken from them, or being cheated by a merchant or employer. There are many other ways in which the government intervenes in the economy to protect people. The government has established rules designed to protect workers from having to work under unusually dangerous conditions and rules to help ensure that products sold to consumers are safe.

Many lives have been lost in the past due to unsafe working conditions, and due to the sale of unsafe products. Today, the government tries to minimize injury and loss of life from such causes. The government has also enacted laws that regulate the amount of pollution that companies may put into the air and waterways, and laws that make it illegal for employers to hire children below certain ages.

Producing Collective Goods and Services

One of the most important areas in which the government is involved in the economy is in the production and distribution of *collective goods and services.* Collective goods and services (also known as public goods and services) are things which tend to benefit large groups of people and would not be available to everyone if each individual had to provide them for himself or herself. National defense, highways, and the public schools, are examples of collective goods and services provided by government. National defense is an example of an item that could not be adequately provided by private enterprise. Individuals and businesses might arm themselves in an effort to protect themselves and their property, but it would be impossible for them to provide adequate defense for the nation as a whole. This is why Americans generally agree that the government should collect tax dollars from the people in order to provide for the nation's defense.

Like national defense, highways are another thing that could not be provided by individuals. In theory, at least, private enterprise could build highways and then charge motorists a fee for each mile driven just like the government does on toll highways. However, in the early days of the automobile, the public began to demand that government build highways upon which they could drive their private automobiles, and the government has been building and maintaining public highways ever since.

In the early days of American history, only the children of wealthy parents were able to get an education. Since there were no public schools, parents who wanted their children to receive an education had to hire a private tutor or enroll their children in a private school where a tuition fee was charged. Eventually, however, our society decided that it was in the nation's best interests to make education available to all, and thus our public school system, which is funded with tax dollars, was born.

Regulating Prices and the Quality of Services

As we saw earlier, competition is very crucial to keeping prices down and quality up. However, there are some areas of our economy in which competition is not always considered an efficient way to accomplish these goals. Public utility companies that provide gas, water and electricity to various local communities usually do not have any competition. The reason is that competition has generally been considered less efficient than government regulation in keeping prices down and the quality of services up in these areas.

For example, a single company can deliver electric power to all the customers in a local community over one set of power lines more efficiently than could three competing firms using three sets of transmission lines. For this reason, economists have long referred to public utilities as "natural monopolies," and traditionally the government has granted a single company the exclusive right to supply electricity to each community. In exchange for the guarantee that it would not face competition, the company was required to accept government regulation of the rates it charged and the quality of service it provided.

However, in the late 1990s efforts were initiated to bring some competition into the public utilities industries and to reduce government regulation. In the future, customers will increasingly be able to choose among competing companies when deciding from whom they will buy their electricity, for example. The various companies that generate electricity will compete with one another in selling the generated power to consumers, but the transmission of the purchased electricity from the power source to individual homes will probably still involve a single company. The same will likely be true also in supplying natural gas and water to households. Thus, we will probably see increased competition gradually replace government regulation in the public utilities industry in the next few years.

Answering the Basic Questions

As we saw in Chapter 1, there are three basic economic questions that must be answered by every economic system. They are: (1) What goods and services shall be produced? (2) How shall they be produced? and (3) For whom shall they be produced? Let us examine how the American economy answers these basic economic questions.

What Shall Be Produced?

The people partly through government and partly through consumer spending answer the question of what shall be produced in the United States. A portion of the nation's limited resources must be used for national defense and other government services, and the people determine what portion will be used for this purpose through their elected representatives in government. Of the remaining productive resources, some will be used for the production of capital goods (things like factories, tools, and machines) that will ultimately be used to produce additional goods and services. The rest of the resources are available for the production of consumer goods and services.

In many nations the government decides how many and what kinds of consumer goods and services will be produced. But in the United States, consumers decide what shall be produced. This process of allowing consumers to determine what shall be produced is called *consumer sovereignty*. It means that people vote with their dollars for the goods they want most. Those items that are bought in large quantities are produced in large quantities. Those items that consumers refuse to buy, or buy in small quantities, will either go out of production or, at the very least, be produced in small amounts.

The kinds of new products produced, the styles of clothing manufactured, the types of books published and movies produced, and the kinds of songs recorded are all determined by consumer tastes as reflected in their buying habits. Whether or not a newly introduced product, or a newly produced movie, will succeed or fail depends upon the number of votes it gets in the market place. If not enough people buy a product to make its production profitable, it will be withdrawn from the market.

A classic example of a new product failing for lack of consumer dollar votes is the Edsel automobile introduced by the Ford Motor Company in 1957. The company spent hundreds of millions of dollars to design, produce, and promote this new car. Some called the launching of the Edsel "The most expensive such venture in the history of commerce." Ford's Edsel division had its own plant with 800 executives and 15,000 workers. And nearly 1,200 automobile dealers across the country gave up profitable franchises for other makes of cars in order to sell Edsels. The Ford Motor Company had left little to chance when it formally introduced the Edsel to the public in September 1957. Extensive market research had been conducted, and the new car was launched with a massive advertising campaign. Yet, the Edsel flopped miserably. In November of 1959, the company discontinued manufacture of the Edsel. During its two years on the market, the Edsel accounted for less than one percent of all cars sold, and it lost its manufacturer hundreds of millions of dollars.

Nobody will ever know for sure why the Edsel was not accepted by the American public. However, it can be said with absolute certainty that the failure of the Edsel demonstrated the enormous power of consumer sovereignty. The spending of hundreds of millions of dollars was not sufficient to make American consumers accept a product they did not want.

In determining the production of consumer goods and services, consumers also indirectly determine the production of the factories, tools, and machines necessary to produce the consumer goods. If people won't buy Edsels, there is no need for Edsel factories. Likewise, if consumers demand some new consumer product, there will be a need for production facilities to produce that product.

How Shall Goods and Services Be Produced?

The methods of production used to produce goods and services in the American economy are determined by the production costs of the various methods of production. Basically, the least cost, most efficient method of production must be used by businesses that have a substantial degree of competition. For example, suppose a business firm has been producing a product for several years, using traditional production methods, and selling the product at a small profit for $30 each. Now suppose that new technology is developed that will enable the product to be produced and sold, at a profit, for a price of only $25. If any of the firm's competitors adopt the new technology and begin selling the product for $25, the firm must also adopt the new technology or be forced out of business. In a competitive market economy, efficiency is the price of survival. Firms are almost continuously pressured to find more efficient, lower cost, methods of production. Consumers generally benefit from this process because it usually means lower prices for the goods and services they buy than would otherwise be the case.

For Whom Shall Goods and Services Be Produced?

"For whom shall goods and services be produced?" This is the most controversial of the basic economic questions. Income distribution, and thus the distribution of the goods and services produced by the economy, has long been a source of heated debate in this country. If the economy alone were allowed to answer this question, goods and services would be distributed strictly on the basis of dollar votes. Those people with the most dollars would receive the most goods and services, and those people with no dollars would receive nothing at all.

The controversy stems from the fact that those people with the most dollars are not necessarily the most deserving or the most in need of the goods and services produced. They are also not necessarily the ones who work the hardest. Some wealthy people receive much of their wealth through inheritance rather than from hard work. On the other hand, some of the hardest working people in our society are some of the poorest. For example, migrant farm workers remain poor despite the fact that they work extremely hard because their pay is low, and their work is usually seasonal. Nevertheless, there must be an important relationship between what people contribute to the economy and what they are entitled to receive. In other words, people must earn what they get. Economic incentives are very crucial to the proper functioning of the American economy, and individuals and businesses must be able to see potential rewards for their work and risks.

The concern is not that everyone should receive the same amount of goods and services. Such a goal is neither possible nor desirable in an economy such as ours. Obviously, some people should receive more than others because they work much harder than others. The concern is to see that people are not denied the basic necessities of life such as sufficient food, clothing, shelter, and medical care. That is why a number of government and private charity programs have been developed to help the very poor obtain at least some goods and services.

Potential vs. Actual
Performance of the Economy

The American economy is potentially a very strong economy. This is true because our economy has an abundance of high-quality productive resources, which are the envy of the world. When fully employed, these resources can provide a very prosperous lifestyle for the American people. We have a highly skilled labor force, and an abundance of natural resources, factories, machines, tools and so forth. However, unfortunately, we don't always fully utilize these resources.

During the late 1920s, the economy was strong and prosperous. However, during the Great Depression of the 1930s, the nation suffered enormous poverty and suffering. The unemployment rate reached 25 percent, and millions of Americans were hungry and homeless. However, while men, women, and children picked through garbage in search of food throughout much of America, sheep farmers in the western states slaughtered sheep by the thousands and destroyed their carcasses. The market price had fallen below the shipping costs, and thus farmers would lose money if they shipped the sheep. At the same time, while millions were without bread, wheat was left in the fields, uncut, because the price was too low to cover the harvesting cost.

In addition, many of the nation's factories, that could have been turning out the goods, and providing the jobs, that Americans wanted and needed so desperately, sat partially or totally idle. The factories didn't operate because they couldn't sell their products, and people couldn't buy the products because they didn't have jobs. The American economic system was simply allowed to break down, and it remained broken down for a decade.

The cost of the Great Depression was astronomical. According to estimates by economic historians, if the economy had fully used all of its resources during the 1930s, the dollar value of the additional production would have been higher than the cost of World War II. This would have been enough money to have covered the cost of a new house, and several new cars, for every American family during the decade.

The real tragedy is that the Great Depression never really needed to happen. The nation had all the productive resources necessary to produce a prosperous lifestyle during the 1930s just as in the 1920s. However, many of the resources were allowed to remain idle while millions were hungry and homeless. The policy makers of the 1930s can be excused to some degree because modern economics was still in its infancy.

There is far less justification for allowing the economy to slip into the severe recession of 1981-82, or the Great Recession that followed the 2008 financial meltdown. During these recessions, long lines of people waited for free food handouts in many cities across the country, and thousands lined up in front of potential places of employment whenever there were reports that some additional workers might be hired. Homelessness, domestic violence, and other socioeconomic problems soared as they always do during severe economic downturns. Much of the nation's industrial capacity lay idle at a time when poverty was on the rise.

If all these idle resources could have somehow been employed during these periods, the nation would have experienced booming prosperity instead of economic stagnation. The lost production resulting from idle productive resources is lost forever. It can never be made up. Our nation will always be poorer because of our failure to fully employ productive resources in the past.

Unlike the Great Depression of the 1930s, failure to avert the severe recession of 1981-82, and the even more severe Great Recession that followed the financial meltdown of 2008, was not the result of a lack of economic knowledge. Instead, it resulted from a failure of politicians to implement sound economic policies. Mainstream economists were cut out of the decision-making process, and economic policymaking was done largely by politicians, who have had no formal training in economics, This economic illiteracy among members of Congress is a major problem. Many of them don't understand macroeconomics, or how the American economy is supposed to work. They need to work closely with competent, mainstream economists in formulating policy.

The American economy is potentially a very strong economy when productive resources are fully employed. However, far too often the economy does not operate at full capacity. Sometimes external events, which are beyond the control of policy makers, are to blame. But, at other times, the fault lies with the policy makers themselves.

The government provides many services ranging from national defense to education. In order to pay for the services, the government collects taxes from citizens. Since taxes are both unpopular and inevitable, some kind of guidelines are necessary to provide as fair a tax system as possible. There is much disagreement over what is a fair tax. Most people seem to think of a fair tax as one that other people pay and they avoid. However, efforts to devise a fair tax system have resulted in two fundamental principles of fairness in taxation. They are the benefit principle and the ability-to-pay principle.

According to the benefit principle of taxation, those people who benefit from any government program or project should pay the taxes to finance that government program or project. The best example of the benefit principle of taxation is the financing of the American highway system. Those people who drive the nation's highways are the ones who pay for highway construction and maintenance. They may pay either directly or indirectly. In the case of toll roads and bridges, motorists pay a direct fee for the use of these public facilities.

In most cases, however, motorists pay indirectly. Whenever they stop to fill up their gas tanks, a portion of the money spent for each gallon of gas is a tax that funds the construction and maintenance of highways. Those people who benefit the most from the system pay the most to keep it operating. The more a person drives, the more gasoline is bought, and thus, the more taxes paid.

Although the benefit principle of taxation works very well for financing the nation's highway system, it is not a practical way to finance most other government programs and projects. First of all, it is not usually possible to determine exactly how much each citizen benefits from most government programs and projects. In addition, programs to aid the poor, by their very nature, must be financed by taxes paid by someone other than the poor.

Since the benefit principle of taxation is not a feasible guide for the financing of most government activities, policy makers have tended to base most taxes on the ability-to-pay principle. According to this principle, the fairest tax is one that is based on the ability of taxpayers to pay it, regardless of the amount of benefits they receive. Under this principle, the more wealth a person has, or the higher his or her income, the more taxes the person would pay. This principle is based on the assumption that each dollar of taxes paid by a wealthy person "hurts" less than each dollar paid by a poor person. The individual income tax is an example of a tax based on the ability-to-pay principle. As income rises, not only do individuals pay more dollars in income taxes, but they also pay higher rates.

Taxes are often classified on the basis of how they

affect a taxpayer as the person's income rises. Taxes may be proportional, progressive or regressive. A proportional tax is one where the percentage of income paid as taxes remains constant as income rises. For example, suppose a taxpayer pays $100 in taxes on an income of $1,000, $1,000 in taxes on an income of $10,000, and $10,000 in taxes on an income of $100,000. In each case, the person is paying a tax rate of 10 percent. Although the amount of tax paid increases as income rises, the rate remains constant at 10 percent.

A progressive tax is one where the percentage of income paid as taxes increases as income rises. For example, suppose a taxpayer is required to pay a tax of $100 on an income of $1,000, $1,500 on an income of $10,000, and $20,000 on an income of $100,000. In this case, the tax rate is 10 percent on $1,000, 15 percent on $10,000, and 20 percent on $100,000. With a progressive tax, both the rate and the amount of taxes increase as income rises.

A regressive tax is one where the percentage of income paid as taxes decreases as income rises. An example of a regressive tax would be one where a taxpayer pays $100 in taxes on an income of $1,000, $900 in taxes on an income of $10,000, and $8,000 in taxes on an income of $100,000. In this case, the tax rate is ten percent on $1,000, nine percent on $10,000, and eight percent on $100,000. With a regressive tax, the amount of tax paid may actually increase as income rises but it increases at a decreasing rate.

Chapter Highlights

- The American economic system is predominantly a market economy that relies primarily on a system of free markets to make basic economic decisions. It is also an example of capitalism. Capitalism is a form of economic organization in which businesses are privately owned and operated and where free markets coordinate most economic activity.

- According to the invisible-hand principle, if individuals were allowed to pursue their own self-interests without interference by government, they would be led as if by an "invisible hand," to achieve what is best for society.

- Although the American economy is very different from the type of economy that Adam Smith described in *The Wealth of Nations*, the principle of the invisible hand still applies to our economy in a modified way. However, for the invisible-hand principle to work, there must be a great deal of competition.

- The price system is the coordination and communication system of capitalism. It communicates messages between buyers and sellers and between employers and employees.

- The government serves as rule maker, referee, protector, provider of collective goods and services, and sometimes as regulator of prices and the quality of services in the American economy.

- American consumers determine what will be produced by voting in the market place with their dollars. This process of allowing consumers to determine what shall be produced is called consumer sovereignty.

- The question of how goods and services shall be produced is determined by competition through the price system. Basically, the least costly, most efficient method of production must be used by businesses that have a substantial degree of competition.

- Goods and services are distributed by the American economic system on the basis of dollar votes. However, a number of government and private charity programs help to ensure that the very poor obtain some goods and services.

- The American economy is potentially a very strong economy when productive resources are fully employed. However, the economy does not always operate at its potential full capacity.

Important Terms

Match each of the following terms with the correct definition:

capitalism	collective goods and services
competition	price system
profit motive	consumer sovereignty
invisible-hand principle	

1. The concept that in a market economy if individuals were allowed to pursue their own self-interests without interference by government, their action would lead to what is best for society.   *I H P*

2. The economic rivalry that controls a market economy.
   competition

3. The coordination and communication system of a market economy.   *price system*

4. Things that tend to benefit large numbers of people collectively and that would not be available to everyone if each individual had to provide them.   *collective goods & services*

5. The process of allowing the people to decide what shall be produced by voting with their dollars for the goods and services they want most.   *consume sovereignty*

6. An economic system in which the businesses are privately owned and operated for profit and where free markets coordinate most economic activity. *Capitalism*

7. The desire to maximize financial gains. *profit motive*

Review Questions

1. What is meant by the invisible-hand principle?

2. How does this principle operate to make sure that the proper combination and quantity of goods and services are available at the right place and time?

3. How does competition enable the invisible-hand principle to work?

4. What is the price system? Why is it referred to as the basic coordination and communication system of a market economy?

5. How are messages communicated between buyers and sellers in the American economy? Between employers and employees?

6. In what ways does the government intervene in the American economy?

7. What are collective goods and services? What role does the government play in the production and distribution of national defense, highways, and the public schools?

8. Why does the government regulate the services and prices in some areas of the economy?

9. How is the question "What shall be produced?" answered in the American economy?

10. What is meant by the term "consumer sovereignty"? How was consumer sovereignty responsible for the failure of the Edsel?

11. How is the question "How shall goods and services be produced?" answered in the American economy?

12. How is the question "For whom shall goods and services be produced?" answered?

Discussion Questions

1. Why is competition so important in the American economy? Give some examples of businesses in your community that have little or no competition. Would the interests of your community be better served if these businesses had more competitors?

CHAPTER THREE

Gross Domestic Product

In order for policy makers to develop and implement the correct economic policies to keep the economy operating properly, they must have accurate measures of the economy's current performance. There are several such measures, but perhaps the three most important ones are the gross domestic product, the unemployment rate, and the inflation rate. We will examine unemployment in Chapter 4, and inflation in Chapter 5. However, let's first examine the most basic and comprehensive measure of the economy's performance, the gross domestic product.

The Concept of GDP

The *gross domestic product*, usually called GDP, is a measure of the total production of goods and services in the economy in a year's time. Specifically, the gross domestic product is defined as *the total dollar value of all goods and services produced in a year's time, within a country's borders, measured in terms of their market prices.* The GDP tells policy makers how well the economy is doing.

Why does the government use the dollar value of all goods and services produced in calculating the GDP, instead of just adding up the physical numbers of all the automobiles, refrigerators, new houses, hamburgers, books, haircuts, and so forth produced? It does so because a tally of the total production in physical numbers would be useless in making comparisons. In order to better understand the need to convert all production into dollar terms, let's look at an example of a single production unit that produces more than one product.

Suppose that a farmer produces three different crops (corn, soybeans, and wheat) on his farm. Now let's suppose that last year he produced 20,000 bushels of corn, 8,000 bushels of soybeans, and 10,000 bushels of wheat. This year, he varied the acreage devoted to each crop, and yields per acre were slightly different from last year. The net result was that this year he produced 18,000 bushels of corn, 10,000 bushels of soybeans, and 11,000 bushels of wheat. Did the farmer have a better year this year or last year? We can't tell with only this much information. Although the farmer produced less corn this year than last, he had an increase in the production of both soybeans and wheat this year. Since the market price per bushel for each of these grains is different, the only way we can tell which year was better for the farmer is to calculate the total dollar value of grain produced in each of the two years.

What is true for this individual farmer is true for the economy as a whole. We must convert the production of each and every good and service produced in the economy into a common measure (dollar value) in order to determine whether the economy as a whole did better last year or this year. Since we use the market price (the actual price that items sell for) to determine their dollar value, we avoid the problem of having to estimate the value of items except for a few rare exceptions that we will consider shortly.

Measuring the GDP

The GDP, which is measured and reported by the United States Department of Commerce, is calculated by adding up the market value of all goods and services produced in the United States by all businesses, and by all levels of government.   In addition, the Commerce Department estimates the value of certain other types of production, that have value but do not enter the market place, and adds this estimated value to the GDP.   One example of a type of production that must be estimated is the rental value of all owner-occupied houses in the nation.

In order to understand the need to add to the GDP such things as the estimated rental value of all owner-occupied houses, let's look at an example.   Suppose you are currently renting your home.   You pay the landlord $500 in rent each month.   He reports this income to the government, and it is included as part of the nation's GDP, because the $500 is considered payment for an economic service.   By providing you with a place to live, your landlord is producing an economic service valued at $500 per month.   If you were to buy the house from the landlord, once you became the owner you would no longer make rent payments.   Thus, the GDP would go down by $500 per month just because you decided to buy the house, if the government did not add the amount to the GDP in the form of estimated rental value.   Your house is providing you with the same living space whether you rent it or own it. Thus, the Commerce Department estimates the rental value of all houses that are owned by their occupants and adds this amount to the GDP.

Although the Department of Commerce estimates the value of some items, such as the example given above, there are many other types of production that have value which are not included in the calculation of GDP because it is difficult to get accurate estimates of their market value. For example, if you hire someone to mow your lawn, do your laundry, and clean your house, the amount you pay for these services will be added to the GDP because an exact market value is determined. However, if you do these jobs yourself, the value will not be included in the calculation of the GDP.

Gross National Product

Prior to 1991, the primary measure of the nation's total production, used by the U.S. Department of Commerce, was the Gross National Product, usually referred to as the GNP. However, since most of the other nations of the world used GDP to measure their output, the United States switched to that measure in 1991 in order to make comparisons between countries easier.

The two measures are very similar. GNP is a measure of the output of the residents of a country regardless of whether the production took place within the country or in foreign nations. GDP, on the other hand, is a measure of the total production that takes place within a country's borders including production by foreign-owned companies operating within the borders of the nation.

Specifically, GNP is equal to GDP plus the value of income earned by U.S. residents from factors of production located outside the United States, and minus the value of income earned by foreigners from factors of production located inside the United States. For some countries, the difference between GNP and GDP may be relatively large but, for the United States, GDP and GNP yield almost the same numbers in dollar terms. They are both good measures of the nation's economic performance. However, since GDP is now the official measure used by the United States Department of Commerce to calculate the nation's output, we will use that term for the rest of our discussion.

Uses of GDP

GDP data is useful in making comparisons over time, such as comparing the GDP of this year with that of last year in order to see how much, if any, the GDP has grown during the past year. GDP figures are also sometimes used to make comparisons between countries. Let's look at these uses of GDP in more detail.

Comparisons Over Time

GDP figures can be used to determine the rate at which the economy is growing. The annual rate of growth of the GDP, adjusted for inflation, can provide policy makers with a good estimate of whether the GDP is growing too fast, too slowly, or at the proper level, just as a speedometer on a car can tell the driver whether he or she is driving above, below, or at the speed limit.

Since GDP figures are calculated and reported on a quarterly basis, new figures are available every three months. This enables economists to project economic growth for at least a year into the future. For example, if the Commerce Department reports that, during the first quarter of the year (January through March), the GDP was growing at an annual rate of 3 percent, adjusted for inflation, this means that, if the economy continues to grow at this rate for the entire year, the dollar value of all the goods and services produced this year will be 3 percent larger than that of the previous year. Of course, the rate of growth in the second quarter may be either higher or lower than that of the first quarter, resulting in an adjustment in the predicted growth for the year.

The rate of growth of the GDP is used to determine what kinds of economic policies are needed. If the GDP grows too slowly, or actually declines, there will be an increase in the unemployment rate. Similarly, if the GDP grows too rapidly, there may be an increase in the inflation rate. The rate of growth of the GDP is one of the major indicators available to economists for use in forecasting the future performance of the economy. If economists believe the GDP is growing too slowly, they will recommend economic policies that will contribute to increased growth. If the GDP appears to be growing too rapidly, on the other hand, policies to slow it down will be recommended. In Chapters 6 and 7, we will examine the policy options available to policy makers for speeding up, or slowing down, the economy's rate of growth.

Comparisons Between Countries

GDP figures are sometimes used to make comparisons between countries. However, such comparisons are often very misleading. It is impossible to get comparable statistics for any two countries because each country has its own way of calculating production and its own monetary unit. Furthermore, lifestyles are very different between countries.

Thus, the fact that the GDP per person in the United States is ten times that of another country does not necessarily mean that the average American's standard of living is ten times as high as that of the average citizen in the other country. The United States is a cash economy in which most people buy almost everything they use. Therefore, a large cash income is essential in this country. However, in some countries, people provide for most of their needs themselves. Therefore, little cash is needed.

The most useful comparisons between countries are comparisons of the rates of growth of GDP between countries with similar economies. For example, we can compare the rate of growth of the GDP in the United States with that of other major industrialized countries to see how well our economy is performing relative to similar economies. If we find that our economy is not doing as well as some other economies, we might want to carefully analyze the differences to see if we can take actions that will improve the performance of our economy.

Determining the Level of GDP

The size and the rate of growth of the GDP are the major determinants of the standard of living. As previously noted, if GDP grows too slowly, or declines, more people will become unemployed, whereas, if it grows too rapidly, increased inflation may occur. What determines the level of GDP? The answer to this question is that the level of total spending in the economy is the primary determinant of the level of GDP.

As a first step in understanding how the level of total spending in the economy determines the level of GDP, let's see how the level of total production is determined in a single factory. Suppose you own and operate a small manufacturing plant that produces quality bookcases. You have a number of distributors for your product and, for quite some time, you have been producing and selling approximately 500 bookcases per week. Since you know that the demand for your product can fluctuate up or down, you maintain an inventory of 400 bookcases in a warehouse. Thus, if there should be a sudden increase in the demand for your product to 600 bookcases per week, you could sell from your reserve inventory, as well as from current production, temporarily. However, the warehouse reserves will last for only four weeks should the demand continue at 600 bookcases per week. Therefore, you will probably hire additional workers and increase current production to 600 bookcases per week if the demand remains at that level for very long.

Now suppose that just the opposite occurs. After being able to sell 500 bookcases per week for more than a year, sales suddenly begin to decline and demand soon falls to only 400 bookcases per week. You will not continue to produce 500 bookcases per week, indefinitely, if you are able to sell only 400 per week. As unpleasant as it may be, you will need to consider laying off some of your workers and reducing production to 400 bookcases per week so that production will again be in balance with sales. In summary, the number of bookcases you will produce per week will be determined by the number you can sell. If customers increase their purchases of bookcases, you will increase production. But, if they reduce purchases, you will reduce production accordingly. Over the long run, you will produce just about as many bookcases as you can sell.

What is true for an individual factory is true for the economy as a whole. Just as you will increase or decrease production, and the size of your work force, depending on the level of sales, the economy as a whole will adjust production, and the number of workers employed, when the level of total spending rises or falls. In other words, if total spending in the economy increases, total production (GDP), and the number of workers employed, will also rise. On the other hand, if total spending decreases, total production (GDP) and employment will decline.

The total spending in the economy is made up of the combined spending of three different sectors of the economy. They are consumer spending, investment spending, and government spending. There is also a foreign sector. However, in order to keep our analysis as simple as possible, we will assume that imports of goods and services from foreign countries are offset by an equal amount of exports of goods and services to foreign countries. In this case, consumer spending, plus investment spending, plus government spending would make up 100 percent of net total spending in the economy. As you probably know, imports and exports are not in balance today. However, over the long run, they have roughly canceled one another out, and hopefully this will become true again in the future. In any case, by making the assumption that exports equal imports, we are able to provide a much clearer analysis of how the economy operates.

Because the three major components of total spending are so important, we want to examine each one in some detail. We will look at the factors that determine the amount of spending in each category as well as the effects of each component on GDP.

Consumer Spending

Consumer spending, usually referred to simply as *consumption* by economists, involves the purchase of consumer goods and services. These are things that consumers buy for their own personal use such as food, clothing, appliances, haircuts, entertainment, and medical care. Consumer spending is the largest of the three components of total spending, accounting for more than 60 percent of GDP. Since consumption is such a large portion of the total spending, changes in consumption have a much greater effect on the level of GDP than changes in the other two components. Let's examine some of the determinants of the amount of consumer spending that will take place.

Income. The most important determinant of consumer spending is income. Increases in income almost always lead to increased consumption, while decreases in income usually result in reduced consumption. If the GDP is rising, and more and more unemployed workers are finding jobs, there will be an increase in income that in turn will lead to an increase in consumer spending. This increase in consumer spending will lead to an even larger GDP and thus more jobs and income. This cycle can continue until the economy reaches the full-employment level of GDP which is the point where all productive resources are being utilized. Any increase in spending beyond this level will lead to increased inflation.

Let's look at the opposite situation. Suppose that, at a time when the economy is operating at the full-employment level, the GDP begins to decline. This decline in GDP will cause workers to lose their jobs and will thus reduce income. The reduction in income will cause a decrease in consumer spending which will cause GDP to decline even more, and will result in still more workers losing their jobs and thus suffering reductions in income. The longer this downward cycle is allowed to continue, the greater the unemployment rate.

Economists use the term, *recession,* to describe periods when the GDP is declining and unemployment is rising. Usually, if the GDP declines continuously for a period of six months, the economy is considered to be in a recession. If the GDP falls and remains at a very low level for a prolonged period, while large numbers of people are unemployed, the term, *depression,* is used to describe the situation.

Expectations. Consumers' expectations about the future of the economy play a major role in determining the amount of money they will spend. If individuals believe the economy will soon go into a recession and they will lose their jobs, they may cut back substantially on their spending. This can be a very dangerous thing. If enough people simultaneously become convinced that a recession is on the way, and if they behave accordingly, they can bring on the very recession that they fear. Why is this true? Because, if people believe there will soon be a recession that will cause them to lose their jobs, they will cut back on spending and begin saving their money for use when the recession occurs. In other words, they will not buy the new automobiles, refrigerators, television sets, and so forth that they were planning to buy. As orders coming into factories for such items decline, employers will reduce production and lay off workers. These unemployed workers will then reduce their spending because of a lack of income and, as a result, still more workers will lose their jobs.

Consumer spending can also be affected by expectations of future inflation. The fear of increased inflation can cause consumers to behave in such a way that they actually contribute to the inflation they fear. If they believe there will be substantial price increases in the near future, they may go on a spending spree in an effort to buy as many consumer goods and services as possible before these items become so expensive they can no longer afford them. However, the increased demand for goods and services will cause prices to rise even higher.

Taxes. Taxes affect consumer spending because they determine the amount of after-tax income people have to spend. An increase in taxes will result in a reduction in after-tax income and thus a reduction in consumer spending. Similarly, a decrease in taxes will give consumers an increase in after-tax income, and will thus result in increased spending. This relationship between taxes and consumer spending provides the government with a potential device for regulating the level of the GDP. By reducing taxes and giving the people more money to spend, the government could raise the level of the GDP. On the other hand, if the government wanted to reduce the rate of growth of the GDP, it could raise taxes and thus reduce the spending power of consumers.

Investment Spending

Investment spending, usually referred to simply as *investment* by economists, refers to business spending for such things as new factories, machines, store buildings, and so forth, which will ultimately increase the productive capacity of the economy. We are using the term, investment, here in a different way than you probably normally use the term. You probably use the term to refer to purchasing stock, bonds, insurance policies, and so forth. This type of investment is personal investment, which may have an important impact on your personal financial future, but which does not affect the productive capacity of the economy. When you buy so many shares of stock, somebody else is selling them. Thus, you have increased your investments, but this is canceled out by the fact that somebody else has decreased his or her investments. By contrast, when the Ford Motor Company builds a new factory, and equips it with the necessary machines and tools to manufacture automobiles, the productive capacity of the economy is increased.

The amount of business spending on investment, during any given period, is largely dependent upon the availability of potentially profitable investment opportunities, and the cost and availability of investment funds. Let's look at each of these factors.

Availability of Investment Opportunities. There are a number of factors that determine the availability of profitable investment opportunities. Consumer demand is the most important of these factors. If manufacturers are unable to sell all of the products that they are currently capable of producing, there are no incentives for them to build new factories or buy additional machines.

Government tax policies also play an important role in determining the amount of investment that will take place. If business tax rates are high, businesses will have less after-tax profits, and thus less incentive to invest. However, if businesses are offered tax incentives to invest, they are more likely to increase their investment.

The invention of new products and the development of new technology often lead to large increases in business investment. Historically, periods of high investment have usually coincided with the development of new products and new technology. The invention of the automobile led to massive amounts of investment in factories, tools, and machines for the mass production of automobiles. More recently, the electronics industry, including computers, has provided good opportunities for new investment.

Since the invention of new products and the development of new industries is rather sporadic, good investment opportunities are more plentiful in some time periods than in others. Since investment spending is one of the three basic determinants of the level of GDP, fluctuations in investment can cause fluctuations in the GDP.

Cost and Availability of Investment Funds. Since much of the business investment that takes place is paid for with borrowed money, the availability of loans and the interest rates that must be paid on these loans are important determinants of the amount of investment that will take place during any given period of time. Both the savings rate and government policies are important in determining interest rates and the availability of loans. When we examine the Federal Reserve System and monetary policy in Chapter 7, you will learn how the government influences interest rates and the availability of loans.

Government Spending

Approximately 20 percent of the total spending is government spending. This includes the spending of federal, state, and local governments. Since government spending is a major determinant of the GDP, changes in government spending can have a substantial effect on GDP, and on inflation and unemployment. If the economy is operating at the full-employment level, with GDP growing so fast that increased inflation is likely, the government can attempt to reduce the danger of inflation by reducing government spending, and thus reducing the rate of growth of the GDP. On the other hand, if the economy is operating below the full-employment level, the government might increase spending in an effort to increase the level of GDP and reduce unemployment.

Equilibrium GDP

Equilibrium GDP occurs when the GDP is exactly equal to the level of total spending. In other words, the total spending for goods and services is exactly equal to the total production of goods and services, such that there is neither a shortage nor a surplus. In terms of supply and demand, consumer spending, plus investment spending, plus government spending is the total demand (aggregate demand) for goods and services. And GDP is the total supply (aggregate supply). Thus, at equilibrium GDP, total supply equals total demand. (Or, in the language of economists, aggregate supply equals aggregate demand at equilibrium GDP.) Since equilibrium is a point of rest, once GDP has reached the equilibrium level, there will be no tendency for it to change until total spending changes.

It is important to understand that equilibrium GDP is not always desirable. Equilibrium GDP simply means that GDP is remaining at its current level, and there is no tendency for it to change in either direction. Equilibrium GDP is good only if the current level of GDP is the most desirable level. It would be possible for the economy to be in equilibrium in the depths of a depression with millions of workers unemployed. Certainly this would not be a good equilibrium. In this case, we would want to implement policies that would increase the level of total spending and throw the GDP out of equilibrium, because during periods of high unemployment we want the GDP to be growing. Only when the economy reached the full-employment level with minimal inflation would we want GDP to be in equilibrium. In other words, the desired goal is for the GDP to be in equilibrium at the full-employment level, and only at the full-employment level.

Economic Growth

In addition to the goal of maintaining equilibrium GDP at the full employment level, another goal is to pursue policies that will enable the full-employment level of GDP to grow over time. In other words, we not only want our economy to produce as many goods and services as possible with our limited resources today, but we also want the capacity of the economy to grow so that we can produce still more goods and services in the future.

Economic growth is extremely important because, without it, there can be no improvements in the standard of living even if the size of the population remains constant. And, if the population grows at a time when we are not increasing the production of goods and services, the standard of living will actually decline.

The rate of economic growth depends primarily on the quantity and quality of productive resources (labor, natural resources, and capital goods), and on the efficiency with which these productive resources are used.

The United States has a highly skilled labor force, and an abundance of most natural resources, compared to many countries, although we do not have an inexhaustible supply. The United States also has a large supply of what economists call capital goods. *Capital goods*, which include such things as factories, machines, tools, railroads, trucks, and business buildings, are human-made resources that are used for the production of consumer goods and services, and additional capital goods. Without capital goods, natural resources are not very useful. Capital goods and labor are needed to turn the natural resources into the products the American people want.

The United States has concentrated much effort on the production of capital goods in the past, but it is necessary to continue to produce as many capital goods as possible if we want to maximize future economic growth. During periods when the economy is operating at full employment, the only way to increase the production of capital goods is to reduce the production of consumer goods temporarily. However, increased production of capital goods will increase the productive capacity of the economy and make possible the production of both more capital goods and more consumer goods in the future.

♦The efficiency with which labor is combined with the other productive resources determines labor productivity, which is an important determinant of economic growth. *Labor productivity* can be defined as the amount of output produced by a given quantity of labor. The more output we can get from our labor force, the greater will be the nation's economic growth. The quantity and quality of capital goods available to the labor force are important determinants of labor productivity.

Chapter Highlights

- The gross domestic product (GDP) is the total dollar value of all goods and services produced in a year's time, within a country's borders, measured in terms of their market prices.

- The GDP is measured and calculated by the United States Department of Commerce. In addition to adding up the market value of all goods and services produced in the United States by all businesses and all levels of government, the Commerce Department estimates the value of certain other types of production that have value but do not enter the market place, and adds this estimated value to the GDP.

- GNP is a measure of the output of the residents of a country regardless of whether the production took place within the country or in foreign nations whereas GDP is a measure of the total production that take place within a country's borders including production by foreign-owned companies operating within the borders of the nation.

- Prior to 1991, the Commerce Department used Gross National Product (GNP) as the primary measure of the nation's total production, but since most other nations used GDP to measure their output, the United States switched to that measure in 1991 in order to make comparisons among countries easier. Although for some countries the difference between GNP and GDP may be relatively large, for the United States, GDP and GNP yield approximately the same numbers in dollar terms.

- The GDP is used to make comparisons of an economy's performance over time, such as comparing the GDP of this year with that of last year in order to see how much the GDP has grown during the past year. GDP figures are also sometimes used to make comparisons between countries.

- The total spending in the economy is made up of consumer spending, plus investment spending, plus government spending, plus the difference between exports and imports. The level of total spending determines the level of total production (GDP) in the economy. If total spending increases, total production (GDP) and the number of workers employed will increase. If total spending decreases, total production (GDP) and employment will decline.

- Equilibrium GDP occurs when the GDP is exactly equal to the level of total spending. In other words, total spending for goods and services is exactly equal to the total production of goods and services, such that there is neither a shortage nor a surplus.

- Economic growth occurs when the productive capacity of the economy grows over time so that more goods and services can be produced in the future than at the present. Economic growth is extremely important because without it there can be no improvements in the standard of living when the population remains constant, and the standard of living will actually decline if population grows at a time when there is no economic growth.

- Labor productivity can be defined as the amount of output produced by a given quantity of labor. Labor productivity is determined by the efficiency with which labor is combined with the other productive resources.

Important Terms
Match each of the following terms with the correct definition:

consumer spending   gross domestic product
economic growth   gross national product
government spending   investment spending
labor productivity   equilibrium GDP
recession   depression

1. The amount of output produced by a given quantity of labor.

2. That level of GDP at which the total supply of goods and services is exactly equal to total spending.

3. An increase in the productive capacity of the economy over time, which enables the economy to produce more in the future than at the present.

4. The purchase of consumer goods and services by consumers for their own personal use.

5. A period when the gross domestic product is declining and unemployment is rising.

6. Business spending for such things as factories, tools, and machines.

7. The total spending by all levels of government.

8. A period when the GDP falls and remains at a low level for a prolonged period while large numbers of people are unemployed.

9. The total dollar value of all goods and services produced in a year's time, within a country's borders, measured in terms of their market prices.

10. The total dollar value of all goods and services produced by a country in year's time regardless of whether the production took place within the country or in foreign nations, measured in terms of their market prices.

△ Review Questions

1. What is the gross domestic product? How is it calculated?

2. What is the difference between the gross domestic product (GDP) and the gross national product (GNP)?

3. What determines the level of GDP?

4. What are the three major components of total spending in the American economy?

5. What are the necessary conditions for equilibrium GDP?

6. Why is equilibrium GDP not always the desirable position for the economy?

7. Under what conditions is equilibrium GDP desirable?

8. What is economic growth? Why is it so important?

9. What are the determinants of economic growth?

10. What is labor productivity? What role does it play in economic growth?

Discussion Questions

1. Why are comparisons between countries based on GDP statistics often very misleading?

2. Why is economic growth so important? What are the consequences of little or no economic growth?

CHAPTER FOUR

Unemployment

One of the most serious and cruel of all economic problems is the problem of unemployment. It not only robs people of their jobs and livelihoods, but it also takes away their dignity and self-esteem. During periods of high unemployment, there is an accompanying rise in mental illness, domestic violence, and even suicide. These social ills result from workers' frustration with being thrown out of work through no fault of their own, and often being almost helpless in terms of doing anything about their economic circumstances.

Unfortunately, there is a tendency for many people to look upon the unemployed as being lazy, incompetent, irresponsible, or in some other way deficient. "If people want jobs badly enough and are willing to work hard, there are jobs out there," is a phrase one often hears from people who are fortunate enough to still have their jobs during severe recessions and depressions.

The sad truth is that, although there are always some lazy people among the unemployed, just as there are some lazy people among the employed, during certain times, and in certain geographic locations, it is virtually impossible for workers to find jobs no matter how hard they try. On the other hand, there are other times when jobs are plentiful and employers have trouble finding enough workers. In late 1999, the unemployment rate dropped to a 30-year low, and "help wanted" signs were seen almost everywhere. The differences between the job market of the early 1980s and that of the late 1990s were so great that young people entering the labor force during the booming 1990s could not have imagined how different their lives would have been if they had been born a decade and a half earlier.

The recession, following the 2008 financial meltdown, brought a sharp decline in consumer spending, which caused a lot of workers to be laid off. In addition, those people who still had jobs and money, became afraid to spend it. As consumers further reduced their spending, employers had to further reduce production and thus lay off still more workers. The jobs, that existed prior to the crisis, were still "potentially available," but only if consumer demand could be restored to its pre-recession level. That's why so many Americans remained unemployed for so long.

Measuring Unemployment

Each month, the Department of Labor releases employment statistics, including the number of people employed and unemployed, as well as the unemployment rate. How are these statistics obtained, and what do they mean? If, for example, the Department of Labor reports that seven million Americans were unemployed last month, does this mean that each and every one of the seven million were actually counted? If you were unemployed last month, can you be sure that you were included in the unemployment count? The answer to both questions is, no. It would be extremely expensive, and virtually impossible, to account for the status of each and every worker every month. Instead, the Labor Department relies on a sample survey to get an estimate of the number of people who are unemployed each month.

Every month, the Bureau of the Census conducts a sample survey of approximately 60,000 households to determine the employment status of these households during the preceding week. The sample is selected scientifically, and includes households in every part of the country so that it will be as representative of the total population as possible. The results of this survey are used by the United States Department of Labor to estimate the employment status of the American population as a whole. The Labor Department classifies each person 16 years of age or older into one of three categories: (1) employed, (2) unemployed, or (3) not in the labor force. The Department of Labor then determines the *unemployment rate* by dividing the number of unemployed persons by the total number of persons in the labor force.

To be classified as *employed* a person must be actively working, or have a job from which he or she is temporarily absent because of a vacation, illness, a labor dispute, or bad weather. Persons officially classified as *unemployed* include only those people who do not have a job and are "actively seeking work." Many people, who do not have a job, are excluded from the unemployed category even though they may desperately need and want a job.

A person who is out of work must be actively seeking work in order to be classified as unemployed. Specifically, a person must have engaged in some type of job-seeking activity, such as having a job interview or filling out a job application, during the past four weeks in order to be officially classified as unemployed. Exceptions to this rule are persons who are waiting to be called back to a job from which they have been laid off, and persons waiting to report to a new job within the next 30 days.

All persons, 16 years of age and over, who do not fit into the classifications of employed or unemployed, are classified as *not in the labor force*. Many people in this category do not want a job. Such people would include full-time students, some mothers with small children, and retired people. These people are not in the labor force by choice. However, many other people in this classification do want employment and consider themselves unemployed. They are not actively seeking work because they believe there are no jobs available in their geographic area or in their line of work.

For example, suppose you lost your job a year ago because the factory where you had been employed for the past 15 years permanently closed down. For ten months you filled out job applications at every imaginable place of employment in your community. However, because there are so many people in your community who were also thrown out of work by the plant closing, it is virtually impossible to find employment. Since you already have applications on file at the various potential places of employment in your community, you see no point in filling out new applications. Therefore, for the past two months, you have not taken any specific "job-seeking activity," as defined by the Department of Labor. Thus, you are no longer classified as unemployed. Instead, you are classified as not in the labor force. The labor department refers to people who are not actively seeking work because they believe no work is available as *discouraged workers.*

Because of the way the Department of Labor classifies workers, during severe recessions, the number of people who are out of work is substantially higher than the official figures suggest. In addition to the fact that many people who consider themselves as "unemployed" are not classified as such by the government, there is also the problem of people who are working only part time but want to work full time. If a person who has lost a full-time job finds a new job that involves working only one afternoon per week, that person is officially classified by the government as employed rather than unemployed. In fact, even a person who works as little as one hour per week is officially classified as employed.

Types of Unemployment

From the point of view of the unemployed, there is only one type of unemployment. It means no job, no paycheck, loss of self-esteem, and lots of worrying about the future. However, from the viewpoint of policy makers who are trying to formulate policies to reduce the unemployment rate, not all unemployment is the same in terms of causation. Economists generally recognize three basic types of unemployment: frictional, cyclical, and structural. There is also the problem of seasonal fluctuations in employment which is sometimes referred to as seasonal unemployment. Let's examine each type of unemployment.

Frictional Unemployment

Frictional unemployment involves people who are temporarily between jobs. During any given month, a certain number of workers will quit their jobs, others will be fired, and still others will leave school and begin seeking employment for the first time. By the following month, many of these people will have found new jobs, but there will be another group of people who will have just left their jobs. These people who are in transition between jobs are experiencing frictional unemployment. Because of frictional unemployment, *full employment does not equal zero unemployment.*

A certain amount of frictional unemployment is necessary in order to allow workers the freedom to change jobs, and employers the freedom to dismiss employees who are not performing satisfactorily. Thus, there will always be some unemployment even when the economy is performing at its best. The amount of frictional unemployment that is necessary has historically been a subject of much debate among economists. During periods when the economy is booming, 4 percent unemployment has generally been accepted as the full-employment level. However, during periods of recession pessimists have argued that a 4 percent unemployment rate is an unreasonable long-term goal. They have typically argued that we should accept a higher unemployment rate as the full-employment goal. Some have argued that 5 percent unemployment should be considered full employment, while others have at times argued that we should consider the economy to be operating at the full-employment level when there is a 6 percent unemployment rate.

With a labor force of more than 150 million people, a one percent reduction in the unemployment rate means approximately 1.5 million additional jobs. Thus, it makes a great deal of difference to a lot of people whether we set an unemployment rate of 4 percent, 5 percent, or 6 percent as the full-employment target.

Cyclical Unemployment

Cyclical unemployment gets its name from the business cycle. The business cycle is the name given to long-term fluctuations in economic activity. Throughout our history, the economy has fluctuated between periods of recession (where GDP was declining) and periods of recovery and prosperity (where GDP was growing). Since recessions are always ultimately followed by a recovery, and periods of prosperity are always eventually followed by a recession, the full course of going from prosperity to a recession, and then through a recovery back to a new period of prosperity, is called a business cycle.

Cyclical unemployment occurs during periods of recession or depression. The actual cause of the cyclical unemployment, as well as the cause of the recession or depression, is insufficient total spending. If total consumer spending, plus investment spending, plus government spending, is not sufficient to buy all the goods and services currently being produced by the economy, workers will be laid off and production will be reduced. Just as an individual business will reduce production when sales decline, production and employment in the economy will decline when total spending falls. The workers who are laid off as a result of the insufficient total spending will then cut back on their spending since they no longer have paychecks. This will lead to a further decline in production and additional layoffs. This process could go on indefinitely and lead the economy into a deep depression if the government did nothing to offset the reduction in total spending.

Structural Unemployment

Structural unemployment occurs when unemployed workers are unable for some reason to fill job vacancies that exist. In other words, there is a mismatch between job openings and job candidates. The mismatch may be a geographic mismatch, or it may be a skill mismatch. Structural unemployment of the geographic-mismatch type exists when there are job openings in some parts of the country, and unemployed workers in other parts of the country. The unemployed workers are unable, or unwilling, to move to the areas where the jobs exist, and the jobs cannot, or will not, move to the areas of high unemployment.

The coal mining regions of Appalachia are an excellent example of structural unemployment of the geographic-mismatch type. For generations, the primary source of employment in these regions was in the coal mines. However, over time, many of the miners lost their jobs as mines, where most of the coal had been removed, closed down. And still other miners lost their jobs to automated methods of coal mining, which used more machines and fewer workers. These unemployed coal miners were structurally unemployed. Most were either unable, or unwilling, to move to other areas of the country where employment prospects might be better, and few potential new employers were willing to locate in the Appalachian region.

Structural unemployment of the geographic mismatch type increased dramatically after the severe recession of 1981-82. As a consequence of the recession, many manufacturing plants throughout various parts of the nation closed down operations permanently, throwing long-time employees out of work. In some communities the major employer, who had provided employment for most of the community's labor force for many years, ceased operations. This posed a very serious problem for workers, especially those who owned homes. Such people could not move to a new community in search of work unless they could sell their homes. However, with many people wanting to leave the community, and few new people moving into the community, it became virtually impossible to sell homes. In such communities, the only viable solution to the problem would seem to be to attract new employers into the community. However, with communities all over the country courting potential employers and offering attractive incentives for the new employers to locate in their area, many impoverished areas found it very difficult to attract new employers.

Structural unemployment of the skill-mismatch type can occur in almost all communities. There may be both job vacancies, and unemployed workers in the same area. However, the unemployed workers cannot fill the job openings because they do not have the proper skills. Sometimes the problem involves job openings that require a college education and unemployed workers who lack such an education. However, it is not uncommon to find college graduates unemployed in communities where there are job openings for college graduates. The problem is that you must have more than just a college education. Your college degree must be in a field that qualifies you for the job openings. For example, an unemployed high school history teacher cannot fill job vacancies for accountants, computer programmers, or paramedics.

Seasonal Unemployment

People who are seasonally unemployed usually have jobs part of the year, but are unemployed at certain times during the year due to seasonal factors. For example, construction workers in the northern states are often out of work during the coldest months of the year when the ground is frozen and conditions are not favorable for starting new building projects. Migrant farm workers are another example of people who suffer seasonal unemployment. During harvest times, they may have more work than they can handle. However, between harvests, they often have no work at all.

Employees of some manufacturing firms suffer seasonal unemployment. For example, if you worked in a factory that manufactured fireworks displays for the fourth of July, you might have a lot of overtime work in the days and weeks preceding the July 4 holiday so that all the orders could be filled in time for the holiday celebration. However, as soon as the orders were all filled, you might be laid off, since the company may not want to begin full-scale operations right away for next year's sales.

Underemployment

Many people who have jobs are underemployed. Underemployment can take two forms. Workers who want to work full time, but have only part-time jobs, are underemployed. This type of underemployment can be easily measured. However, the other kind of underemployment is not so easily measured. It involves people who are working at jobs below their educational and skill levels. For example, a college graduate who is pumping gas or bagging groceries is underemployed because he or she is not using his or her college training. A skilled welder who is frying hamburgers in a fast food restaurant is also underemployed.

The Great Recession, that followed the 2008 financial meltdown, caused underemployment to soar. In August 2011, the official unemployment rate was a staggering 9.1 percent with 14 million Americans officially counted as unemployed. In addition, another 8.8 million, who wanted to work fulltime, were able to find only part-time work, and an additional 1.6 million "discouraged workers" were excluded from the count because they had not actively sought work during the previous month.

Costs of Unemployment

The costs of unemployment include both economic and social costs, and they can be enormous during periods of prolonged unemployment. As you learned in Chapter 2, economic historians have estimated the dollar cost of the Great Depression of the 1930s as being greater than the cost of World War II. They estimate that the dollar value of the lost production during the 1930s would have been a large enough sum to have covered the cost of a new house, and several new cars, for each and every American family during the decade.

The high unemployment, resulting from the Great Recession, which officially began in December 2007, had already taken a heavy toll by the end of 2011, and nobody knew just how many more years the high unemployment would continue.

The economic cost of the Great Depression would have been even greater if the government had not intervened and employed many of the unemployed workers to do constructive work, much of which we are still benefiting from today. There are few communities in the United States that do not have one or more public buildings still in use that were built by unemployed workers as part of the public works projects of the 1930s. Many public library buildings, city halls, and buildings on college campuses were constructed during this period. Although many people were critical of the 1930s public works projects at the time, the fact remains that labor, which would have otherwise been wasted, was put to good use for construction projects that would benefit many future generations.

By the end of 2011, many economists were advocating a similar program to rebuild the nation's badly deteriorated infrastructure, which could provide jobs for millions of the unemployed. It just did not make sense to allow millions of unemployed workers to remain idle when there was so much work that needed to be done.

The social costs of unemployment can also be enormous. When the economy slips into recession and unemployment begins to rise, domestic violence, mental illness, and even suicide rates rise right along with the unemployment rate. When a person is suddenly thrown out of work through no fault of his or her own, and becomes unable to provide for the needs of his or her family, the humiliation and loss of self-esteem can be devastating.

Methods of Controlling Unemployment

There is no way of eliminating all unemployment. In a dynamic economy such as ours, with people continually shifting jobs, there will always be some frictional unemployment. Also, periodic recessions seem to be inevitable in our economy, thus causing some degree of cyclical unemployment. And, some degree of structural unemployment is probably unavoidable. However, there are a number of things that can be done to minimize unemployment. Let's examine some of them.

Fiscal Policy

Fiscal policy is the deliberate use of the government's spending and taxing powers to accomplish desired objectives. Fiscal policy can be used to combat cyclical unemployment. As you already know, cyclical unemployment results when there is insufficient total spending to buy up all the goods and services that the economy is capable of producing. Workers are laid off because the things they produce are not being bought. Thus, the obvious solution to cyclical unemployment is an increase in total spending. If more goods and services are bought, laid off workers will be called back to work to produce the additional goods and services that are being demanded.

Total spending is made up of consumer spending, plus investment spending, plus government spending. An increase in any or all of these spending components will help to reduce cyclical unemployment. By using fiscal policy, the government can increase the level of total spending and thus reduce cyclical unemployment. For example, the government could increase total spending by increasing its own spending. Any increase in government spending, whether for domestic programs or for national defense needs, should increase the number of jobs available in the American economy.

In addition to increasing its own spending, the government can indirectly influence the levels of consumer spending and investment spending. By lowering taxes, the government provides consumers with more after-tax income, thus increasing their purchasing power. Also, by lowering business taxes, or by providing special tax incentives for investment, the government can encourage increased business investment.

Although fiscal policy has been used successfully to reduce cyclical unemployment in the past, there are serious obstacles to using it today. As a result of the gigantic budget deficits of recent years, and the skyrocketing national debt, government policy makers today find themselves facing a "deficit trap" which prevents them from successfully using fiscal policy.

The skyrocketing rise in the national debt, from $1 trillion in 1981 to more than $14 trillion in 2011, has greatly restricted the government's ability to stimulate the economy back to prosperity. The actions that would be needed for stimulating the economy are just the opposite of the actions that would normally be used to reduce the deficit. It is a Catch 22 scenario. Actions to restore prosperity will increase the deficit and debt. But actions to reduce the deficit will cause unemployment to rise.

Monetary Policy

In Chapter 7, we will examine the Federal Reserve System in detail, and you will learn how it conducts monetary policy in an effort to accomplish desired economic objectives. However, for our present purposes, suffice it to say that monetary policy involves changes in interest rates and the availability of loans. By lowering interest rates and making loans more readily available, the Federal Reserve attempts to encourage businesses and consumers to borrow money and increase their spending. If there is increased investment and consumer spending as a result of lower interest rates and an increased availability of loans, more jobs will become available, and cyclical unemployment will be reduced.

Other Methods of Controlling Unemployment

As you have just learned, fiscal policy and monetary policy are used to reduce cyclical unemployment. We will now look at the problems of structural and seasonal unemployment to see if anything can be done about these types of unemployment. There are some things that could be done to reduce structural and seasonal unemployment, but little has actually been done in recent years to combat these problems. Let's look at some potential remedies.

Frictional Unemployment. As you will remember, frictional unemployment involves people who are in transition between jobs. They have recently left one job, and have not yet found a new job. The length of time it takes for an unemployed worker to find a new job plays a major role in determining the level of frictional unemployment. If the time required for a worker to find a new job, after leaving a previous job, could be substantially reduced, then the level of frictional unemployment, and thus the unemployment rate used to determine full employment, could be substantially reduced.

The way in which most people go about finding jobs in this country leaves much to be desired, especially in today's modern computer age. For example, suppose you are an unskilled factory worker who has suddenly been thrown out of work. How would you go about finding a new job? Your first step would probably be to look at the "help-wanted" ads in the classified section of your local newspaper. However, your chances of finding suitable employment through this source are not good, especially if the economy is in a recession and the unemployment rate is high. Very few good jobs are advertised in the newspapers.

Your next step might be to go to the nearest state employment service office. There is a slim chance that you might find employment through this source, but your chances of getting a good job through the state employment service are not good. The problem is that most employers do not list their job vacancies with the state employment service.

Next you will probably hit the streets and begin going door-to-door, asking potential employers if they have any job openings. This is not a very efficient way of finding a job. However, it is the way most unskilled workers find employment. It would be so much easier if there was a single place where unemployed workers could find out about all the job vacancies that existed in their geographic area and line of work.

If a way could be found to get all employers to list their job vacancies with the state employment service, such a place would exist. State employment service offices have modern computer equipment that enables them to match job applicants with the qualifications stipulated by employers. For example, an employer could state that he or she wanted only applicants who had a college degree in accounting and a certain number of years of work experience. Thus, the employment service could provide information about this particular vacancy only to candidates who met the stipulated requirements.

Structural Unemployment. Efforts to solve structural unemployment of the geographic-mismatch type usually involve attempts to attract new employers into areas of high unemployment. Many local communities provide strong incentives for new employers to locate in their areas. They may offer special tax breaks and free land to potential new employers. In some cases, local communities may even offer to construct buildings to house the new employment facilities. Competition between communities for new employers is so keen that some poor communities are unable to successfully compete. Unfortunately, those communities with the greatest unemployment, are often the ones least able to provide the financial incentives necessary to attract new employers.

Some nations have national programs for encouraging employers to locate in those areas where unemployment is highest. For example, in Sweden there is a program called the special investment reserve which exempts a portion of a corporation's profits from taxes when the profits are used for investment under certain conditions stipulated by the government. Usually these funds can be invested tax free only at times of rising unemployment, and in those regions of the country where there is a surplus of labor. Thus, new jobs are created in those areas which need them most.

Solutions to the problem of structural unemployment of the skill-mismatch type involve better career guidance and retraining programs. The best method of preventing this type of structural unemployment is to provide high school and college students with comprehensive career guidance programs that will help them to select career fields that have labor shortages, and avoid those fields where there are labor surpluses.

Seasonal Unemployment. There are few solutions to the problem of seasonal unemployment. Unemployment that exists in the construction industry during bad weather, and causes migrant farm workers to be unemployed during part of the year, is probably unavoidable.

Chapter Highlights

- Employment statistics are based on a sample survey of approximately 60,000 households conducted each month. The Department of Labor classifies each person 16 years of age and older into one of three categories: (1) employed, (2) unemployed, or (3) not in the labor force. The unemployment rate is the number of unemployed persons divided by the number of persons in the labor force.

- Economists generally recognize four types of unemployment: frictional, cyclical, structural, and seasonal. Frictional unemployment involves people who are temporarily between jobs. Cyclical unemployment results from insufficient total spending in the economy. Structural unemployment occurs when there is a mismatch between job openings and job seekers. Seasonal unemployment involves workers who have jobs for part of the year but who are without work at times because of seasonal factors.

- The costs of unemployment involve both direct costs to those who are unemployed and costs to the economy in terms of lost production.

- Methods of controlling cyclical unemployment include the use of monetary policy and fiscal policy to stimulate additional spending in the economy.

- Better programs to match unemployed workers with job openings could help reduce frictional unemployment.

- Incentives for employers to locate in those areas where unemployment is highest could help reduce structural unemployment of the geographic-mismatch type, and better career guidance can help to combat structural unemployment of the skill-mismatch type.

Important Terms

Match each of the following terms with the correct definition:

discouraged workers   frictional   unemployment
underemployment   seasonal   unemployment
employed   structural unemployment
cyclical unemployment   unemployed

1. Those people who are actively working or have a job from which they are temporarily absent because of a vacation, illness, a labor dispute, or bad weather.

2. Unemployment caused by a mismatch between job seekers and job openings.

3. A term used to describe workers who are either working only part time when they want to work full time, or are working at jobs below their educational and skill levels.

4. Unemployment that involves people who are temporarily between jobs.

5. People who are not actively seeking work because they believe that no work for which they are qualified is available.

6. Unemployment caused by insufficient total spending in the economy.

7. Those people who do not have a job and are actively seeking work.

8. Temporary unemployment caused by seasonal factors.

Review Questions

1. How is unemployment measured?

2. What are the three categories the government uses to classify the employment status of individuals?

3. Describe frictional unemployment. What are its causes? What are some possible solutions?

4. What is cyclical unemployment? What are its causes? What can be done to reduce it?

5. Describe structural unemployment. What are its causes? What can be done to combat it?

6. What is seasonal unemployment? How does it differ from other types of unemployment?

7. What is meant by underemployment?

8. What are the costs of unemployment to the economy and to the unemployed workers and their families?

Discussion Questions

1. Why is unemployment described as "one of the most serious and cruel of all economic problems"?

2. If you were in charge of economic policy, what would you do to combat the various types of unemployment?

CHAPTER FIVE

Inflation 通貨膨脹

Inflation is defined as *a general rise in the price level* or, to put it another way, *a decline in the purchasing power of the dollar.* In simple terms, during periods of inflation most prices are rising and, thus, it takes more dollars to buy the same quantity of goods and services this month than it took last month. If it is allowed to get out of control, inflation can become a very serious problem, and there are historical cases of "hyperinflation" becoming a catastrophic problem. For example, after World War I, prices in Germany rose so high and so fast that money become almost worthless. A story is told of a man who was robbed on his way to the store with a wheelbarrow full of money during this period. The robbers allegedly dumped the money on the ground and made a fast get away with the wheelbarrow, which had a great deal more value than the money it was carrying. Prices increased one trillion-fold in Germany from 1920 to 1923, meaning that an item that cost one German mark in 1920 would have cost one trillion marks three years later.

Unfortunately, as you will learn later in this chapter, there is a tradeoff relationship between unemployment and inflation such that efforts to reduce the unemployment rate usually lead to higher inflation. Likewise, efforts to reduce the inflation rate usually result in more unemployment.

Thus, policy makers are constantly facing the dilemma of whether greater emphasis should be placed on lowering unemployment or inflation.

Measuring Inflation

The most commonly used measure of the general inflation rate is the *consumer price index*, which is also sometimes called the "cost-of-living index." The consumer price index is based on approximately 400 frequently purchased items considered by the U.S. Department of Labor to be a "typical market basket" of consumer goods and services. Each month the Department of Labor checks the prices of these 400 items in 85 urban areas which include every major part of the nation. If the total cost of the 400 items remains constant, there is no inflation, even if the prices of several specific items rise, but are offset by corresponding price decreases of other items. Almost always, some prices are rising while other prices are falling. Thus, just because the prices of some items are rising does not mean that we have inflation. For inflation to exist, average prices must be rising. This means that the rising prices for some items must more than offset falling prices for other items such that the total cost of the 400 items is higher than it was during the previous months. The percentage increase in the price of the 400 items from one year to the next year is the annual inflation rate.

Types of Inflation

Although all inflation involves rising prices, economists generally recognize two different types of inflation. They are *demand-pull inflation,* and *cost-push inflation.* Since the causes of these two types of inflation are different, the solutions must also be different. Let's examine each type of inflation.

Demand-Pull Inflation

Demand-pull inflation occurs when the total spending in the economy rises more rapidly than the available supply of goods and services. In other words, the total of consumer spending, plus investment spending, plus government spending exceeds the total supply of goods and services available at current prices. Thus, there would be a shortage of many items throughout the economy if prices remained constant. However, prices will not remain constant. Common sense tells you that when there is a shortage of anything, prices will rise unless there is some artificial constraint on prices such as government price controls. Thus, the prices of the various items in short supply will rise until shortages no longer exist. This will result in a rise in average prices thus causing inflation.

Actually, demand-pull inflation is just the opposite of cyclical unemployment. Cyclical unemployment occurs when there is not enough total spending to buy up all the goods and services the economy is capable of producing. Thus, cyclical unemployment is caused by too little total spending. Demand-pull inflation, on the other hand, is caused by too much total spending. Demand-pull inflation occurs when total spending exceeds the dollar value of all goods and services that the economy is capable of producing at the full-employment level of operation. If the economy is operating at the full-employment level of GDP, there can be no increase in the total supply of goods and services. Thus, any increase in total spending must lead to higher prices. Just as an increase in the demand for a single item, relative to the supply, will cause the price of that item to rise, an increase in the total demand for all goods and services, at a time when the economy is operating at the full-employment level, will cause average prices for the economy as a whole to rise.

Cost-Push Inflation

Cost-push inflation occurs when sellers raise their prices in an effort to pass increased production costs on to their customers. The increased production costs may be in the form of higher prices for raw materials, capital goods, energy, or any other item that producers use in the production process. They may also be in the form of higher wages for employees. Regardless of the source, any increase in production costs will lead to lower profits unless producers raise their prices. Since a reduction in profits is never an attractive option, many producers simply try to pass increased production costs on to their customers in the form of higher prices. If production costs are rising in many industries throughout the economy, and if producers are successful in passing the costs on in the form of higher prices, average prices in the economy will rise, and cost-push inflation will occur. Some economists use the term *wage-push* inflation to refer to cost-push inflation that results from higher labor costs.

Cost-push inflation can occur during periods when the economy is operating below the full-employment level as well as when the economy is operating at full employment. A major factor in the high inflation of the 1970s was the rapidly rising energy prices. From 1973 to 1980, the world market price of crude oil increased from $3 a barrel to about $33 a barrel. This eleven-fold increase in crude oil prices, in a seven-year period, created a great deal of cost-push inflation. It is easy to see how the rising energy costs affected the gasoline and home heating components of the consumer price index. However, many people overlook the fact that most prices went up because of the energy crisis. A part of the production cost, and much of the transportation cost, of all manufactured items and all food products is energy cost. Also, crude oil is used as a raw material in the production of many synthetic fibers and other products.

Effects of Inflation

Although everyone is affected by inflation to some degree, some people are affected far more severely than others.   Let's examine the various negative effects of inflation.

Effects on People With Fixed Incomes

People living on fixed incomes are especially hard hit by severe and prolonged inflation. Such people have the same amount of income to spend month after month, year after year. If prices held steady over the long run, these people would maintain their standard of living, but it would not increase over time.   However, if prices are rising, the fixed income will buy less and less each month. If a person's income is fixed over a period of many years, and if there is substantial inflation during this period, that person will see his or her income eroded away by the inflation, and will experience a continual decline in the standard of living as time passes.

For example, prices more than tripled during the twenty-year period, 1970-1990. This means that if a person retired in 1970 on a fixed income of $9,000, he or she would need more than $27,000 in 1990 just to buy the same amount of goods and services that the $9,000 bought in 1970. However, if the person's income remained fixed over the period, he or she would still have only $9,000 in income in 1990. This $9,000 would buy less in 1990 than $3,000 would have bought when the person retired in 1970. Although Social Security benefits are adjusted for inflation, many elderly people depend on money they saved during their working years as the major source of their retirement income.   Since this money is now worth considerably less than it was worth when it was earned, these people have in a sense been cheated out of a financially secure retirement by inflation.

Effects on Long-Term Lending

ᴌ   Inflation benefits borrowers at the expense of lenders. ⸢Suppose you borrow $20,000, which you promise to repay at the end of five years. If prices were to double during the five-year period, you would, in effect, be paying back only $10,000 in purchasing power. Although you repay $20,000 in actual dollars, this sum will purchase only as much as $10,000 would have bought at the time you borrowed the money. Thus, you have⸢experienced a substantial benefit at the expense of the person who loaned you the money⌟ He or she, in effect, lost $10,000 in purchasing power over the five-year period as a result of the doubling in prices.⸥

Although this may seem like an extreme example, the problem is very real. The high inflation of the 1970s and early 1980s had a disastrous effect on many lending institutions, and it resulted in major changes in long-term lending policies. In 1980, when the inflation rate was 13.5 percent, a fixed-rate loan which had been made at 8 percent would have resulted in a net loss of 5.5 percent for the lender. Even a loan with an interest rate of 13.5 percent would have, in effect, earned the lender zero interest in real terms, because the interest rate was just high enough to offset the loss in purchasing power resulting from the 13.5 percent inflation rate.

Prior to the prolonged period of high inflation during the 1970s and early 1980s, lending institutions were willing to make long-term home mortgage loans at fixed rates of interest. However, as a result of the losses incurred during that long period of inflation, some lending institutions changed their lending policies. Instead of long-term fixed rate mortgages, some lenders began offering adjustable-rate mortgages with provisions that would allow interest rates to rise or fall with interest rates in general.

This practice contributed to the foreclosure crisis of 2008 and after. Loans were offered with very low initial rates. Later, the rates were adjusted upward to a level so high that many homeowners were unable to make the monthly payments, resulting in foreclosure of the homes.

Effects on Savings

Individual savers are affected by inflation in the same way that lenders are affected, because savers are really lenders. When you deposit money in the bank in a savings account you are really lending the money to the bank, which will in turn lend the money to someone else at a higher interest rate than they are paying you.

Suppose you deposit money in a bank at an interest rate of 5 percent at a time when the inflation rate is 4 percent. In effect, you are receiving a "real interest rate" of only 1 percent. Now suppose the inflation rate is 5 percent. In this case, you are receiving zero percent real interest rate. The rate at which your money is losing purchasing power through inflation is equal to the rate of interest so that you make no net gain. Even worse, if the inflation rate is higher than the interest rate, your real interest rate is negative.

Effects on International Trade

If the inflation rate in the United States is higher than that in other countries with which we engage in international trade, the inflation can have an adverse effect on our balance of trade. For example, if American prices are rising faster than those in Japan, Americans will tend to buy more Japanese-made goods since they are cheaper than American-made goods. At the same time, the people of Japan will tend to buy fewer American-made goods because they are becoming more expensive. This will lead to a larger deficit in the international trade balance of the United States. There are, of course, many other factors besides inflation that affect international trade. We will examine these other factors in Chapter 8. However, for the moment, suffice it to say that high inflation usually has a negative effect on international trade.

Effects on Income Distribution

Inflation has a tendency to redistribute income from the poor to the rich. While the poor tend to experience only negative effects from inflation, wealthy people often benefit from it. For example, during periods of high inflation, the prices of most things are rising, including real estate values. Individuals who own substantial amounts of real estate may see their net worth rise significantly because their real estate has increased in value. However, the very poor are usually renters who discover that the rising real estate values mean only higher rent for them. Since the poor usually own little or nothing that rises in value during periods of inflation, they have no gains to offset the losses from the higher prices they must pay for almost everything.

On the other hand, wealthy individuals pay more for their food, clothing, and other purchases, just like everyone else. However, if they own substantial assets and the value of these assets increases along with the general rise in prices, the gains from the increased value of their assets can more than offset the rising prices they pay for purchases.

The Unemployment-Inflation Tradeoff

As you can see, both unemployment and inflation are very serious economic problems that most people would like to see eliminated, or at least kept to a minimum. However, it is impossible to eliminate either of these problems, and efforts to reduce one usually lead to an increase in the other. As you know, cyclical unemployment is caused by insufficient total spending, and demand-pull inflation is caused by too much total spending. Thus, the solution for cyclical unemployment is to increase total spending, while the solution for demand-pull inflation is to decrease total spending. However, ⌐usually when policy makers attempt to increase total spending in an effort to reduce unemployment, there will be some increase in the inflation rate./ Likewise, efforts to reduce inflation by reducing total spending will usually result in some increase in unemployment. There are some exceptions to this rule. ⌐If the economy is in a deep recession with very high unemployment, the unemployment rate can usually be reduced somewhat through increased total spending without setting off increased inflation. ⅃ However, it is usually not possible to bring the economy all the way back to the full-employment-level without causing some increase in inflation.

Because of the unemployment-inflation tradeoff, policy makers are always faced with the dilemma of having to decide which is worse, inflation or unemployment. Should they attempt to reduce the inflation rate even though it will cause an increase in the unemployment rate? Or should they put their emphasis on maximizing the number of jobs available and thus cause increased inflation? There are no easy answers to these questions, and different groups in our society have different ideas about which of the two problems is worse. For example, bankers, who are seldom unemployed, and who place a high value on price stability, may favor putting more emphasis on fighting inflation than on combating unemployment if a choice must be made. On the other hand, labor unions, who often have automatic adjustments for inflation built into their union contracts, will probably put more emphasis on keeping unemployment as low as possible in order to maximize the number of jobs available to their members.

Methods of Controlling Inflation

Numerous things can be done to help control inflation. However, some are more effective than others. Let's look at some of the policy options available for combating inflation.

Fiscal Policy

As you already know, ⌐fiscal policy is the deliberate use of the government's spending and taxing powers to accomplish desired economic objectives.⌐ Fiscal policy can be effective in combating demand-pull inflation which is inflation caused by too much total spending in the economy. By reducing its own spending, the government can reduce the level of total spending. It can also reduce total spending by raising taxes, thus leaving consumers with less after-tax income to spend. Although, these solutions sound good in theory, they are not always feasible in actual practice because of political considerations. It is never politically popular to raise taxes, and few politicians have the guts to propose, or vote for, higher taxes.

This is, of course, the major reason that the giant federal budget deficits have been allowed to continue for so long. Thus, it is very difficult to get a tax increase to fight inflation, especially considering the fact that most voters could not see the relationship between higher taxes and lower inflation. Cutting government spending may be a little easier than raising taxes, but history has shown that it is also very difficult to enact government spending cuts. Thus, fiscal policy remains more of a theoretical way to fight inflation than an actual practical tool.

Monetary Policy

⌐Monetary policy, which involves deliberate changes in interest rates and the availability of loans by the Federal Reserve System, is usually more effective than fiscal policy as a tool for combating inflation⌐ Monetary policy is under the control of the Federal Reserve Board of Governors, who are appointed for 14-year terms of office, and are thus far better insulated from political pressures than are members of Congress and the president. Thus, the Federal Reserve Board is often able to take unpopular actions for the good of the economy without the fear of political consequences.

By forcing interest rates artificially high, and making it very difficult to obtain loans, the Federal Reserve Board can reduce the amount of spending that takes place on credit. Since a great deal of both consumer spending and business investment spending are done with borrowed money, by forcing interest rates up and making it difficult to obtain loans, the Federal Reserve can substantially reduce the level of total spending and thus reduce demand-pull inflation. We will have an in-depth look at the Federal Reserve System and its operation in Chapter 7.

Wage-Price Controls

During periods of high inflation, there are always many advocates of wage-price controls as a method of bringing the inflation under control. During such periods, many people come to believe that the solution to rapidly rising prices is to simply make it illegal for wages and prices to continue to rise. However, most professional economists are vigorously opposed to the use of wage-price controls under most circumstances.

The problem is that ⌐you cannot solve basic economic problems simply by passing laws against them.⌐It would be wonderful if you could. Wouldn't it be great if we could eliminate poverty simply by making poverty illegal? Yes, but it is an unrealistic approach to the problem. In order to solve the problem of poverty, it is necessary to solve the basic underlying economic problems that contribute to poverty. The same is true for inflation.

Not only do wage-price controls usually fail to

solve the problem of inflation, but they create additional problems.   Rising prices for products usually reflect shortages of the products. In other words, at current prices, the quantity demanded exceeds the quantity supplied. If prices were not allowed to rise, many people would be unable to buy the things they wanted due to the shortages. However, as prices rise, fewer and fewer people are willing to buy the expensive items. At the same time, increased quantities may be made available at the higher prices so that once again the quantity demanded is equal to the quantity supplied.

Wage-price controls were imposed during World War II, when there were critical shortages of many items. The shortages were so severe, that it was believed that allowing the price system to do the rationing would result in such high prices for some items that they would be affordable only to the rich. Thus, the government imposed strict wage-price controls and developed an elaborate system of rationing the goods so that everyone would have the opportunity to buy their "fair share" at the government-controlled prices.

Peacetime wage-price controls were tried in the United States during the early 1970s. On the evening of August 15, 1971, President Nixon, in a dramatic nationally televised address to the nation, announced a ninety-day freeze on wages, prices, and rents. This was the beginning of an attempt to control the U.S. economy artificially which would last for two years and eight months. On November 14, 1971, the price freeze was replaced with Phase II of the wage-price control sequence. Phase II was replaced by Phase III on January 11, 1973. Phase III was followed by a second price freeze on June 13, 1973, and this was followed by Phase IV on August 12, 1973. Phase IV was the last stage of the control sequence which finally ended in April 1974.

The controls did not bring inflation under control,

and many economists argued that the controls made the problem even worse. They contended that the controls caused distortions in the economy, and resulted in many shortages which then further contributed to inflation. Even President Nixon's own economic advisers expressed serious doubts that the control program had made much of a contribution in the fight against inflation.

Chapter Highlights

- Inflation is defined as a general rise in the price level or a decline in the purchasing power of the dollar.

- The consumer price index, which is based on approximately 400 frequently purchased items considered by the U.S. Department of Labor to be a "typical market basket" of consumer goods and services, is the most commonly used measure of inflation.

- Economists generally recognize two basic types of inflation: demand-pull inflation and cost-push inflation. Demand-pull inflation occurs when the total spending in the economy rises more rapidly than the available supply of goods and services. Cost-push inflation occurs when sellers raise their prices in an effort to pass increased costs on to their customers.

- Although everyone is affected by inflation to some degree, some people are affected far more severely than others. People on fixed incomes, long-term lenders, and savers are all hurt by inflation. Inflation also has a negative effect on international trade.

- Both unemployment and inflation are serious economic problems that most people would like to see eliminated or at least kept to a minimum.

However it is not only impossible to eliminate either unemployment or inflation, but there is a tradeoff relationship between the two. Efforts to reduce unemployment usually lead to an increase in inflation, and efforts to reduce inflation usually lead to an increase in unemployment.

- Fiscal policy, the deliberate use of the government's spending and taxing powers to accomplish desired economic objectives, can be useful in combating demand-pull inflation.

- Monetary policy, which involves the deliberate changes in interest rates and the availability of loans by the Federal Reserve System, can be an effective tool for combating inflation.

- Wage-price controls have been used in the past in an effort to fight inflation. However, most economists believe wage-price controls usually do more harm than good, and are opposed to the use of such measures under most circumstances.

Important Terms
Match each of the following terms with the correct definition:

demand-pull inflation   cost-push inflation
wage-price controls   consumer price index
inflation

1. A general rise in the price level or a decline in the purchasing power of the dollar.

2. The most commonly used measure of the general inflation rate.

3. Inflation caused by too much total spending in the economy.

4. Inflation resulting from sellers' raising their prices in an effort to pass increased costs on to their customers.

5. Government imposed restrictions on the free movement of prices.

Review Questions

1. What is inflation? How is it measured?

2. Describe the two basic types of inflation. What are the causes of each?

3. How does inflation affect people on fixed incomes? How does it affect lenders and savers? Why does inflation have a negative effect on international trade?

4. What is meant by the unemployment-inflation tradeoff? Explain what happens to inflation when efforts are made to reduce unemployment. What happens to unemployment when efforts are made to reduce inflation?

5. Explain how fiscal policy and monetary policy can be used to combat inflation.

6. Why do most economists oppose the use of wage-price controls as a method of controlling inflation?

Discussion Questions

1. Who is hurt most by inflation? Who is hurt least? If you had to choose between high unemployment and high inflation, which would you choose? Why?

CHAPTER SIX

Government Fiscal Policy
政府财政政策

Economists usually define _fiscal policy_ as the deliberate use of the government's spending and taxing powers to influence economic activity. When the government raises or lowers taxes, or changes its spending levels, in order to bring about a desired change in the level of total spending, and thus the performance of the economy, it is practicing fiscal policy. Fiscal policy can also be defined more generally as simply the government's taxing and spending policies regardless of whether or not it is trying to bring about changes in the level of total spending in the economy.

Fiscal Policy in Theory

The origin of fiscal policy as a tool to bring about deliberate changes in the performance of the economy dates back to 1936 when a British economist, named John Maynard Keynes, published a monumental book, _The General Theory of Employment, Interest, and Money._ In this book, Keynes set forth a new economic theory that became known as _Keynesian economics._

Keynesian economics soon became the predominant body of economic theory in the Western world. Although his theories have undergone substantial refinement and revision, much of modern Keynesian economics is still rooted on the ideas set forth by Keynes. The belief that the government should play an active role in maintaining the proper level of total spending is a central part of Keynesian economics. Keynes argued that, in order to minimize both unemployment and inflation, the government needed to be involved. He believed that, with the proper use of the government's spending and taxing powers, the extremes of the business cycle could be avoided.

The extremes of the business cycle, which result in high unemployment or high inflation, can be very costly. During a severe recession, millions of workers become unemployed, and billions of dollars' worth of potential production are permanently lost. In addition, prolonged periods of high inflation can have a devastating effect on both the economy and the people.

The objectives of deliberate fiscal policy are to minimize the levels of both unemployment and inflation by using the government's taxing and spending powers to assure the correct level of total spending. Total spending should be approximately equal to the full-employment capacity of the economy. If total spending is insufficient to buy all of the goods and services that the economy is capable of producing at the full-employment level, workers will be laid off and production will adjust downward to the level of spending.

On the other hand, if total spending is greater than the capacity of the economy to produce at current prices, there will be a shortage of goods and services and prices will be bid up. Since the actual Gross Domestic Product (GDP) will be determined by the level of total spending, it is important that the level of spending be approximately equal to the economy's capacity to produce when all resources are fully employed. At least in theory, fiscal policy can be used to regulate the level of total spending, and thus the level of production. If GDP could be maintained at the appropriate level, it would be possible to avoid both high inflation and serious unemployment.

Fiscal Policy in Practice

Most mainstream economists believe that fiscal policy, if used properly, can be a strong tool for managing the economy. The best example of successful use of fiscal policy is the long period of economic expansion during the 1960s. When President John F. Kennedy took office in 1961, the economy was suffering from a recession that had begun in 1958. Kennedy brought into his administration economic advisers who were determined to use fiscal policy to bring the economy out of the recession. The first fiscal-policy measures included increased federal spending on highways, and legislation that allowed businesses to subtract from their taxes a part of the cost of new investment in factories and machines.

When these measures proved insufficient, the President proposed a major tax cut. Although President Kennedy was assassinated before the tax cut was enacted, his successor, Lyndon Johnson, signed an $11 billion tax cut into law in February 1964. This large tax cut, along with substantial increases in spending for the Vietnam War, fueled the longest economic expansion in American history. The expansion lasted from February 1961 to December 1969—106 consecutive months.

Fiscal policy does not have such a good track record in combating inflation, however. The problem is not that proper fiscal policies cannot successfully control inflation. The problem is the political feasibility of getting the President and Congress to support the proper fiscal policies during periods of inflation. Many economists believe that when inflation began to rise in 1966, at a time of full employment, the government should have raised taxes and reduced government spending in order to lower the level of total spending and nip the inflation in the bud. But higher taxes and cuts in government programs are never popular with the public, and many politicians do not have the guts to do what is right for the economy because such unpopular actions might cost them votes in the next election.

If fiscal policy is to be used successfully for managing the economy, it must be possible to raise taxes as well as lower them, and to decrease government spending as well as increase it. If the general public and government officials had a clear understanding of basic economics, it might be possible to pursue sound fiscal policy in both controlling unemployment and inflation. But, as long as the majority of people cannot see how higher taxes will help to reduce inflation, it is unlikely that they will support the higher taxes when they are needed. Thus, fiscal policy is not very practical for fighting inflation.

Keynesian economics was the predominant body of economic theory for nearly half a century. Much of the content in the economics textbooks used at both the high school and college levels today is derived from Keynesian economics. And most mainstream economists are still strong supporters of the basic ideas set forth by Keynes and revised and refined by later Keynesian economists. In addition, prior to the Reagan administration, most government economic policies were based on Keynesian economics.

Supply-side Economics

In 1981, President Reagan abandoned Keynesian economics and launched the nation in a new direction based on a new, untested theory called *supply-side economics*. This new theory received most of its support from non-economists, with only a small fraction of professionally-trained economists supporting it. Usually, new economic theories require years of debate and testing before they stand a chance of being implemented as a part of government economic policy. But, because the ideas of the supply-side supporters were so compatible with the political philosophy of Ronald Reagan, this new, untested theory, was to become the cornerstone of Reagan's economic policy.

The proponents of supply-side economics argued that taxes had risen to such a high level that they served to discourage work and investment. They contended that a sharp reduction in tax rates would provide strong incentives for workers to work harder and longer, and for businesses to produce more goods and services. The supply-side advocates argued that there would be so much additional work and production, as a result of the tax cut, that the government would actually collect more tax dollars than before, even with the lower tax rates. This was like having your cake and eating it too. According to supply-siders, the government could lower tax rates and at the same time collect more tax dollars.

In 1981, Congress enacted the president's tax-cut proposal. The proposal had been reduced by Reagan's budget director from a 30 percent cut to a 25 percent cut in personal income tax rates over a three-year period. Although inflation did come down as the nation plunged into recession, the unemployment rate climbed to 10.7 percent in December 1982, the highest level since the Great Depression of the 1930s. And, instead of the promised balanced budget by 1984, the federal government ran a budget deficit of $207.8 billion in fiscal year 1983, and the deficit had risen to $221.2 billion by fiscal year 1986. The previous record deficits, prior to the Reagan presidency, were $73.7 billion in 1976, and $73.8 billion in 1980. In 1970, just ten years before Reagan's election, the federal budget deficit was less than $3 billion.

Although President Reagan abandoned Keynesian economics, Keynesian economics can be used to explain much of what happened during the Reagan presidency.

First of all, the severe 1981-82 recession, which caused millions of Americans to lose their jobs might have been prevented. When President Reagan took office in January 1981, the economy was weak because it was still recovering from the mild recession that occurred during the Carter administration. In terms of fiscal policy, the economy needed a boost in the form of a substantial tax cut and/or increased government spending. If President Reagan had carried out his original plan to cut tax rates by 10 percent effective January 1981, the severe recession might have been avoided. But Budget Director, David Stockman, convinced the president to reduce his first year tax cut from 10 percent to 5 percent, and to delay its implementation from January 1 to October 1, 1981 in order to reduce the size of the deficit for that year.

Thus, instead of the planned 10 percent tax cut that was to have taken place in January 1981, there was no tax cut at all for the first 9 months of that year, and only a 5 percent cut for the last three months of the year. At the same time, the president was making substantial cuts in federal spending for domestic programs. The fragile economy simply could not stand the shock of such a stringent budget in 1981.

Budget Deficits

In January 1982, a full 10 percent cut in tax rates was added to the 5 percent cut of October 1981 and, in January 1983, the final 10 percent tax-rate cut took effect. Thus, effective January 1983, tax rates were 25 percent lower than just 15 months earlier. Some economists believe that if there had been a 10 percent cut in tax rates in January 1981, and no further cuts after that, the economic history of the 1980s might have been radically different. The nation might have avoided both the severe recession of 1981-82 and the huge budget deficits that sent the national debt soaring.

The 25 percent tax cut, implemented over a 15-month period between October 1981 and January 1983, was more medicine than the ailing economy could handle. The patient was harmed a great deal more than it was helped with this prescription. The large tax cut resulted in a substantial loss in revenue, and thus contributed to the gigantic budget deficits.

The huge tax cuts of 1982 and 1983 did help the economy to recover from the severe recession. There is no surer way to bring about a strong economic expansion than for the government to spend billions of dollars more into the economy than it pulls out in taxes. The huge deficits made the strong recovery and expansion possible, but the nation paid a terrible price for this expansion. In a sense, we mortgaged our future.

The 1968 budget deficit of $25.2 billion during the Vietnam War was, at the time, the largest budget deficit since World War II, and it was followed by the small budget surplus of 1969. In 1976 and 1980, the government ran budget deficits close to $74 billion dollars, but in both of these years the economy was in recession and the deficits were due largely to the high unemployment that existed. When workers are laid off, they stop paying income taxes to the federal government and, in most cases, the government begins to pay them money in the form of unemployment compensation. This automatically increases the deficit.

According to Congressional Budget Office calculations, if the economy had been operating at the full-employment level during these two years, there would have been no deficits. It is in 1982 that the federal government begins to run exceptionally large and sustained budget deficits on a regular year-by-year basis. In 1982, the deficit was $128 billion. The following year it soared to $207.8 billion. Although, the deficit fell slightly to $185.4 billion in 1984, it rose to $212.3 billion in 1985, and $221.2 billion in 1986. In 1987, with unemployment continuing to decline, the deficit fell to $149.8 billion. But the fiscal 1990 deficit was $221.2 billion, and by 1992 it had soared to $290.4 billion.

The large deficits of 1982, 1983, and 1984 can be attributed partly to the high unemployment resulting from the severe recession of 1981-82. However, the huge budget deficit of $212.3 billion in 1985 was at least partly caused by the excessive cuts in tax rates in 1982 and 1983. If we compare 1985 with 1980 (years with identical unemployment rates of 7.1 percent), we can see the change in the potential of the tax structure to generate sufficient revenue as a result of the cuts in tax rates. The 1980 deficit was only $73.8 billion, about one-third of the $212.3 billion deficit of 1985.

Clearly, there was a basic structural problem with the federal budget. In the past, most deficits had been due almost totally to unemployment. Thus, they were called cyclical deficits because they resulted from a downturn in the business cycle. When the economy again reached full employment, most of the deficit disappeared. However, by early 1990, the unemployment rate had fallen to its lowest level since the early 1970s, but large deficits remained. Only a small amount of the fiscal 1990 deficit was due to the unemployment rate. Most of the deficit was a structural deficit. The structural deficits resulted from the fact that the 25 percent cut in tax rates, during the early part of the Reagan presidency, created a situation where, even at full employment, the tax structure could not generate nearly enough revenue to provide a balanced budget.

The large deficits of the 1980s and early 1990s resulted in huge increases in the national debt. Every dollar that is spent by the government, above and beyond the amount of revenue it receives, must be borrowed. So each time the government borrows money to cover the deficit, this borrowed money is added to the national debt.

Clinton and a Return to Traditional
Economic Policies

During the Clinton administration, there was a return to more traditional economic policies, and the structural component of the budget deficit was at least partially eliminated with selective increases in income taxes that were combined with government spending cuts.

The spending cuts, included some cuts in entitlement programs, and the collapse of the Soviet Union also allowed the United States government to make especially large cuts in defense spending. The budgetary policy reforms, along with the booming economy, permitted the deficits to diminish during the last half of the nineties. There was a tiny operating budget surplus of $1.9 billion in 1999 and a more respectable $86.4 billion surplus in 2000. Unfortunately, the budget returned to deficit territory in 2001 and there were large annual deficits in the years that followed.

Fiscal Policy Under George W. Bush

George W. Bush was elected president in 2000 largely on the basis of his promise to implement major tax cuts. Despite the warning of professional economists and many members of his own political party, Bush pushed through a huge tax cut in 2001 that the nation could not afford unless government spending was cut by the same amount. By 2003, Bush had racked up a huge deficit of $317.5 billion for fiscal year 2002, and the projected deficit for 2003 was an estimated all-time record of $467.6 billion. Instead of admitting that his 2001 tax cut had been a mistake, and calling for its repeal, Bush called for yet another large tax cut. Ultimately a $350 billion additional tax cut was approved in 2003.

Bush disregarded the advice of mainstream professional economists who did everything in their power to warn the public about his irresponsible fiscal policies. When more than 400 of the nation's top economists placed a full-page ad in the *New York Times* to warn the public about the dangers of the second proposed tax cut, President Bush totally ignored their warnings and campaigned against them and anyone else who opposed his latest tax cut. He also traveled around the country trying to convince the American people to put pressure on Congress to pass his proposal.

On Friday, May 23, 2003 the Senate took two actions so contradictory that historians will have trouble understanding the political mindset of Congress during that troubling period. First, the Senate voted to raise the nation's debt limit by nearly $1 trillion because, in less than a week, the Treasury Department was expected to run out of borrowing authority and risk default on the nation's debt.

What was so extraordinary about the May 23, 2003 vote to raise the debt ceiling was the fact that it came on the very same day that the Senate also passed a $350 billion tax cut. If the financial condition of the United States government was so dire as to require almost a trillion-dollar increase in the debt ceiling, how could a single senator justify voting for a $350 billion tax cut?

The economic policies of George W. Bush were not based on either Keynesian economics or supply-side economics, although his tax policies did resemble those of Reagan. In fact, they were not really economic policies. They were political policies. Bush seemed determined to cut taxes by as much as possible.

The National Debt
When Ronald Reagan took over the reins of government in 1981, the total accumulation of debt by the previous 39 administrations over 192 years of our history had not yet reached $1 trillion. Although a trillion dollars is not an insignificant amount, the fact that it had taken 192

years to approach the first $1 trillion of debt was somewhat comforting, so the national debt was not seen as one of the major problems facing America at that time. That all changed very quickly. In just a little over five years, the national debt doubled to $2 trillion and was headed skyward. During the 12 years that Reagan and George H. W. Bush occupied the White House, the national debt quadrupled from $1 trillion to more than $4 trillion.

In 1992, the first President Bush was defeated by Bill Clinton, primarily because of the massive deficits, the soaring national debt, and the weak economy. Shortly after taking office, Clinton pushed a major deficit-reduction package through Congress, which included both higher taxes and reduced government spending. The net result was a reversal in the trend. The deficits became smaller and smaller during Clinton's first six years and the government experienced true budget surpluses in 1999 and 2000 for the first time in 40 years. Although the national debt rose to $5.7 trillion during Clinton's presidency, it held steady during his last two years because of the elimination of the deficits.

The two large tax cuts during George W. Bush's first term, along with massive new spending on wars in Afghanistan and Iraq, sent the national debt skyrocketing again. In just six years (2001-2007), the national debt increased by approximately 50 percent. By 2012, the debt had soared to $15 trillion. Thus, the national debt, which took nearly 200 years to reach the first $1 trillion in 1981, increased fifteenfold during the next 30 years.

TABLE 6-1
National Debt In $Trillions and as a Percent of GDP, 1981-2012

Year	Total Debt in $Trillions	Debt as Percent of GDP
1986	2.121	48.1
1987	2.346	50.5
1988	2.601	51.9
1989	2.868	53.1
1990	3.206	55.9
1991	3.958	60.6
1992	4.002	64.1
1993	4.351	66.2
1994	4.643	66.7
1995	4.932	67.2
1996	5.182	67.3
1997	5.369	65.6
1998	5.478	63.5
1999	5.606	61.4
2000	5.629	58.0
2001	5.770	57.4
2002	6.198	59.7
2003	6.760	62.5
2004	7.355	63.9
2005	7.905	64.4
2006	8.451	64.7
2007	8.951	64.4
2008	9.986	69.4
2009	11.876	84.2
2010	13.529	93.2
2011*	15.476	102.6
2012*	16.654	105.3

Source: *Economic Report of the President,* 2011. * Estimates

Some people, who are looking for a silver lining in the dark cloud that the national debt represents, try to focus on the debt as a percent of GDP. They say that as a nation's GDP rises, it is better able to handle a larger debt. But, as you can see in Table 6-1, the debt looks even worse when we consider it as a percent of GDP. By late 2011, the dollar amount of the debt had soared to $15 trillion, and the debt, as a percent of the GDP, was more than 100 percent for the first time since the Civil War!

Another reason for increasing concern about the skyrocketing national debt is that, unlike the distant past, when almost all of the debt was owed to American citizens, a great deal of the debt today is owed to foreign nations. Approximately 47 percent of America's publicly held debt, at the beginning of 2011, was held by foreigners. China held 9.8 percent of the U.S. debt, and Japan held 9.6 percent. The balance of the foreign-held debt is owed to many nations around the world, including the United Kingdom. As a result, when the United States government pays interest on the debt, much of the interest flows out of the American economy and into the economies of foreign nations. At the beginning of 2012, the total interest on the national debt was more than $20 billion per month.

Balancing the Budget

The government, like any individual or business, cannot spend more than it takes in year after year without serious consequences. However, it is probably not possible to balance the federal budget each and every year as some people advocate. Most economists favor balancing the budget under the right circumstances, but few support the idea of a balanced budget every year. There are basically three alternative balanced-budget policies: the annually balanced budget; the cyclically balanced budget; and the full-employment balanced budget.

An *annually balanced budget* would be one where total government revenue is exactly equal to total government expenditures each and every year. Although an annually balanced budget may seem attractive in theory, few economists would support such a policy.

Since most of the federal government's revenue comes from the individual and corporate income taxes, the government's revenue is very much influenced by the business cycle. During periods of recession, when unemployment is high and many corporations are losing money instead of making profits, government revenue falls off sharply. At the same time, government expenditures for unemployment compensation and other social programs rises in response to the increased unemployment. The combined effect of reduced tax revenue and increased spending will inevitably lead to a larger budget deficit.

If the government attempted to balance the budget during a severe recession by increasing taxes and/or reducing government spending, the resulting decline in total spending would lead to still more unemployment and an even larger deficit. Raising taxes and/or reducing government spending during a period of high unemployment will cause still more workers to lose their jobs. As this happens, the newly unemployed workers will stop paying income taxes, and will begin receiving unemployment compensation payments from the government. Thus, the deficit will be driven still higher. It is inevitable that the nation will experience budget deficits during periods of recession and high unemployment. The only way to reduce these deficits is to pursue policies that will restore full employment to the economy. Therefore, an annually balanced budget is not feasible.

With a *cyclically balanced budget*, the government would attempt to balance the budget over the course of the business cycle. During periods of recession, there would be deficits because of the loss of tax revenue from unemployed workers and the increased spending for such programs as unemployment compensation. However, as the economy recovered from a recession, the government would receive additional tax dollars from the newly employed workers who are recalled to their jobs and would spend decreasing amounts on unemployment compensation and similar programs. The net result would be a decline in the deficit.

During periods of economic prosperity, when total spending is so high that it threatens to increase the inflation rate, the government would spend less than it collected in taxes, thus creating a budget surplus. Under such a policy, during some years there would be balanced budgets, during other years there would be deficits, and during still other years there would be a surplus in the budget. If the surpluses offset the deficits, over a period of years, total government spending would be approximately equal to total revenue, and thus, there would be a balanced budget over the long run.

The cyclically balanced budget is a far sounder budget policy than the annually balanced budget, and it is much closer to the way family budgets operate. Very few families operate on an annually balanced budget every year throughout their entire lives. Usually, when a young couple gets married and begins a family, they run deficits for the first several years of their married life. They borrow money to buy such things as a car, a home, and furniture. When they purchase these items, they are spending far more than they are earning, so they are running budget deficits. However, after a period of 20 or more years, the home mortgage and other loans should be paid off. At this point, a wise couple will begin saving toward retirement. Therefore, for many years they will be spending less than they earn which will result in surpluses in their budget to offset the deficits of earlier years.

Once they retire, most families will again begin

running deficits in the sense that they are now living off the surpluses they built up over the years when they were saving for retirement. At the end of their lives, most couples will have spent just about as much as they have earned, thus balancing their budgets over a lifetime. Some will have accumulated a surplus which they will leave behind as inheritance for their children, and still others will leave debts behind, meaning they have spent more during their lifetimes than they have earned.

In theory, a cyclically balanced budget would help to even out the high and low points of the business cycle and, at the same time, lead to a balanced budget over the long run. However, in actual practice, the results would be different. Since business cycles are not uniform or predictable, it would be highly unlikely that the surpluses and deficits would exactly cancel one another out in any given time period, even if the government restrained itself and accumulated surpluses during periods of high prosperity. But the big problem is the political feasibility of following such a policy. The government has no problem with running deficits during recession years, but it also runs deficits during the boom years. There is not sufficient political will and discipline to cut back on spending just because that would be good for the economy. Unfortunately, our government has for years spent beyond its means in both recession years and during periods of prosperity.

The other budget alternative is the *full-employment balanced budget.* Under this policy, the federal budget would be balanced when, and only when, the economy is operating at or near the full-employment level. The government would estimate the total revenue that it would receive when the economy was operating at the full-employment level. The budget would then be structured so that spending would not exceed this full-employment revenue. When the economy was operating at the full-employment level, there would be a balanced budget. But, if the economy slipped into a recession, there would be a decline in tax revenue, an increase in government spending for unemployment compensation, and a budget deficit.

This is the budget policy that is probably supported by the largest number of economists. Almost all economists believe the government should have a balanced budget, or perhaps even a small surplus, when the economy is operating at the full-employment level. But, when the economy is operating below the full-employment level, it is necessary for the government to put more money into the economy than it takes out. Thus government spending will exceed tax revenue, resulting in a budget deficit. Under these circumstances, the deficit is actually beneficial to the economy because the excess government expenditure, over the amount of tax revenue collected, will help the economy to recover from the recession. When the economy has recovered from the recession and is once again operating at the full-employment level, the deficit will disappear, and the economy will again have a balanced budget. If the budget is structured so there will be a small surplus, instead of a balanced budget, at the full-employment level, the surpluses might approximately offset the deficits so that an approximately balanced budget could be attained over a period of several years.

In summary, a nation cannot continue to have large budget deficits year after year, indefinitely. The United States government has lived beyond its means during most years for the last quarter century, and the time of reckoning has come. However, we must steer clear of the temptation to try to balance the budget on an annual basis. Such a policy is unworkable. Instead, we need to think in terms of roughly balancing the budget over a period of years.

Chapter Highlights

- Economists usually define fiscal policy as the deliberate use of the government's spending and taxing powers to influence economic activity. The government is practicing fiscal policy when it raises or lowers taxes or changes its spending levels in order to bring about a desired change in the level of total spending and thus the performance of the economy.

- The idea of fiscal policy originated with the publication of *The General Theory of Employment, Interest, and Money*, in 1936, a monumental book written by British economist, John Maynard Keynes. In this book, Keynes set forth a new economic theory that became known as **Keynesian economics**.

- Keynesian economics soon became the predominant body of economic theory in the Western world. Although his theories have undergone substantial refinement and revision, much of modern Keynesian economics is still rooted in the ideas set forth by Keynes. Fiscal policy is a central part of Keynesian economics.

- In 1981, President Reagan abandoned Keynesian economics and launched the nation in a new direction based on a new, untested theory called **supply-side economics**. In a sense, supply-side economics is just the opposite of Keynesian economics. The proponents of supply-side economics argued that policy should be focused on the total supply of goods and services instead of on the total spending for those goods and services.

- Budget deficits occur when the government spends

more money than it collects in the form of tax revenue. The United States ran large budget deficits during the 1980s and early 1990s

- The national debt, which increases every time the government borrows money to cover budget deficits, first reached $1 trillion in 1981, and it had soared to $15 trillion by early 2012.

- Most economists favor balancing the budget under the right circumstances, but few economists support the idea of a balanced budget each and every year. There are basically three alternative balanced-budget policies: the annually balanced budget, the cyclically balanced budget, and the full-employment balanced budget.

Important Terms

Match each of the following terms with the correct definition:

annually balanced budget   Keynesian economics
full-employment balanced budget   fiscal policy
cyclically balanced budget   supply-side economics

1. The deliberate use of the government's spending and taxing powers to influence economic activity in order to accomplish desired economic objectives.

2. Economic theory that emphasizes aggregate supply as a means of increasing production and reducing unemployment.

3. A budget policy under which the federal budget would be balanced when, and only when, the economy is operating at the full-employment level.

4. A body of economic theory based on the belief that the

government should play an active role in maintaining the proper level of aggregate demand.

5. A budget policy under which the government would attempt to balance its budget over the course of the business cycle.

6. A budget policy under which the government would attempt to have a balanced budget each and every year.

Review Questions

1. What are the objectives of fiscal policy? How can fiscal policy be used to reduce unemployment and inflation?

2. What are some of the reasons for the failure of fiscal policy to solve the problems of unemployment and inflation?

3. What are the main ideas behind supply-side economics? How does it differ from Keynesian economics?

4. How successful was supply-side economics in accomplishing the objectives promised by its advocates?

5. Identify three budget policies. How do they differ from one another?

6. How do budget deficits affect the national debt?

Discussion Questions

1. Why is it often difficult for the government to follow consistent and sound fiscal policies?

2. Do you believe the government should have a balanced budget? If so, which budget policy do you believe is best? Give reasons for your answer.

CHAPTER SEVEN

Money and Banking

Money is one of the most crucial and fascinating things in modern society. To a small child, money is magic—pieces of green paper and metal coins that can be exchanged for all sorts of wonderful things. To adults, money is an important item that is needed to buy a home, food, clothes, a car, and many other things. Money is also one of the most misunderstood things in modern society. In the first part of this chapter, we will learn about the functions of money, the characteristics of money, and the kinds of money used in this country. The latter part of the chapter will be devoted to the nation's banking system and monetary policy.

What Is Money?
First we must ask and answer the question, "What is money?" Most Americans would probably answer this question by saying that money consists of coins and paper bills of various denominations. But that would only be a description of some of the things that are used to represent money in this time and place. At various other times and places in history, stones, whale teeth, boar tusks, woodpecker scalps, fishhooks, pearls, sheep, pigs, salt, rice, sugar, and a host of other unlikely materials have served as

money. One of the most interesting units of money in the world is found on the tiny island of Yap in the Pacific Ocean. Large stone wheels or discs—one of them 12 feet in diameter—with holes in the center serve as money for the inhabitants of this 46 square-mile island. The wealthiest people on the island are those who own the most of these heavy stones.

In its broadest definition, *money* is anything that is generally accepted and generally used as a medium of payments. It doesn't matter whether money is made from gold, silver, whale teeth, or just simple pieces of paper. As long as people are willing to accept an item as payment for whatever they have to sell, that item is money.

Functions of Money

Money has three important functions: It serves as a medium of exchange, a measure of value, and a store of value. When we use money both as a medium of exchange and as a measure of value, we are using it as a standard of deferred payments.

A medium is anything that serves as a go-between and makes it easier for something to happen. Therefore, when we say that money is a *medium of exchange*, we mean that money makes it easier to exchange or trade things. Without money people would have to resort to *barter*—a form of trade in which people directly trade goods and services for other types of goods and services without using money. Barter is a very cumbersome form of trade that is not practical in a modern, complex society.

Money also serves as a *measure of value*. This means that money is used to compare the worth of various things. Without money, it would be necessary to state the price of each item in terms of all of the products for which it might be exchanged.

In addition to serving as a medium of exchange and

a measure of value, money also serves as a *store of value*. This means that people can use money as a means to store their wealth. In other words, instead of spending money immediately for some tangible item, the money can be deposited in the bank.

Sometimes we refer to money as serving a fourth function called a *standard of deferred payment*. This involves the use of money both as a medium of exchange and as a measure of value. When we buy something on credit, we use money as a measure of value in that the amount that we will have to pay in the future is stated in dollar terms. When we actually make the payments, we are using money as a medium of exchange.

Characteristics of Money

In order to be effectively used as money, an item must have certain characteristics. It must be durable, accepted, portable, and divisible. Anything used for money must be *durable* so that it can stand the wear and tear that results from it being passed from person to person over a long period of time. It is no wonder that gold and silver were often used as coins. Many ancient coins are still in existence today, thousands of years after they were first created. Paper money is considered durable today only because old bills can be replaced easily when they wear out.

Acceptability means that the item is recognized as money by the general public and will be accepted as payment by almost everyone within the borders of a given country. Just because something is called money doesn't necessarily mean that it will be accepted in that capacity. Although we all take American money for granted, knowing that it will always be accepted in this country, there are many places outside the United States where American money would not be accepted. Likewise, few American merchants would accept another nation's "money."

In order to serve well as a medium of exchange, objects used as money must be able to be carried easily from place to place. Paper money and coins are very *portable* and are commonly used as money in most nations of the world. The huge stones that serve as money on the island of Yap are not very portable and would not be viable as a source of money in a modern economy.

Money must be easily *divisible* so that purchases of any size or price can be made. The American dollar is divisible into coins of different denominations—pennies, nickels, dimes and so forth. The coins can be combined in varying amounts to make change for any purchase.

Types of Money

In the United States, there are basically three types of money: coins, paper money, and checking account money. Let's examine each of these plus some related concepts including debit cards and credit cards.

Coins

Coins—pennies, nickels, dimes, quarters, 50-cent pieces, and dollar coins—make up the smallest part of the nation's money supply. Only about 2 or 3 percent of the nation's total money supply is in the form of coins. Coins are made by the Bureau of the Mint—a part of the U.S. Treasury Department. At one time, all denominations of coins from dimes up contained 90 percent silver and 10 percent copper. The value of the silver in these coins was at least equal to the purchasing power of the coins. In other words, the value of the silver in a quarter was worth at least 25 cents. Today, however, no coins produced for circulation contain silver. Pennies are made of copper and zinc, and all other coins are made of a combination of copper and nickel.

Coins have value today not because of their metal

content but because they are generally accepted in payment and because the government has officially established them as *legal tender*. This means that they must be accepted for all debts, public and private.

Paper Money

Paper money makes up approximately 25 percent of the nation's money supply. Such money consists of Federal Reserve notes issued by the Federal Reserve Banks. Federal Reserve notes are printed by the Bureau of Engraving and Printing in Washington D.C., and then shipped to the Federal Reserve Banks. Like coins, Federal Reserve notes are legal tender. Printed on the front of each Federal Reserve note is the statement, "This note is legal tender for all debts, public and private." This means that, by law, they must be accepted as payment for any and all debts.

Some people have the mistaken notion that paper money is backed by gold or silver. This is not true today, although at one time it was. Until 1933, paper money in the United States was convertible into gold and silver. The Treasury Department kept a substantial amount of gold and silver available so that people could exchange their paper money for the precious metals if they wished to do so. In 1933, however, the United States government abandoned the gold standard, and citizens no longer could convert paper money into gold. (Up until 1968, the government did require that a certain amount of gold be held as partial backing for Federal Reserve notes, but that requirement was also suspended.) Today, there is no gold or silver backing paper money up, and there is nothing magic about these precious metals that requires them to be used to back up paper money. Paper money is money because the United States government has decreed that it is legal tender for all debts, public and private.

Checking Account Money

Checking account money is the largest component of the money supply in the United States. In terms of dollar value, the vast majority of all transactions are carried out by transferring balances between checking accounts. People deposit money in checking accounts, and then write checks against those deposits. Because checking account money is payable on demand to the depositor, or to anyone else, to whom, the check is written, checking accounts are called *demand deposits*. Demand deposits are considered money because they are used as a medium of exchange. In addition to writing checks, payment can be made from checking accounts by online banking. Online banking involves using the internet to transfer balances from one account to another account. Some people do most of their banking online, so they rarely actually write checks or use cash.

Debit Cards and Credit Cards

Debit cards are just a modern alternative to writing checks. When you use a debit card to make a purchase, the money is electronically transferred from your checking account to the account of the business from whom you are making the purchase. You can also withdraw cash from your checking account electronically from automatic teller machines (ATMs) throughout the country. When you use a debit card, you must enter a personal identification number (PIN) into a device, which verifies that you are authorized to make transactions with the debit card.

Credit cards do not serve directly as money. They are simply a means of buying things on credit. When you use a credit card to make a purchase, you are not paying for the purchase with the credit card. The credit card is simply proof that you do have an approved line of credit with the issuer of the credit card. You actually pay for the items purchased on credit with a check when you make your payment to the credit card company on a monthly basis.

The Federal Reserve System

The Federal Reserve System (or the "Fed" as it is usually referred to by the news media) serves as the nation's central monetary authority or "central bank." The central policy-making body of the Federal Reserve System, the Board of Governors, is responsible for supervising the overall operation of the Fed and for formulating and carrying out monetary policy. The seven members of the Board of Governors have enormous economic power. Back when Paul Volker was still chairman of the Federal Reserve Board, *Newsweek* magazine did a cover story on him. The cover of the magazine carried a full-length photograph of the very tall, Mr. Volker, and the words, "The second most powerful man in America." *Newsweek* was not exaggerating, and the statement applies just as much to Volker's successors, Alan Greenspan and Ben Bernanke, as it did to Volker. The chairman of the Federal Reserve Board of Governors has more power than the Vice President, or any other government official except for the President.

Many Americans are probably not even aware that there is such a body as the Federal Reserve Board of Governors, and few would be able to name any member of the board. Yet, these seven people have an enormous impact on the lives of each and every American. They determine how much money banks have available with which to make loans, and they determine overall interest rates. The interest rate you will get on your savings, the interest rate you will pay on your home mortgage or auto loan, and even whether or not you will be able to get such loans, is strongly affected by the decisions and actions of these people. Let's begin our coverage with a look at the organization of the Federal Reserve System.

Organization of the Federal Reserve System

The Federal Reserve System has three levels of organization. At the very top of the organizational structure are the *Board of Governors*, the *Federal Open Market Committee*, and the *Federal Advisory Council*. The second level of organization consists of twelve *Federal Reserve Banks* scattered throughout the United States. And the third level is made up of thousands of *member banks*. Let's examine each of these organizational units of the Federal Reserve System.

Board of Governors

The Board of Governors consists of seven members (prominent bankers, economists, and business executives) who are appointed by the President of the United States and confirmed by the Senate. Each member is appointed for a 14-year term and is ineligible for reappointment. The terms of the seven members are staggered so that a new member is appointed by the President every two years. The President also appoints one of the seven members as chairperson of the Board for a term of four years. Although the chairperson has only one vote on the Board, he has substantially more power than the other members. He meets frequently with Congress to brief them on the state of the economy and what needs to be done in terms of monetary policy.

The Board of Governors is the central policy-making body of the Federal Reserve System. It is responsible for supervising the overall operation of the Fed, and for formulating and carrying out monetary policy. The members of the Board of Governors are seven of the most powerful people in the nation, in terms of the effect their decisions have on the economy. Thus, it is very important that their decisions not be influenced by partisan politics. Fortunately, the creators of the Federal Reserve System took precautions to prevent this from happening. First of all, the Federal Reserve System is an independent government agency. Decisions made by the Board of Governors do not have to be approved by either the President or by Congress. In addition, because Board members serve 14-year terms and are ineligible for reappointment, they do not have to fear losing their jobs because a new President or Congress has been elected. Basically, the Board of Governors remains relatively independent of politics. They can do what they think is best for the economy without worrying about how the voters will react.

Federal Open Market Committee

The Federal Open Market Committee is responsible for directing the buying and selling of government securities in the open market in order to influence interest rates and the availability of credit. This committee consists of the seven members of the Board of Governors plus five presidents of Federal Reserve Banks, for a total of 12 members. We will examine the activities of the Open Market Committee in more detail later in this chapter when we discuss monetary policy.

Federal Advisory Council

The Federal Advisory Council is made up of 12 commercial bankers with one member selected by each of the 12 Federal Reserve Banks. The duties of this council are strictly advisory. It meets periodically with the Board of Governors to report on general business conditions throughout the nation, and to give the Board advice about future banking policies. This council performs an important service by providing a link between bankers and the Board. However, in reality, it has virtually no power, and little impact on the way the Fed carries out its day-to-day activities.

The Federal Reserve Banks

The 1913 Federal Reserve Act, which created the Federal Reserve System, divided the United States into 12 districts and established a separate Federal Reserve Bank for each district. This is in sharp contrast to many nations that have a single central bank. For example, the Bank of England, which was founded in 1694, is a single central bank which serves the entire nation. The 12 Federal Reserve Banks are located in Boston, New York, Philadelphia, Cleveland, Richmond, Atlanta, Chicago, St. Louis, Minneapolis, Kansas City, Dallas, and San Francisco. Some of the 12 Federal Reserve Banks have branch offices in other cities so that transactions between the Federal Reserve Banks and member banks can be carried out more speedily. The activities of the 12 Federal Reserve Banks are coordinated by the Board of Governors, and each individual Federal Reserve Bank is responsible to the Board of Governors. However, the Board may allow individual Federal Reserve Banks to adopt policies designed to deal with special economic conditions existing within their districts.

Member Banks

Commercial banks fall into two categories: national banks, and state banks. National banks are chartered by the federal government, and they are required by law to become members of the Fed. However, state banks are chartered by the individual states, and these banks have the choice to join or not join the Fed.

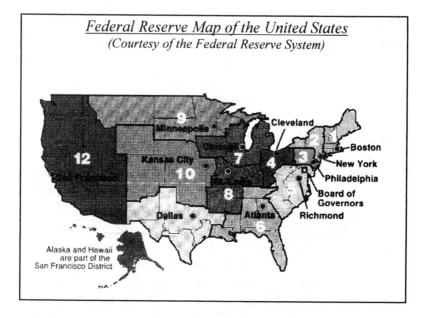

Federal Reserve Map of the United States
(Courtesy of the Federal Reserve System)

The Federal Reserve Banks are "bankers' banks" that deal only with banks and other financial institutions, and with the government. They do not deal directly with the public. You could not walk into a Federal Reserve Bank and open an account or cash a check. Each Federal Reserve Bank is owned by the member commercial banks in its district, which are required to buy shares of stock in their Federal Reserve Bank when they become members of the Fed. Although the Federal Reserve Banks are privately owned, the primary objective of the Federal Reserve Banks is to carry out the monetary policies established by the Board of Governors. In addition, most of the earnings of the Federal Reserve Banks are returned to the U.S. Treasury each year.

Prior to 1980, nonmember state banks were not subject to the control of the Fed. This is a major reason why many chose not to join. State banks at that time were subject to control by state agencies with controls far less strict than those of the Fed. However, the 1980 changes in the banking laws eliminated much of the distinction between member banks and nonmember banks. Today, all state banks, including those that are not members of the Federal Reserve System, must abide by the rules and regulations of the Fed. In addition, nonmember banks as well as member banks have access to the services that are provided by the Fed.

Functions of the Federal Reserve System

The most important function of the Fed is controlling the nation's money supply. It is so important that we will devote much of the remainder of this chapter to an examination of how and why the Fed makes changes in the money supply. However, first let's briefly examine some of the other functions.

A very important function of the Fed is the clearing of checks. Each year, billions of checks are written by individuals, businesses, and the various agencies of government. Each of these checks represents an order to transfer funds from the account of the check writer to the recipient of the check. Sometimes the check clearance process can be very simple. However, at other times, it can be quite complicated.

For example, suppose you order an item from a catalog mail order store in Sacramento, California. Since you live in central Illinois, you will write a check on your local bank and send it, along with your order, to Sacramento. What this check represents is simply a message on a piece of paper instructing your bank to pay a certain amount of money from your account to the Sacramento store. How does this message (check) get from the Sacramento store back to your local bank in Illinois so they can actually pay for your order?

First of all, when the Sacramento store receives

your check along with the order, it will deposit the check in its account at a Sacramento bank. The Sacramento bank will then deposit the check in its account at the Federal Reserve Bank in San Francisco. The next step will be for the Federal Reserve Bank of San Francisco to send the check to the Federal Reserve Bank of Chicago which will deduct the amount of the check from the account of your bank and then forward the check to your bank. Finally, when your bank receives the check it will deduct the amount from your account.

Another important function of the Fed is to serve as a fiscal agent for the federal government. The United States Treasury collects huge sums of money through taxation, and it deposits much of this money in Federal Reserve Banks in checking accounts that are used for such things as tax refunds, Social Security payments and government purchases of goods and services. In addition, the Fed helps the Treasury in its efforts to borrow money by selling government securities, such as U.S. Treasury bonds.

The Fed also performs various supervisory functions intended to ensure that the member banks are in compliance with the banking laws and that they are engaging in sound banking practices. Among these functions are making sure that member banks have adequate funds, overseeing bank mergers, and setting limits for loans by member banks. The Fed also works closely with the Federal Deposit Insurance Corporation, in making sure that all bank deposits are insured.

In addition, the Fed has the responsibility of holding *required reserves.* Banks and other financial institutions are required by law to keep a certain percentage of the money they receive as deposits as required reserves to back up the deposits. One of the important functions of each Federal Reserve Bank is to hold the required reserves of the depository institutions within its district. The Fed has the power to change the percentage of deposits that must be kept as required reserves. This is one of the ways the Fed can increase or decrease the money supply.

Still another very important function of the Fed is to supply paper currency. Paper currency in the United States consists of Federal Reserve Notes that are issued by the Federal Reserve Banks. Although the actual printing of the notes is done by the Bureau of Engraving and Printing in Washington, D.C., each Federal Reserve Note has a seal on the left side of the front indicating which of the 12 Federal Reserve Banks issued it. For example, Federal Reserve Notes issued by the Federal Reserve Bank of New York have a capital letter B printed on them with the name of the bank indicated in the circle that surrounds the B.

Many of the new Federal Reserve Notes are issued to replace old ones that are taken out of circulation because they are torn or worn out. However, the public demands more paper currency at certain times of the year than at others. For example, Americans withdraw large amounts of cash from the banks during the Christmas shopping season each year. In order to meet the increased demand for paper money, commercial banks must withdraw additional Federal Reserve Notes from their accounts with the Federal Reserve Banks. After Christmas, much of the currency is returned to commercial banks. They in turn redeposit that currency with the Federal Reserve Banks.

The most important function of the Fed is regulating the amount of money in circulation. This function is especially important to each and every American because the amount of money in circulation affects the cost and availability of credit as well as the level of business activity in the economy. As a first step toward understanding monetary policy, let's see how banks create money.

How Banks Create Money

In this section, we will examine how banks as a group are able to create money and how the Fed regulates the capacity of banks to create money. We will begin with a look at the relationship between demand deposits and the money supply.

Demand Deposits and Money Creation

Demand deposits are checking accounts. They are called demand deposits because they are payable on demand. You can go to your bank and demand all the money from your checking account without paying any penalty for early withdrawal. When you write checks to other people against your checking account, you are ordering the banks to pay these people the money on demand. By contrast, some types of savings accounts are not payable on demand, in the sense that you cannot write a check against these accounts. You must go to the bank to get your money and, in some cases, such as certificates of deposit, you cannot withdraw the money prior to the maturity date without paying a substantial penalty.

Since demand deposits (checking accounts) are payable upon demand, and since you can buy things and make payments by writing checks against these accounts, they are considered a part of the nation's money supply. The money supply is the total amount of money in circulation. The total money supply consists of coins and paper money (Federal Reserve Notes) in circulation, plus demand deposits (checkbook money.) Coins make up only about 2 or 3 percent of the nation's total money supply. Federal Reserve Notes make up approximately 25 percent of the nation's money supply. And demand deposits make up more then 70 percent of the money supply in the United States. Approximately 90 percent of the dollar value, of all transactions in the United States, involve balance transfers between checking accounts. Thus, demand deposits are the most important component of the money supply.

Demand deposits can originate or change in size in two ways. One way involves the deposit of cash or checks in demand deposits. This practice does not change the nation's money supply. When you deposit $100 of cash in your checking account, you are just trading one kind of money for another. However, the other way in which demand deposits can originate, or change in size, does change the nation's money supply. It involves borrowing money and having it deposited in demand deposits.

If you go into your bank, borrow $1,000, and have it deposited in your checking account, when you walk out of the bank you will have $1,000 more in checkbook money than when you entered the bank. Nobody else's account was decreased in order for you to obtain the $1,000 loan. Thus, not only do you have $1,000 more in money, but the nation's money supply has grown by $1,000. By loaning you the $1,000, your bank has increased the nation's money supply by that amount.

Banks, and our banking system as a whole, create money by making loans. However, the amount of money that banks can create by making loans is not unlimited. The amount of money that banks can lend out is restricted by reserve requirements imposed on them by the Fed.

Reserve Requirements

When you deposit money in your bank, the bank can lend out a portion of it. But the bank must keep a certain percentage of the money as reserves to back up your deposit. Reserves must be kept either in the form of cash in the bank's vault, or as deposits with its Federal Reserve Bank. The percentage of deposits that must be kept to back up these deposits is called the *reserve requirement*. If the reserve requirement is 10 percent, a bank that holds deposits totaling $100 million must keep $10 million in reserves. If the reserve requirement is 14 percent, the bank would have to hold $14 million in reserves. Because banks are required to keep only a fraction of their deposits as reserves, the rest of the money can be invested or loaned out.

Most banks have actual reserves (deposits with the Federal Reserve Banks plus vault cash) in excess of the amount of required reserves that they must hold. The difference between actual reserves and required reserves is known as *excess reserves*. A bank can lend only as much as it has in excess reserves. For example, if a bank has $15 million of actual reserves, of which $12 million is required reserves, it would have $3 million of excess reserves with which it could make loans. When the bank makes loans from its excess reserves, it creates money and increases the nation's money supply.

Deposit Expansion by the Banking System

You have just learned that a single bank can lend only as much as it has in excess reserves. However, the banking system as a whole (all the nation's banks together) can make enough loans to increase the money supply by a multiple of excess reserves. Let's look at a hypothetical example to see how this multiple expansion occurs.

Suppose that your bank, Bank A, has no excess reserves with which to make loans, and assume the reserve requirement is 10 percent. Now suppose you deposit $100,000 in your checking account at Bank A. How much money can be created as a result of this transaction? The answer may surprise you.

First of all, your bank must set aside $10,000 (10 percent of the $100,000) as required reserves to back up your deposit. The remaining $90,000 is excess reserves and can be loaned out. Suppose Bank A loans Arnold Alexander the $90,000 so he can purchase a home from Steve Stoner. As soon as Steve Stoner receives the money, he takes it to his bank, Bank B, and deposits it in his checking account. Bank B now has new lending power. It must set aside $9,000 as required reserves (10 percent of $90,000), but the other $81,000 is excess reserves which Bank B uses to make a loan to Joyce Johnson.

When Joyce Johnson uses the money to purchase a home from Richard Robinson, Mr. Robinson immediately takes the $81,000 to his bank, Bank C, and deposits it in his account. Bank C must now set aside 10 percent of the new money ($8,100) as required reserves, but it has $72,900 in new excess reserves which it lends to Dale Deaver.

Let's now see how much money has been loaned out and how much the nation's money supply has grown simply because you decided to deposit $100,000 in your account at Bank A. Because of the $90,000 of new excess reserves that Bank A acquired when you made your deposit, it was able to loan $90,000 to Arnold Alexander. This loan ultimately enabled Bank B to loan $81,000 to Joyce Johnson. And, when Joyce Johnson spends the $81,000, it ends up in Bank C, enabling Bank C to lend $72,900 to Dale Dever. Thus, a total of $243,900 has already been loaned out, and the nation's money supply has grown by $243,900 simply because you made your deposit of $100,000 in Bank A, thus providing it with $90,000 in excess reserves. As amazing as this may seem, it is only the beginning. The multiple expansion process can continue indefinitely throughout the banking system with a potential of $900,000 in new loans and, thus, an increase of $900,000 in the money supply resulting from the initial $90,000 in excess reserves.

The amount of new loans, and the increase in the money supply that can result from a given amount of excess reserves, depends on the deposit multiplier. The deposit multiplier is the reciprocal of the reserve requirement. In simpler terms, the deposit multiplier can be calculated by expressing the reserve requirement in hundredths, instead of in percentage terms (10 percent = 10/100) and then turning it upside down. For example, a 10 percent reserve requirement equals 10/100. Turn the 10/100 upside down and you get 100/10 or 10. Thus, when the reserve requirement is 10 percent, the deposit multiplier is 10. This is how we know that the initial $90,000 in excess reserves can generate a potential growth in the money supply of $900,000 ($90,000 x 10 = $900,000).

Suppose that when you made your $100,000 deposit the reserve requirement had been 20 percent, instead of 10 percent. In this case, your bank would have been required to set aside $20,000 as required reserves (20 percent of $100,000). This would have left the bank with $80,000 of excess reserves. With a reserve requirement of 20 percent, the deposit multiplier would have been 5. This is calculated by taking 20/100 and turning it upside down (100/20 = 5). Since 5 x $80,000 = $400,000, the $80,000 in excess reserves could have generated a potential increase in the money supply of $400,000 as compared to the $900,000 generated when the reserve requirement was 10 percent.

You should now begin to see how the Fed regulates the nation's money supply. The Fed has the power to change the amount of excess reserves held by banks, and it also has the power to change the reserve requirements. Changes of this type are a part of the Fed's monetary policy. Let's now examine monetary policy in more detail.

Monetary Policy

The Federal Reserve System attempts to control the nation's money supply and interest rates in order to achieve desired economic objectives. The various actions taken by the Fed in order to accomplish its goals are called monetary policy. The economic objectives that the Fed attempts to achieve through monetary policy are economic growth, low unemployment and relatively stable prices. When unemployment is low and inflation is rising, the Fed would want to restrict the growth in the money supply. A decline in the growth of the money supply would make it more difficult to obtain loans, and would cause interest rates to rise. This would cause businesses to reduce investment spending, and consumers to cut back on consumption spending. Thus, by making credit more difficult to obtain, and more costly, the Fed can reduce the level of total spending in the economy and thus reduce inflationary pressures. ⌈During periods when the Fed is restricting the availability of credit, and forcing interest rates higher, economists say that it is pursuing a *tight-money policy.*⌋

On the other hand, when the economy is in severe recession with unemployment rising, the Fed would want to increase the money supply in order to make loans more readily available, and to force interest rates down. Lower interest rates would tend to cause an increase in consumer and business spending. This increase in the level of total spending would help to bring the economy out of the recession because, as people spend more money on goods and services, laid-off workers will be recalled and production will increase. ⌈During periods when the Fed is expanding the money supply and reducing interest rates, economists say that it is pursuing an *easy-money policy.*⌋

The Fed has three major instruments that it can use in its attempt to control the money supply and interest rates. They are (1) changing reserve requirements; (2) changing short-term interest rates; and (3) open-market operations. Let's examine each of these instruments of monetary policy.

Changing Reserve Requirements

As you have already learned, the amount of money that a bank, or the banking system, can lend out depends upon the amount of excess reserves held, and the reserve requirement. The Fed has the power to change the reserve requirements within stipulated limits established by law. By increasing reserve requirements, the Fed can decrease the banks' excess reserves and thus their lending capacity. Likewise, by decreasing reserve requirements, the Fed can increase banks' excess reserves and their lending capacity. Remember that excess reserves are the difference between actual reserves and required reserves, and that banks can lend only the amount of their excess reserves. Thus, by changing reserve requirements, the Fed can change the lending capacity of banks and the money supply of the nation.

If the economy were in a recession with high unemployment, the Fed might want to reduce the reserve requirement. This would give banks more excess reserves and lending capacity. This would result in an increase in the money supply and a reduction in interest rates. These two changes, in combination, could help to bring the economy out of a recession.

However, if the problem was demand-pull inflation, instead of unemployment, the Fed would probably increase reserve requirements, which would reduce excess reserves and the lending capacity of banks. This would cause a decrease in the money supply and an increase in interest rates. Since people would spend less under such a policy, demand-pull inflation should be reduced.

Changing Key Interest Rates

Usually banks obtain most of the funds which they use for loans from depositors. However, banks do occasionally borrow emergency funds from their Federal Reserve Banks or other banks. For example, if a bank should experience large unexpected withdrawals, it might have to borrow funds just to meet its reserve requirement. The rate of interest that Federal Reserve Banks charge banks and other financial institutions for such loans is called the *discount rate*, and the interest rate that banks charge each other on overnight loans is called the *federal funds rate*. A change in these key short-term interest rates by the Fed sends a signal to the banking and business communities about the kind of monetary policy the Fed plans to pursue. If the Fed lowers interest rates, it probably indicates that the Fed is pursuing an easy-money policy. On the other hand, an increase in rates usually indicates a tight-money policy.

An increase in the key rates is usually followed by a similar increase in the rate of interest that banks and other lending institutions charge their customers. The *prime rate* (the rate of interest that large city banks charge their best business customers) usually follows changes in the discount and federal funds rates. For example, if the Fed should increase the key rates by 1/2 percent, most large banks would probably increase the prime rate by the same amount within a short period of time. Thus, an increase in the key rates usually signals a rise in general interest rates. This affects borrowing and thus credit spending.

Open-Market Operations
The monetary policy most often used by the Fed is open-market operations, which are directed by the Federal Open Market Committee that was described earlier in this chapter. Open-market operations involve the buying and selling of United States government securities by the Fed in the open market. The term, open market, refers to the fact that the buying and selling takes place in the same securities markets that are open to ordinary citizens and businesses. The purpose of open-market operations is to increase or decrease the reserves, and thus the lending capacity, of banks and other financial institutions. When the Fed buys securities in the open market, the reserves of banks and other financial institutions are increased. The Fed buys securities in the open market from whomever is

selling them. It might be banks, or private individuals, or businesses. It doesn't matter from whom the Fed buys. The point is that the Fed must pay for these securities, and the money the Fed spends on them will end up in the nation's banks as additional reserves, thus increasing the lending capacity of the banks. In short, when the Fed buys securities in the open market, it pumps additional money into the economy. The net result will be lower interest rates, increased availability of credit, and thus an increase in total spending which will create additional jobs.

When the Fed sells securities in the open market, the buyers must pay the Fed money for the securities. Thus, the reserves held by the banking system are decreased. As the reserves are reduced, so is the lending capacity of banks. This causes a decrease in the nation's money supply which will result in higher interest rates, a reduction in the availability of credit, and a reduction in total spending.

Usually, the Fed would want to buy securities and pump additional money into the economy during periods when total spending is not sufficient to provide full employment in the economy. The increase in the money supply and lower interest rates may result in additional total spending, and thus more jobs. On the other hand, if the economy is operating at the full-employment level, and is experiencing demand-pull inflation because there is too much total spending, the Fed would probably want to sell securities in the open market in order to pump money out of the economy and thus reduce the level of total spending.

Monetarism

Although most economists believe that the money supply plays an important role in the American economy, some economists place much greater emphasis on the relationship between the money supply and economic activity than others. A school of economic thought called, *monetarism*, takes the position that the money supply is the key factor in determining the economic health of the nation. Economists who believe in the doctrine of monetarism are called monetarists. These economists argue that the erratic changes in the money supply are the dominant cause of business cycles. They believe that the economy would be relatively stable if we did not have the large fluctuations in the rate of growth of the money supply that are caused by the Fed's monetary policy.

Because they believe that changes in the money supply are the chief determinant of economic activity, monetarists generally oppose the use of fiscal policy to regulate the level of total spending. Monetarists also oppose the use of monetary policy as a means of attempting to increase or decrease the level of total spending. Instead, the monetarists believe that the money supply should grow at a fixed rate of about 3 to 4 percent per year, because they believe the economy's long-term potential rate of sustainable growth in GDP is about 3 to 4 percent. The monetarists believe such a policy would permit the economy to stabilize itself and avoid both high inflation and high unemployment.

Monetarists got their first opportunity to put their theories into practice when the Fed decided in October 1979 to base monetary policy on money supply targets rather than on manipulating interest rates to desired levels. The Fed's change in policy was inspired by the then new Fed Chairman, Paul T. Volker, who argued that control of the money supply was necessary to control the rate of inflation. The Fed's experiment with strict money-supply targeting did not last long. Their strict constraint on the growth of the money supply drove the prime interest rate up to 18 1/2 percent in 1981. And, although the Fed's policy did reduce the inflation rate, the tight-money policy also contributed to the worst recession and the highest unemployment since the Great Depression of the 1930s.

Thus, in 1982, with the unemployment rate averaging 9.5 percent, the Fed suspended its experiment with money-supply targeting.

Most economists believe the view of the monetarists is too narrow and too simplistic. They believe that both monetary and fiscal policy can be used to smooth out the extremes of the business cycle. Mainstream economists believe that the failure to use fiscal policy to stimulate the economy during periods of severe recession or depression results in unnecessary, prolonged unemployment that imposes a heavy cost on society in terms of individual suffering as well as lost production.

Chapter Highlights

- The Federal Reserve System, which was established by the 1913 Federal Reserve Act, consists of three levels of organization. The first level consists of the Board of Governors, the Federal Open Market Committee, and the Federal Advisory Council. The second level consists of 12 Federal Reserve Banks, and the third level is made up of thousands of member banks.

- The Board of Governors is responsible for supervising the overall operation of the Fed and for formulating and carrying out monetary policy. It consists of seven members, appointed by the President and confirmed by the Senate for 14-year terms.

- The Federal Open-Market Committee consists of the seven members of the Board of Governors plus five presidents of Federal Reserve Banks for a total of 12 members. This committee is responsible for directing the buying and selling of government securities in the open market in order to influence interest rates and the availability of credit. The Federal Advisory Council consists of 12 commercial bankers who advise the Board of Governors about banking policy.

- The Federal Reserve Act divided the United States into 12 districts and established a separate Federal Reserve Band for each district. The Federal Reserve Banks are "bankers' banks" that deal only with financial institutions and the government. They are owned by the member banks in the districts but their primary objective is to carry out the monetary policies established by the Board of Governors.

- Important functions of the Federal Reserve System include clearing checks; serving as the fiscal agent for the federal government; supervising member banks: holding required reserves of banks and other financial institutions; supplying the nation's paper currency; and regulating the money supply.

- Banks as a group can create money in the form of demand deposits by making loans. The capacity of banks to create money depends on the amount of excess reserves—actual reserves minus required reserves—they hold and the Fed's reserve requirements.

- Monetary policy can be defined as actions taken by the Fed to control the nation's money supply and interest rates in order to achieve low unemployment and relatively stable prices. The three major instruments of monetary policy are changing reserve requirements, changing the discount rate, and open-market operations.

- A school of economic thought called monetarism takes the position that the money supply is the key factor in determining the economic health of the nation.

- Monetary policy affects the entire economy, but in particular it affects investment in factories and equipment, the housing market, and consumer spending. It also has an enormous impact on individual borrowers and savers.

Important Terms

Match each of the following terms with the correct definition:

Federal Advisory Council   easy-money policy
Federal Open Market Committee   monetarism
Board of Governors   discount rate
open-market operations   required reserves
member banks   monetary policy
Federal Reserve System   tight-money policy
Federal Reserve Banks   excess reserves
prime rate

1. Commercial banks that are members of the Federal Reserve System.

2. The nation's central monetary authority or "central bank."

3. A school of economic thought that takes the position that the money supply is the key factor determining the economic health of the nation.

4. The amount of reserves that a bank is required to hold as backing for money that has been deposited with it.

5. The buying and selling by the Fed of government securities in the open market.

6. The rate of interest that Federal Reserve Banks charge banks for loans.

7. The central policy-making body of the Federal Reserve System.

8. The Board of Governors plus five presidents of Federal Reserve Banks.

9. Actual reserves minus required reserves.

10. Twelve commercial bankers who advise the Board of Governors on banking policy.

11. Twelve banks established by the Federal Reserve Act of 1913.

12. The rate of interest that large banks charge their best business customers.

13. A policy of expanding the money supply and reducing interest rates.

14. Actions taken by the Fed to control the nation's money supply and interest rates.

15. A policy of restricting the availability of credit and forcing interest rates up.

Review Questions

1. How is the Federal Reserve System organized?

2. What functions are performed by the Board of Governors? The Federal Open Market Committee?

3. How many Federal Reserve Banks are there? What functions do they serve?

4. What are the primary functions of the Federal Reserve System? Which is the most important?

5. Describe the check-clearing process.

6. In what two ways do demand deposits originate or change in size? Which of these ways changes the money supply? Why?

7. What are excess reserves? How are they calculated?

8. How does the banking system as a whole increase the money supply?

9. Define monetary policy. What is meant by a tight-money policy? An easy money policy?

10. How do changes in the reserve requirements affect the lending capacity of banks?

11. What is the discount rate? Why does the Fed change it from time to time?

12. What are open-market operations? What is their purpose?

Discussion Questions

1. Do you think the actions of the Board of Governors should be regulated by the President and Congress? Why or why not?

2. Which instrument of monetary policy do you think is most effective in regulating the money supply?

CHAPTER EIGHT

International Trade and Finance

Have you ever felt guilty about buying a foreign-made automobile, appliance, or article of clothing? There are some people in this country who still feel it is unpatriotic to buy foreign-made products. During the recession of 1981-82, when American automobile sales were down, Japanese automobiles were placed in front of American auto plants by company officials who supplied workers with sledge hammers to smash the foreign-made cars. As workers vented their frustration by pounding on the foreign-made automobiles with sledge hammers, the implication was that the foreign products were the enemy that was causing the high unemployment in this country. Many people seemed to think that, if only we could prevent the sale of foreign-made products in this country, our unemployment problems would be over.

People who think in these terms simply do not understand how the world economy operates. They fail to see that many American jobs are dependent on sales to foreign countries. If we restrict imports to save the jobs of some Americans, we will lose export sales that will cost other American workers their jobs. Furthermore, many of those people who condemn others for buying foreign products are doing the very same thing themselves. It is almost impossible to avoid buying some foreign-made products today.

For example, suppose you buy a new small American-brand automobile, and your neighbor buys a new Japanese-brand car. Who is most patriotic, in terms of supporting American workers? It may turn out to be your neighbor. His foreign-brand automobile may have been manufactured in the United States by American workers while your American-brand automobile may have been manufactured in a foreign country by foreign workers. American automobile companies have many manufacturing plants in foreign countries today where they hire foreign workers to produce the cars. At the same time, a number of new plants have been built in the United States by foreign automobile manufacturers who hire American workers. Even if you buy an American-brand automobile that was assembled in the United States, it is very likely that some of the parts used to assemble the car were manufactured in other countries.

In this chapter we will try to clarify some of the confusion that exists with regard to international trade and finance. Let's begin by looking at why countries trade.

Why Countries Trade

Countries engage in international trade for the same reasons that individuals specialize in specific careers. They do it because specialization increases total output. Suppose you decided to try to become totally self-sufficient. You would have to build your own shelter, grow your own food, make your own clothing, build your own source of transportation, take care of your own medical problems, and so forth. If you attempted to do this, you would not live nearly as well as you do now because you would have so many jobs to do that you would not be very good at any of them. Thus, your standard of living would not be very high.

Doesn't it make more sense to specialize in a specific career so that you can become very good at the work you do? This will enable you to earn enough money to buy other things you need from other "specialists." You will have skilled carpenters, plumbers, and electricians construct your home, and you will allow professional farmers to grow your food. By doing this, you will have a much higher standard of living than if you tried to produce everything yourself. With all people specializing in what they do best, more goods and services are produced, and everyone is better off.

Differences in Resources of Nations

Just as a single nation is able to produce a great deal more when individuals specialize in what they can do best, total world production of goods and services is much greater when nations specialize in producing the things they can produce most efficiently. There are substantial differences in the resources that various nations possess. Thus, by specializing in the production of things that they can produce most efficiently with the resources they have, the nations of the world can produce a great deal more than if each nation tried to be self-sufficient.

For example, Canada has huge forests that make possible the production of lumber and paper products for sale to foreign nations. Ecuador has an ideal climate for the production of bananas, and it exports more bananas than any other nation. Both Columbia and Brazil have ideal growing conditions for coffee, and thus they are the world's leading producers of that crop. Some countries have large oil reserves, and many coastal nations have rich fishing grounds off their coasts.

The United States does not have the right resources for the efficient production of coffee or bananas. However, our country has an abundance of many very important, and valuable, productive resources. We have a highly skilled labor force, considerable technological knowledge, and large quantities of capital goods (factories, tools, machines, and so forth). Thus, the United States is well suited for the production of many complex manufactured products, such as computers and other electronic equipment, as well as farm machinery. In addition, the United States has some of the best soil and growing conditions found anywhere in the world. Since we are able to produce much more food than our people can eat, we are a major food exporter.

The Concept of Absolute Advantage

Because the various nations have different kinds and quantities of resources, some countries can produce certain products more efficiently than other countries. A nation that can produce a particular product more efficiently than another nation is said to have an *absolute advantage* in the production of that product. This means that, given a set amount of resources, the country can produce more of the product than the other nation can. In other words, one country has an absolute advantage over another country in producing a product when it can use fewer resources than the other country to produce the same quantity of the product.

Certainly Ecuador has an absolute advantage over the United States in the production of bananas because Ecuador has the ideal climate for growing bananas naturally. Although a few people in southern Florida raise bananas in their gardens, most of the United States is not suitable for growing this tropical fruit. The only way the United States could produce large quantities of bananas would be in expensive, heated greenhouses with controlled environments. Thus, it would take substantially more resources in the United States to produce a given quantity of bananas than would be required to produce an equal quantity in Ecuador. In fact, producing bananas in an artificial environment would be so expensive that the price of bananas would be so high that few people would be able or willing to buy them.

It usually does not make good economic sense for a country to produce a product that will cost a lot more than would be the case if it imported the product from another country. It is usually best for each nation to produce what it is most efficient at producing and then trade with other nations for the products it cannot produce efficiently.

Although Ecuador has an absolute advantage over the United States in the production of bananas, the United States has an absolute advantage over Ecuador in the production of wheat, corn, soybeans, beef, steel, and most other items. Actually, the United States has an absolute advantage over most nations in the production of most commodities. Does this mean that the United States cannot benefit from trading with other nations, except for products in which other nations have an absolute advantage? No, because a country can benefit from international trade even when it has an absolute advantage in the production of most products. This is true because the United States has a greater absolute advantage in the production of some products than it has in the production of other products.

The Concept of Comparative Advantage
Suppose that a lawyer is more efficient in general office skills than his or her assistant. This means the lawyer has an absolute advantage over the assistant in both office skills and in the practice of law. Does this mean that the lawyer should do the office work in addition to practicing law? No. The lawyer can earn a great deal more per hour by practicing law than by doing office chores. Suppose the lawyer can earn $200 per hour practicing law and pays an assistant $20 per hour for the work he or she does. In other words, the lawyer can earn ten times as much per hour practicing law as can be earned by doing office work. Therefore, the lawyer should specialize in

practicing law and pay the assistant to do the office work.

In economic terms, the lawyer has a *comparative advantage* in the practice of law because the absolute advantage of practicing law is greater than the absolute advantage of doing office work. Whenever an individual, or a nation, has an absolute advantage in the production of two goods or services, the individual or nation has a comparative advantage in the production of that good or service where the absolute advantage is greater.

Let's suppose the United States has an absolute advantage over another country in the production of both product A and product B. However, the absolute advantage is much greater in the production of product A than in the production of product B. In fact, the United States can produce five times as much of product A as the other nation, with a given amount of resources. However, the United States can produce only twice as much of product B as the other nation, with a given quantity of resources. Although the United States has an absolute advantage in the production of both products, its absolute advantage is much greater in the production of product A than its absolute advantage in the production of product B. Therefore, the United States has a comparative advantage in the production of Product A.

Anytime a nation has an absolute advantage in the production of two products, it has a comparative advantage in the production of the product where the absolute advantage is greater. Likewise, in the case of a country which has an absolute disadvantage in the production of two products, it has a comparative advantage in the production of the product where the absolute disadvantage is least.

If all nations of the world specialize in the production of those products in which they have a comparative advantage, the world's resources will be used more efficiently, and total world production will be much greater than if all nations tried to become self-sufficient. In short, the main reason that countries engage in international trade is that, when each nation specializes in the production of those things it can produce most efficiently, and then trades with other nations for the products that other nations can produce most efficiently, all nations benefit.

Barriers to Trade

Most people have a very poor understanding of international trade, and thus they cannot see how we are benefiting by importing products from foreign nations. Thus, there are always many people, including some members of Congress, who advocate restrictions on international trade. The most common barriers to trade are *tariffs* and *import quotas*. A tariff is a tax imposed by the government on imported products. Tariffs raise the price of imported products, making it easier for domestic producers to compete with imports. While the tariffs may benefit American producers who compete with foreign-made products, they hurt American consumers who must pay more for what they buy because of the tariffs.

An import quota places a precise legal limit on the number of units of a particular product that can be imported into the country during a specific time period. For example, the United States government might establish an import quota on the number of automobiles that could be imported from Japan per year. Once the quota had been reached, no more autos from Japan could be imported during that time period even though there might be many American consumers wanting to buy them.

Most economists oppose tariffs and import quotas. They believe that both do more harm than good. Usually, when the United States imposes new tariffs or import quotas, other nations retaliate by imposing similar trade barriers against American products sold in their markets. The net result is that none of the nations have improved their economic situation. Generally, economists believe that the more trade that takes place, the better off all nations of the world will be, including the United States.

Arguments For and Against Trade Barriers

Trade barriers are always very controversial because they usually help some people and hurt others. Let's briefly examine some of the arguments used by supporters of trade barriers, as well as the responses given by their opponents.

National Security Argument

The national security argument is based on the assumption that a country should be as self-sufficient as possible in the production of goods needed for war and national defense. For example, proponents of this viewpoint argue that the United States should not become too dependent on foreign-made steel because steel is a crucial ingredient in the manufacture of military weapons. If the United States were to become involved in a war, these people argue that foreign supplies might be interrupted. The same argument is used for many other products, but critics believe that some industries have overstated their case in seeking protection on these grounds.

Infant Industry Argument

The infant industry argument is most relevant to the underdeveloped countries of the world. It is based on the belief that certain new industries (infant industries) should be protected from foreign competition until they have developed sufficient technological efficiency and large-scale production to enable them to compete in world markets. For example, if one of the developing countries wanted to develop a domestic automobile industry, it would need protection from foreign imports for a few years in order to stand any chance of survival. This is true because, during the first few years of such an industry, the costs of producing automobiles would probably exceed the cost of importing automobiles from other nations. This argument might have merit in some of the developing countries of the world, but it is difficult to make a case on these grounds for protection of American industries.

Employment Protection Argument

The employment protection argument is probably the most emotionally charged and most frequently used of all arguments in favor of trade barriers. This argument is based on the notion that a reduction in imports would lead to more American jobs, or at least provide protection for existing jobs. Those who argue for employment protection often attempt to appeal to people's sense of patriotism by urging them to buy American-made products, and they often suggest that people who buy foreign-made products are contributing to the nation's unemployment problem. Economists, however, emphasize the fact that many American jobs are dependent on sales to foreign countries and, in international trade, goods pay for goods. A nation that exports goods must also import goods, and any attempt to reduce imports probably will result in a similar reduction in exports. Thus, although trade barriers may help to protect the jobs of some workers, they tend to cost other workers (those who produce goods for export) their jobs.

Wage Protection Argument

The basis of the wage protection argument is that, because wages are higher in the United States than in most other industrialized countries, tariffs or import quotas are needed to protect wages of American workers from the threat of "cheap labor" from abroad. Advocates of this argument contend that a high-wage nation cannot compete successfully with low-wage nations. However, economists point out that many products produced in this country do compete quite successfully with products made elsewhere because labor is only one component of production costs. In many American industries, labor is combined with highly efficient equipment that is not available in many other countries. As a result, the prices of American products are often comparable to similar foreign-made products from low-wage countries.

The Inevitability of Trade Barriers

Economists generally agree that trade barriers benefit some groups at the expense of the rest of society. In one study, 97 percent of economists agreed that tariffs and import quotas lower real income. Thus, if the only goal of society was to maximize world production of goods and services, all nations would produce those products in which they have a comparative advantage, and there would be no trade barriers.

Life, however, is not that simple. Nations must worry about national security, and politicians must worry about getting reelected. As a result, many prominent people, including some business executives, labor leaders, and politicians, continue to support restrictions on international trade. Thus, there will probably always be some trade barriers, although most economists will continue to argue that it is in society's best interest to keep such barriers to a minimum.

International Finance

International trade involves international financial transactions because different countries have different units of money. When Americans wish to buy goods from other nations, they usually must pay for the goods in the currency of the exporting country. In other words, Japan will probably demand yen, France will demand francs, West Germany will want deutsche marks, Great Britain will insist on pounds, and Mexico will demand pesos in payment for the goods they sell. Foreign currencies are called *foreign exchange*, and they are bought and sold in *foreign exchange markets,* which are markets that deal in the buying and selling of foreign currencies. Some banks specialize in financing international trade, and they are the major participants in foreign exchange markets. If an American importer wishes to buy automobiles from a Japanese manufacturer, the importer will go to a bank that specializes in financing international trade, and will exchange dollars for yen.

Exchange Rates

The *foreign exchange rate* is the price of one currency in terms of another. For example, the British pound might be worth $1.70 in American money. Historically, there have been two major types of foreign exchange rates: fixed exchange rates and flexible exchange rates.

Under the *fixed-exchange-rate* system, the price of one currency was fixed in terms of other currencies so that the rate did not change. The advantage of such a system is that importers and exporters know exactly how much foreign currency they can purchase with a given quantity of their own nation's currency today, next week, or six months from now. Foreign exchange markets operated under a fixed-exchange-rate system from 1944 until the early 1970s. Prior to 1971, the value of the United States dollar was tied to gold at the rate of $1 equals 1/35 of an ounce of gold. In other words, one ounce of gold was equal to $35 in American money. Since the value of other currencies was also fixed in relation to gold, the dollar price of each foreign currency remained constant.

The disadvantage of the fixed-rate system was that it did not make allowances for changing economic conditions in various countries. For example, if the United

States was experiencing high inflation at a time when Japan was experiencing little or no inflation, American-made goods would become increasingly expensive in relation to goods made in Japan. As a result, Japan would purchase fewer American-made goods while Americans would tend to buy more goods made in Japan. This in turn would lead to a serious imbalance in imports and exports between the two countries.

With a *flexible-exchange-rate* system, the type of system under which world trade operates today, the forces of supply and demand determine the value of a country's currency in terms of the value of other currencies. Therefore, under this system, the price of a country's currency can fluctuate up and down daily in response to market conditions.

The supply and demand for foreign exchange usually are largely determined by the supply and demand for goods and services. For example, if United States importers wish to import increased quantities of goods from Japan, there will be a strong demand for the Japanese yen. This could force the price of the yen up substantially unless Japan was at the same time providing a large supply of yen in order to increase their imports from the United States.

The demand for goods and services is not the only factor that determines the demand for a nation's currency. Political or economic instability in other countries may cause people in those countries to exchange their currency for a more stable currency, such as the United States dollar. In addition, high interest rates in a particular country may cause foreign investors to convert their currencies into the currency of that nation. This happened in the United States during the early 1980s. Interest rates became so high in this country that many foreign investors were prompted to exchange their currency for American dollars for investment purposes. This increased demand for dollars caused the value of the dollar to increase in terms of other currencies. The "strong" dollar made American-made products more expensive in world markets. As a result, Americans bought more foreign-made products, and foreigners bought fewer American-made products.

Balance of Trade

The amount of goods and services that a nation sells to other nations, and the amount it buys from other nations, are not always equal. The difference between the dollar value of exports and the dollar value of imports is called the *balance of trade*. If the United States exports more goods to foreign nations than it imports from foreign nations, it has a *trade surplus*. However, if the United States imports more than it exports, it has a *trade deficit*. In 1971, the United States recorded its first trade deficit of the century. In all the years since then, except in 1975 when there was a modest surplus, the United States has imported more than it has exported, and the trade deficits of recent years have been so large that they have caused major concern among some economists.

However, not all economists agree on how serious a problem the trade deficits are, or even on their causes. Some believe that, in the long run, market adjustments will correct the problem. Others are not so sure. Some economists believe that the high trade deficits are linked to the large deficits in the federal government's budget in the past two decades. They argue that heavy government borrowing to finance high budget deficits helps to keep interest rates high and encourages foreign investors to exchange their foreign currencies for dollars. However, so many things influence the trade deficits that it is not always clear which factors are playing the biggest role in the deficit at any specific time. The one thing that is clear is that the United States must increase its competitiveness in world markets. Like it or not, the world is moving rapidly toward a global economy. The volume of international trade is bound to grow rapidly in the decades ahead. Competition is still the name of the game, but the number of players has increased.

Balance of Payments

Economic relations between nations involve much more than just imports and exports. There are many different kinds of transactions that involve the exchange of money between nations. For example, American businesses invest funds in foreign nations, and American banks make foreign loans. In addition, the United States government spends money for foreign aid and to support military personnel stationed abroad. Americans spend money for goods and services when they travel abroad, and American citizens often send money to relatives living in other nations. On the other hand, money flows into the United States from other countries when foreign citizens travel in the United States, when foreign businesses make investments in the United States, when Americans receive dividends on foreign investments, and so forth.

Each nation keeps an accounting record of all its monetary transactions with other countries. This accounting record is called the *balance of payments*. A nation's balance of payments account includes all payments that it makes to other nations, and all payments it receives from other nations during a year. A country's balance of payments includes imports and exports, flows of investment funds into and out of the country, loans between nations, and all other transactions that involve payments between countries. The balance of payments is a broader measure of the financial transactions between countries than the balance of trade.

Chapter Highlights

- International trade is very important to most nations of the world. Without international trade, many countries would be unable to feed their people. Even in the United States, we are dependent on the other countries for certain products.

- There are substantial differences in the resources of the various nations of the world. Therefore, the more each nation engaged in trade specializes in the production of those products that it can produce most efficiently, the more the total world production of products will increase.

- One nation has an absolute advantage over another nation in producing a product when it can use fewer resources than the other nation to produce the same quantity of the product.

- Any time a nation has an absolute advantage over another nation in the production of two products, it has a comparative advantage in the production of that product in which the absolute advantage is greater. Similarly, when a nation has an absolute disadvantage in the production of two products, it has a comparative advantage in the production of that product in which the absolute disadvantage is less.

- Despite the benefits of specialization and international trade, most nations put some restrictions on trade in order to protect home industries from foreign competition. These restrictions usually take the form of tariffs or import quotas.

- Arguments used in support of trade barriers include the national security argument, the infant industry argument, the employment protection argument, and the wage protection argument. Although most economists believe it is in society's best interest to keep trade barriers to a minimum, there will probably always be some trade barriers.

- When Americans wish to buy goods from other nations, they usually must pay for the goods in the currency of the exporting country. Foreign currencies are known as foreign exchange, and they are bought and sold in foreign exchange markets.

- The foreign exchange rate is the price of one currency in terms of another. There are two major types of foreign exchange rates: fixed rates and flexible rates. The foreign exchange markets have operated under a flexible-exchange rate system since the early 1970s.

- The difference between the dollar value of exports and the dollar value of imports is called the balance of trade. If the United States exports more goods to foreign nations than it imports from foreign nations, it has a trade surplus. However, if the United States imports more than it exports, it has a trade deficit.

- In addition to imports and exports, there are many other kinds of transactions that involve the exchange of money between nations. The accounting record of all of a nation's monetary transactions with other countries is called the balance of payments.

Important Terms

Match each of the following terms with the correct definition:

foreign exchange	balance of payments
absolute advantage	import quota
balance of trade	import
trade surplus	tariff
trade deficit	export
comparative advantage	flexible exchange rates
foreign exchange rate	
fixed exchange rates	
foreign exchange market	

1. The ability of one nation to produce a product with fewer resources than another nation.

2. A tax imposed by the government on imported products.

3. To buy a product from another nation.

4. Foreign currencies.

5. A situation in which a country has a greater absolute advantage or less of an absolute disadvantage in the production of one of two products.

6. A situation in which a country's imports exceed its exports.

7. To sell a product to another nation.

8. A government policy that places a precise legal limit on the number of units of a particular product that can be imported into a country during a specified time period.

9. An exchange rate system under which the forces of supply and demand determine the value of a nation's currency in terms of the value of the currencies of other nations.

10. The price of one currency in terms of another.

11. The difference in the dollar value of exports and imports.

12. An accounting record of all of a nation's monetary transactions with other countries.

13. A situation in which a country's exports exceed its

imports.

14. An exchange rate system under which the price of one currency is fixed in terms of other currencies so that the rate does not change.

15. Market in which foreign currencies are bought and sold.

Review Questions

1. Why do countries engage in international trade?

2. Explain the concept of absolute advantage.

3. Explain the concept of comparative advantage.

4. Who gains from international trade? Explain.

5. Why do nations put restrictions on international trade?

6. What is a tariff? Explain how tariffs give domestic producers a competitive advantage.

7. What is an import quota? Explain how import quotas operate.

8. Give four arguments that are frequently used in support of trade barriers. Do economists generally favor or oppose trade barriers? Explain.

9. What is foreign exchange? What are foreign exchange markets?

10. What is meant by the term "foreign exchange rate"? Describe two types of foreign exchange rates. Which type is used for world trade today?

11. What is the balance of trade? What is the balance of payments? Explain the difference between the two.

Discussion Questions

1. Suppose the United States were to suddenly halt all trade with other countries. How would such an act affect your life and that of other Americans? Do you think the United States should have more or fewer restrictions on international trade? Why? Who benefits from trade barriers? Who is hurt by them?

CHAPTER NINE

Business Organization and Market Structures

Businesses play a vital role in our lives. We depend on them not only for our livelihood, but also for the goods and services we use in our daily lives. Nearly everything we own and use—from our food and clothing to our automobiles and homes—is produced by businesses.

In this chapter, we will examine business organization and market structures in the United States. We will examine the various ways in which a business can be organized and consider the advantages and disadvantages of each. We will also explore the various types of market structures under which businesses operate in America and examine government efforts to promote and maintain competition. Let's begin by examining the characteristics of business firms.

Characteristics of Business Firms

A **business firm** is an organization that brings together the factors of production—natural resources, capital goods, and labor—for the purpose of producing and/or distributing goods and services. Business firms purchase the factors of production, transform them into goods and services, and sell the goods and services to consumers and other firms. For example, a furniture-manufacturing firm purchases lumber and equipment from other firms and labor in the form of its employees. It then uses these resources to produce furniture, which is sold to consumers and to other business firms.

One of the major characteristics of business firms is specialization and division of labor. Workers are trained in specific tasks and perform only a small part of the production process. For centuries, people have been aware of the advantages of specialization and division of labor. Even when early households produced many of their own basic necessities, at least some goods and services were produced by specialized workers outside the household. Today, most commodities are produced by outside business firms.

Specialization and the division of labor result in increased efficiency in the production process. Economists refer to the savings resulting from this increased efficiency as economies of scale. **Economies of scale** occur when a large volume of output can be produced at a lower cost per unit than can a small volume of output. In other words, whereas it might cost an individual person $5 to produce each of five small products if he or she worked alone, a business firm that utilized mass production techniques, including specialization and the division of labor, might be able to produce 5,000 of the same item for 25 cents each.

Another important characteristic of the business firm centers around risk. There is always the possibility that a business will fail and the money invested in it will be lost. Despite this possibility, the owners of business firms are willing to invest substantial sums of money in the hope that their business ventures will be profitable. If the businesses fail, of course, the owners suffer the consequences. Needless to say, not all people are willing or able to take such risks, so many instead choose what they consider to be more secure ways of earning a living.

Forms of Business Organization

Business firms may be classified in various ways. One way is to group them according to the products they produce. Firms that produce identical or similar products are said to be in the same **industry**.

For example, General Motors, Ford, and Chrysler are all part of the automobile industry. Similarly, General Electric, Whirlpool, and Westinghouse are all part of the home appliance industry. However, many major companies produce products in more than one industry. In addition to producing automobiles, General Motors also produces trucks, buses, diesel locomotives, and home appliances. Therefore, it would be correct to say that General Motors is also in the truck industry, the bus industry, the diesel locomotive industry, and the home appliance industry.

Another way to classify firms is by their legal form of organization. There are three basic forms of business organization that we will consider: (1) the individual proprietorship; (2) the partnership; and (3) the corporation. Let us briefly examine the special characteristics of each.

Individual Proprietorships

An **individual proprietorship** is a form of business organization in which the business firm is owned by a single individual (the individual proprietor) who makes all the business decisions, receives all the profits earned by the firm, and is responsible for any losses incurred by the firm. It is the simplest, oldest, and most common type of business firm in the United States. More than 75 percent of all business firms are individual proprietorships. Most, however, are very small, and they account for only about 7 percent of all **business receipts**. Typical individual proprietorships include neighborhood grocery stores, barbershops, auto repair shops, and farms. Individual proprietorships have both advantages and disadvantages. We have already mentioned the risks involved when considering a business venture. Let us now further examine the pros and cons of starting an individual proprietorship.

One of the major advantages of an individual proprietorship is the ease with which it can be started. There are few formalities, relatively little red tape, and few fees to pay. Anyone who wants to start an individual proprietorship can do so as long as he or she has the money. These factors are especially significant when the business to be started is very small and has limited profit potential.

A second advantage of an individual proprietorship is that the owner gets all the profit, assuming the business is successful. This is especially appealing to people who believe that the chance of phenomenal success is worth the risk of failure. Although the odds of turning a very small investment into a business empire are small, there have been enough amazing success stories to entice others to try.

A third advantage of this form of business organization is that an individual proprietor is his or her own boss. Although individual proprietors may hire salaried employees to help them operate the business, they are still the final decision makers. They decide such things as what items to stock, the hours of operation, and how the business should be run. For people who dislike working for and having to take orders from someone else, the prospect of owning their own business is very attractive.

Despite these advantages, there are also some important disadvantages of the individual proprietorship. One of the most serious disadvantages involves **unlimited liability**, the potential for a business owner to incur and have to pay unlimited business debts. Every potential proprietor should give serious consideration to this problem before going into business. Let us take a hypothetical example.

Suppose a person who has had a successful career as an employee decides to quit his or her job to launch a small business with $50,000 worth of savings. This person has a mortgage-free home worth $300,000, and a new car worth $25,000, in addition to the $50,000 in cash. How much can this person lose if the business venture fails? The answer is almost everything, including the home and the car, depending on the bankruptcy laws in his or her state. In short, people who launch individual proprietorships are liable for far more than the amount of money they invest.

A second disadvantage centers around the limited fund-raising ability of individual proprietorships. Individual proprietors themselves are unlikely to have sufficient funds with which to start or expand a business. They are also less likely than a group of people to get substantial bank loans. Therefore, it is often difficult for individual proprietors to raise enough money to experience the economies of scale that result from increased size. If the individual proprietor is competing with larger firms that, because of economies of scale, are able to produce goods and/or services for a lower cost per unit, he or she ultimately may be forced out of business.

A third disadvantage of individual proprietorships involves a limited life. When the proprietor dies, or decides that he or she no longer wants to remain in business, it is possible that the business firm will cease to exist. This limited life feature may result in the loss of potential customers who are concerned about service for the products they buy. For example, suppose you are buying a microwave oven with a ten-year warranty. Would you rather buy it from a firm that is likely to be in business for years or from an individual proprietor who may go out of business in the near future? Chances are you'll deal with the more-permanent firm.

Partnerships

A **partnership** is a form of business organization that is collectively owned by two or more people (called partners) who jointly make the business decisions, share the profits of the business, and bear the financial responsibility for any losses. Partnerships are the least common form of business organization in the United States, accounting for only 8 percent of all business firms and 4 percent of all business receipts. Essentially, partnerships are expanded proprietorships in which all decisions and responsibilities are shared by the partners. Because of their structure, they have the same advantages and disadvantages as individual proprietorships, except on a different scale. Let us examine these advantages and disadvantages.

Like the individual proprietorship, a partnership is also relatively easy and inexpensive to start up, with the owners collectively getting all the profits and making all the decisions. In addition, in a partnership there is the opportunity for some specialization in management. For example, one partner might concentrate most of his or her efforts on sales while another partner specializes in production. The partnership also has better fund-raising abilities than an individual proprietorship, although the ability of the business to raise cash is still very limited.

On the negative side, a partnership has limited life, lasting only as long as the partnership agreement is in force. There are many things that can put an end to the agreement. For example, suppose a senior partner who owns a substantial portion of the business decides to leave the business over a disagreement. In order to remain in business, the other partners must buy this person's share of the business or find a new partner willing to do so. If they cannot do either, the partnership has to be dissolved. Other factors that might cause a partnership to end are changing interests and the death of a partner.

In addition, partnerships face unlimited liability of a far more serious nature than for an individual proprietorship. In a partnership, a business debt incurred by any of the partners becomes the responsibility of the partnership. As a result, each partner stands to lose substantial personal wealth if the business fails.

To take an extreme example, suppose that an individual decides to invest $90,000 in a partnership with a friend who is investing only $10,000. The first individual owns 90 percent of the business, and the second individual owns 10 percent. As long as the business succeeds, there is no problem. The first individual reaps 90 percent of the profits, while the other reaps 10 percent. However, suppose that the partner with only 10 percent ownership incurs $150,000 of business debts. If this partner has no other assets, the other partner could end up liable for the entire $150,000. This problem of unlimited liability justifiably causes many people to think long and hard before entering a partnership.

Corporations
Corporations are the third form of business organization. A **corporation** is a form of business organization that is collectively owned by a number of individuals but has the legal status to act as a single fictitious person. The corporation is by far the most important form of business organization in the United States. Although corporations make up less than 25 percent of all business firms in this country, they employ more than 60 percent of the labor force and account for approximately 90 percent of all receipts. Corporations completely dominate many major industries, including manufacturing, transportation, and public utilities. In manufacturing, for example, corporations account for approximately 98 percent of all business receipts; in the transportation and public utilities industries,

this figure exceeds 90 percent.

Unlike the minimal paperwork required to establish individual proprietorships and partnerships, setting   up a corporation requires obtaining a corporate charter.   A **corporate charter** is a legal document granted by a state government that gives a business the authority to operate in that state.   Each state has its own set of rules and regulations governing the establishment of corporations.   However, obtaining a charter is usually relatively easy and inexpensive.

The corporate charter establishes the corporation as a "legal person," separate from the actual owners of the corporation.   As a legal person, the corporation can enter into contracts and make commitments in its own name for which the corporation alone is responsible.   Thus, the corporation as a whole can be sued, although the individual owners cannot.

A corporate charter also authorizes the corporation to issue and sell shares of **stock**, or ownership in the corporation, to enable the corporation to raise money. The people who buy the shares of stock are called **stockholders**. There are two major types of stock that people may buy: preferred stock and common stock. **Preferred stock** gives the shareholder a prior claim on dividends but no voting privileges. **Dividends** are cash payments made to stockholders out of a corporation's profits. Thus, assuming a corporation is profitable, owners of preferred stock are the first to receive dividends after all interest obligations are paid. This dividend payment is always a fixed amount, regardless of how profitable the corporation is. However, should the corporation fail, preferred stockholders are the first to receive payment for their investment after all creditors have been paid.

Common stock gives stockholders voting privileges but no prior claim on dividends. In addition, common stockholders are the last to be paid if the corporation fails. However, there is a potential for greater earnings over the long run if the corporation is successful because the dividends paid can be increased in years when the corporation is very profitable. Also, common stock gives investors some voice in the operation of the corporation through their voting privileges.

In addition to issuing shares of stock, corporations can also raise financial capital by selling bonds to investors. Corporate **bonds** are IOUs of the corporation that bind the corporation to pay a fixed sum of money when the bonds reach maturity. The corporation must also pay a fixed sum of money to bondholders annually until the maturity date. This fixed annual payment is called the **interest** or the **coupon payment**. Unlike stockholders, bond owners do not own shares in the corporation. When people buy bonds, they are simply lending money to the corporation for which they will receive interest payments.

The stockholders of a corporation elect a board of directors who is responsible for the management of the corporation. Each stockholder gets one vote for each share of common stock owned. In large corporations, the board of directors hires a president and other officers to carry out the corporation's day-to-day management operations. The employed officers are responsible to the board of directors, who is in turn responsible to the stockholders. In smaller corporations, one or more members of the board of directors may also serve as officers of the corporation.

In addition to voting for the board of directors, stockholders also have the right to vote on other matters affecting the corporation, such as proposed mergers with other companies. They do this at an annual stockholders meeting, where they may cast their votes in person or vote by **proxy** (sign over their voting privileges to the current management or to some other group). In practice, most stockholders in large corporations choose the latter option and play little or no role in corporate decision making. They often live far from the meeting place and are too involved in their own lives to devote much attention to corporate affairs. Moreover, few stockholders own enough shares to have much influence on corporate policies.

As with other forms of business organization, corporations have both advantages and disadvantages. The advantages include limited liability, ability to raise large sums of money, and unlimited life. The drawbacks include separation of ownership and management, and double taxation. Let us look at each of these.

Perhaps the most important advantage of the corporation from the standpoint of potential investors is its limited liability. Unlike individual proprietorships and partnerships, investors in a corporation can lose no more than the amount of money they invest. The stockholders of a corporation cannot be held personally liable for the debts of the corporation. If a corporation is successful, the stockholders may reap large profits. If the corporation fails and goes bankrupt, the stockholders' loss is limited to the value of the shares of stocks owned.

The limited liability feature of corporations contributes significantly to the second advantage of the corporation form of organization—the ability to raise large sums of money. Since potential stockholders will share in large profits if the corporation succeeds and face only limited losses if the corporation fails, they are more willing to invest in stocks than in other more risky ventures. Corporations can raise large sums of money by issuing stock, by selling corporate bonds, and by borrowing from lending institutions. This ability to raise large sums of money is the primary reason that almost all large business firms are corporations.

Another important advantage of corporations is the fact that they have an unlimited life. Unlike individual proprietorships and partnerships, the death or resignation of the current president does not alter the legal status of the corporation. Similarly, when owners (stockholders) die, their heirs simply inherit the shares of stock and the corporation is unaffected. Few major corporations today have the same owners and officers they had when they were founded. Many corporations, in fact, are over a hundred years old. This unlimited life feature contributes to a corporation's ability to raise money. Banks and other lending institutions are willing to make long-term loans to corporations because they know the corporations will outlive their current owners and officers. Also, new stockholders can more easily be brought into a corporation because they know that the existence of the corporation does not depend on the individuals who currently run it.

The first corporations set up in the United States were small firms whose founders had simply chosen the corporate form of business organization over that of the proprietorship or partnership. The people who set up the corporation owned most or all of the stock, and they managed the firm. However, as corporations grew larger and larger, ownership passed from the hands of the founding owner-managers into the hands of millions of stockholders, and management was turned over to salaried officers who were hired to manage the day-to-day operations of the corporation. Only a very few of the large corporations today are privately owned by those who are responsible for their management.

This separation of ownership and management may pose some problems. Since the owners and managers of many large corporations are two separate groups of people, their views of what is best for the company may not always coincide. Most hired managers have been trained in business administration, and they are likely to feel that their training and their familiarity with day-to-day operations put them in a better position than the stockholders to know what is best for the corporation.

Generally, both groups are interested in maximizing profits, but they may not agree on the best way to do so. For example, there is the question of short-term profits versus long-term profits. Managers who are only five years away from retirement may be most interested in maximizing profits during that five-year period. Their personal income may be linked to the annual profit of the corporation, and certainly their status will be enhanced if their corporation shows relatively large profits. Maximizing profits during that five-year period, however, may not be in the best interest of either the corporation or the stockholders. It might be better to forgo large profits during that period in order to invest in new technology that will enable the company to earn even greater profits over a longer period of time.

The problem of double taxation is considered by some to be a disadvantage of the corporate form of business organization. **Double taxation** refers to the fact that corporations have to pay taxes on their profits even though stockholders later pay a tax on some of these same profits when they are distributed as dividends that are subject to personal income taxes. However, there is considerable disagreement over just how much of a disadvantage this problem of double taxation really is. Some argue that many large corporations with substantial market power are able to pass the corporate income tax on to their customers in the form of higher prices. When this happens, it is the consumer, not the corporation or the stockholders, who is actually paying the corporate income tax.

Other Forms of Business Organization

In addition to individual proprietorships, partnerships, and corporations, there are two other forms of business organization that provide goods and services. They are nonprofit organizations and cooperatives. Let us briefly examine each of these forms of business organization.

Nonprofit Organizations

Nonprofit organizations are dedicated to providing public services. They may not and do not earn a profit. Any revenue in excess of operating costs is used to further the purposes of the organization. Churches and many other private charity organizations, as well as cultural organization such as opera or museum associations, are nonprofit organizations.

Some nonprofit organizations are engaged in production in much the same way as are other business firms. For example, Goodwill Industries, which is devoted to helping the handicapped, employs handicapped workers who repair clothing, furniture, and other household items that have been donated. The repaired items are then sold to the public through stores operated by the organization. The earnings of the organization are used to pay the workers and to help train them for jobs in the private sector.

Cooperatives

A cooperative is a voluntary association of people formed for the purpose of providing economic benefits for its members. The three most common types of cooperatives are consumer cooperatives, producer cooperatives, and credit unions.

Consumer cooperatives are formed for the purpose of collectively buying consumer products in large quantities at low prices. The objective of consumer co-ops is to offer their members lower prices than those charged by regular businesses. Members usually pay regular prices to the co-op at the time they make their purchases but receive rebates at the end of each year.

Producer cooperatives are voluntary associations of producers of certain products that attempt to obtain higher prices than the members could get by selling individually. Most producer co-ops in the United States are made up of farmers. Some farm co-ops have meat-processing plants or facilities for processing grain, and they often help transport and advertise their members' products. The primary objective of producer cooperatives is to eliminate middleman charges and pass the savings on to their members in the form of higher prices.

Credit unions, which are very common in large cities, are often created by employees of a large company or by other large groups of people. They accept deposits and make loans. Their purpose is to help their members get a better deal instead of making a profit. Thus, compared to other financial institutions, they usually pay higher interest rates on members' savings and charge lower interest rates on members' loans.

The Importance of Competition

As we have already seen, competition is extremely important to the proper functioning of the American market economy, especially if we want to keep government intervention to a minimum. In Chapter 2, we examined the invisible-hand principle, which was first described by Adam Smith, the founder of economics, more than 200 years ago. According to this principle, if individuals were allowed to pursue their own self-interests without interference by the government, they would be led, as if by an invisible hand, to achieve what is best for society.

In Smith's hypothetical economy, there were many small sellers engaged in such strong competition with one another that none were able to take advantage of consumers. Any efforts by a business to take advantage of customers by raising prices arbitrarily high were doomed to failure because consumers would simply abandon the seller and buy the product from another seller at a lower price. In Smith's economy, there were no patent laws, no giant corporations, or other barriers to entry into an industry.

There was no government regulation, no advertising, and no brand names. In addition, Smith's hypothetical economy was different in several other ways from today's American economy. It had built-in safeguards to prevent individuals and businesses from taking advantage of one another that are not always present today.

The key to the successful operation of the invisible-hand principle is a high degree of competition. Some areas of the American economy do have a great deal of competition; whereas, other areas have very limited competition. We will now examine the various market structures that exist in the American economy and the degree of competition that exists in each.

Market Structures and Competition

Market structures are determined primarily by (1) the number of firms selling in the market; (2) the extent to which the products of the different firms are different from one another; and (3) the ease with which firms enter or leave the market. Based on these criteria, economists group market structures into four basic categories: (1) **pure competition;** (2) **monopoly;** (3) **oligopoly**; and (4) **monopolistic competition**. Let's see how these market structures differ.

Pure Competition

In order for pure competition to exist there must be (1) many sellers; (2) a standardized product; (3) easy entry and exit; and (4) no artificial restrictions. Let's examine each of these conditions briefly.

Many Sellers. There must be many sellers, and each seller must be so small relative to the entire market that its actions will have no effect on the price of the product. Instead, each firm must accept the going market price that has been established by the freely operating forces of supply and demand. In other words, if one of the sellers tried to raise its price even slightly above the going market price, it would be unable to sell any of its product because consumers would buy from other firms.

A Standardized Product. The products of all the sellers must be so nearly identical that buyers do not prefer the product of any one firm over that of any other firm. In other words, there are no brand names. Buyers consider a bushel of wheat from farmer Brown identical to a bushel of wheat from farmer Jones. Likewise, a ton of coal from the ABC Coal Company is considered identical to a ton of coal from the XYZ Coal Company.

Easy Entry and Exit. There are no significant barriers to prevent new firms from entering the market or to prevent existing firms from leaving the markets. This means there are no patent laws that would prevent new firms from producing any product they wish, no firm has exclusive control of the raw materials necessary to produce a product, and enormous sums of money are not required to enter a business. Under these conditions, firms are free to enter and leave the market at will.

No Artificial Restrictions. There are no labor unions, minimum wage laws, or wage and price controls on the free movement of wages and prices up and down.

After reading the above conditions that are necessary for pure competition to exist, it should be clear to you that pure competition is rare, if not nonexistent, in the American economy. As you know, many markets are dominated by a few giant firms, and the products produced are not identical. Also, it is difficult, if not impossible, for new firms to enter some markets because of patent laws, shortages of crucial raw materials, and other reasons. In addition, labor unions, minimum wage laws, and other artificial restrictions prevent the free movement of prices and wages.

Although pure competition is rare in the American economy, it is regarded by some economists as the ideal market structure that, if it actually existed, would result in maximum freedom and the most efficient allocation of scarce resources. It is the type of market structure that Adam Smith had in mind when he described his famous "invisible-hand" principle where individuals could achieve what is best for society simply by following their own self-interests without interference by government. Under such a market structure, competition would prevent firms from taking advantage of either their customers or their employees.

Thus, pure competition gives us a useful standard against which to compare other market structures. Furthermore, some industries do come close to the market structure of pure competition. Agriculture is an example of one industry in the United States that comes close to meeting the conditions of pure competition. There are hundreds of thousands of small farmers, and each one produces only a small percentage of the total agricultural output. Thus, no single farmer is able to influence the prices of farm products and take advantage of consumers. Farm prices are determined by the forces of supply and demand, and any farmer who tries to raise his price above the going market price will be unable to sell his product. In addition, the products produced by farmers are almost identical. A bushel of wheat from one farmer is very similar to a bushel of wheat from any other farmer. Also, entry into agricultural markets is much easier than in most other industries. Although the high costs of land and machinery make it difficult for new farmers to enter agriculture, existing farmers can enter new agricultural markets rather easily because they already have the necessary machinery and land. For example, farmers who normally produce only corn and soybeans could easily produce wheat on their land if it became more profitable to do so.

Monopoly

Monopoly is the extreme opposite of pure competition. With monopoly, there is a single seller who sells a product for which there are no close substitutes. Also, there are barriers to entry that prevent competitors from entering the market. Thus, without competition, a monopolist can control the price of his or her product within limits.

Cases of pure monopoly are rare in the United States today. There are few products for which there are no close substitutes, and permanent barriers to entry generally are not permitted. However, there are numerous markets that come close to being pure monopoly because the available substitutes are not considered adequate by many people, and certain barriers restrict entry of new firms into the market. Let's briefly consider these two factors that contribute to the existence of monopoly power for many sellers.

Availability of Adequate Substitutes. In the broadest sense of the word, General Motors has a monopoly on General Motors' automobiles. No other company can produce cars that are exactly like Chevrolets, Cadillacs, and so forth. However, since most people consider automobiles manufactured by the Ford Motor Company, Chrysler Corporation, and a number of foreign automobile manufacturers adequate substitutes for General Motors' cars, there is little market power in such a monopoly. To have true monopoly power, General Motors would need to be the only producer and seller of all automobiles so that potential car buyers would have no alternative options. As long as there are adequate substitutes available for a product produced by a monopolist, that monopolist can make only limited use of its monopoly power.

An example of monopoly power where there are not adequate substitutes is in the distribution of electricity. In order to avoid duplication of services and increased production costs, the government grants a single company the exclusive right to supply electricity in each community. If three or four separate companies were competing for the business of consumers of electricity in each community, there would be three or four sets of electrical lines running down every road and street, an equivalent number of maintenance crews, and many other duplications. This would clearly lead to higher costs for consumers of electricity than the current system. Thus, the government gives monopoly power to a single utility company in each area and then regulates both prices and the quality of service in order to prevent the monopoly companies from taking advantage of consumers.

Since competition has been eliminated, if the government did not regulate prices and the quality of service of utility companies, these companies could take advantage of consumers since there are no good substitutes for electricity. There are some substitutes. Gas, oil, and wood are substitutes for electricity for heating purposes, and candles, kerosene lamps, and battery-powered lights could serve as substitutes for electricity for lighting. In addition, there are portable gasoline-powered electrical generators available for sale that could be used to operate electric lights and appliances. But many people would not consider these items adequate substitutes for electricity. Thus, the electric companies could make extensive use of their monopoly market power if they did not face government regulation.

Barriers to Entry. For monopoly to exist for any extended period of time, it must have strong barriers to entry that prevent potential competitors from entering the market. In the case of electricity, the barriers to entry are provided by the government who grants a single company the exclusive right to serve a specific community.

Control of essential raw materials needed for the production of a product also can be an important barrier to entry. For example, until 1945 the Aluminum Company of America (ALCOA) manufactured more than 90 percent of the aluminum produced in this country. ALCOA was able to prevent competitors from entering the market because it owned most of the nation's bauxite, the ore from which aluminum is made.   However, the government broke ALCOA's monopoly power in 1945 by requiring it to make some bauxite available to other companies.

Patents provide another important barrier to entry. When a seller develops a new product and obtains a patent from the government, the patent prohibits potential competitors from producing or selling the patented product without the permission of the patent owner. Thus, the patent owner becomes a monopolist for that product. The positive side of patent laws is that patents encourage potential investors to create new products by assuring them the profits from their inventions. The negative side is that patents, by eliminating competition, often enable companies to charge excessively high prices for their patented products.

Sometimes the government intervenes to break up monopolies resulting from patent rights. For example, Xerox Corporation had a monopoly on photocopying equipment in the United States for many years because of patents it owned.   However, in 1975, the government required Xerox to make some of its patent rights available to competitors in order to create competition in the market.

The size of a potential market is another barrier to entry. In many small communities, there is only enough business to support a single bank, hardware store, drugstore, and so forth. If a second firm entered the market, there would not be enough business for both firms, and it is likely that neither firm would earn a satisfactory profit. Monopolies of this type may exist indefinitely.

Oligopoly

Many industries in the United States, operate under a market structure known as oligopoly. It is the market structure under which most large corporations operate, and it has the following characteristics: (1) a few sellers; (2) substantial barriers to entry;   (3) either standardized or differentiated products; and   (4) substantial nonprice competition. Let's examine each of these characteristics.

A Few Sellers. Instead of a single seller, as is the case with monopoly, oligopoly is characterized by a small number of sellers. For oligopoly to exist, the number of firms in the market must be small enough so that the actions of any one firm will affect the other firms in the market and vice versa. In such a market structure, a firm would not change the price of its product, the quality of its product, or its advertising without first taking into consideration the possible reaction of its competitors.

The American automobile industry is a good example to illustrate how oligopoly works. Suppose, for example, that Chrysler Corporation is contemplating offering a much improved, long-term warranty on automobiles in order to pull customers away from Ford and General Motors. The warranty will cost Chrysler a great deal of money, but it hopes to more than cover the increased costs through increased profits from a larger sales volume. Whether or not Chrysler's strategy will work depends on whether or not Ford and General Motors match the new improved warranty. If they do not match it, Chrysler will probably sell more cars. However, if Ford and General Motors offer comparable warranties, Chrysler will end up with a more costly warranty program but little or no increase in sales. Thus, before plunging into action of this type, Chrysler would carefully consider how Ford and General Motors would react.

Likewise, when an oligopolist is contemplating a price increase, it must consider whether or not its chief competitors will follow its lead and also increase prices. For example, suppose General Motors decides to increase prices by 10 percent on its new models. If its competitors increase their prices by a similar amount, the effect of the price increase on sales will probably be small. However, if General Motors' competitors fail to match the price increase, GM will be forced to either roll back its price increase, or risk losing many of its customers. Thus, when there are so few sellers in a market that each one worries about the actions and reactions of its competitors, the market structure is oligopoly.

Not all oligopolies are national in scope. There are many local communities where oligopoly is common. If there are only two or three grocery stores, or gas stations, in a given community, each owner will almost always consider the reactions of his or her competitors when changing prices, advertising strategies, and so forth.

Barriers to Entry. The barriers to entry in markets characterized by oligopoly are not as strong as those where a monopoly exists. Nevertheless, there are usually substantial barriers to entry in oligopolistic markets. In the case of national oligopolies such as the automobile industry, the high cost of acquiring the resources necessary to establish a new firm, and the inability to begin producing on a sufficiently large scale to take advantage of the economies of scale that the established firms are experiencing, can be strong barriers to entry. It would be very difficult for a new firm to raise enough money to enter the automobile industry.

In addition, a new firm would probably be unable to sell enough cars during its first few years in business to enable it to take advantage of the cost savings that result from mass production. Since its production costs per unit would be higher than that of its competitors, it would have to charge a higher price for its cars than the established firms. It is highly unlikely that consumers would be willing to pay a higher price for an automobile produced by a new, unproven company than for one produced by an established firm. Thus, the new automobile firm would probably be doomed to failure from the very beginning.

As in the case of monopoly, control of important raw materials can be a strong barrier to entry into oligopolistic markets. If a few large firms own most of the raw materials necessary for the production of a product, potential new competitors will be prevented from entering the market.

Market size may be the primary barrier to entry in the case of local oligopolies. If two existing grocery stores are able to supply all the needs of a community, it is unlikely that a third store would be very profitable. Also, customer loyalty to established firms may be a difficult obstacle for new firms to overcome in the case of both local and national oligopolies.

Standardized or Differentiated Products. In some oligopolistic markets the products sold are standardized while in others the products are differentiated. In industries such as steel and aluminum, the products are almost identical. However, in industries such as breakfast cereals, laundry detergents, home appliances, and automobiles, the products are differentiated.

Nonprice Competition. Oligopolistic firms, in those industries where the products are differentiated, engage in vigorous nonprice competition. In other words, they attempt to persuade consumers to buy a particular product for reasons other than price. Have you ever seen a breakfast cereal commercial on TV in which viewers are asked to buy the product because it is less expensive than those of competitors?   How about soap and laundry detergent commercials?   Commercials for these types of products attempt to convince consumers that the product is better, not less expensive, than those of competitors. Most commercials for such products attempt to convince consumers that the breakfast cereal is tastier or more nutritious, or that the detergent gets clothes cleaner than competing brands.

Oligopolists seldom engage in price wars because, if a firm operating in an oligopolistic market lowers its price, its competitors will be forced to match the price cut. As a result, all firms will suffer a reduction in profits. Therefore, prices tend to remain relatively stable in oligopolistic markets, with most competition being of a nonprice nature.

Monopolistic Competition

Monopolistic competition is characterized by: (1) many sellers; (2) differentiated products;   (3) non-price competition; and   (4) relatively easy entry and exit.   It has similarities to both pure competition and oligopoly.

Like pure competition, there are many sellers and no strong barriers to entry in the market structure of monopolistic competition.   Firms can and do enter and leave markets on a regular basis.   Also, the amount of investment necessary to start a business is relatively small, and there are few government regulations restricting those wishing to enter a market.   In addition, unlike oligopoly, each firm operating under monopolistic competition controls such a small share of the market that each believes its actions will bring no reactions from competitors.

The most important characteristics that distinguish monopolistic competition from pure competition are product differentiation and non-price competition.   Firms operating under monopolistic competition do extensive advertising in an effort to convince consumers that their products are better than those of their competitors. Often there is little or no actual difference in the products, but advertising campaigns lead some consumers to believe otherwise. For example, all brands of aspirin contain very similar ingredients that are stipulated by federal law. However, many consumers believe that some highly advertised brands are better than others, and they are willing to pay a premium price for them.

Most retail stores in medium-to-large-sized cities operate under the market structure of monopolistic competition. They advertise heavily and try to convince consumers that their products and services are superior to those of other competitors. Stores may emphasize such things as convenient location, ample parking space, courteous service, and a large selection of merchandise, in addition to low prices, in their advertising campaigns.

Government Efforts to
Promote and Maintain Competition

Since competition is so essential to the proper functioning of a market economy, the promotion and maintenance of competition have long been important goals of American government. Business firms, though, sometimes have tried to reduce competition in an effort to increase their profits.

One way that firms operating in an oligopolistic market have avoided competition among themselves is by entering into secret agreements in which each firm agrees to charge a certain fixed price. Through such "price-fixing" agreements, the firms have achieved almost as much market power as if they were one giant monopoly. Although price-fixing agreements are illegal in the United States, they have occurred in the past and probably will occur in the future. The larger the number of firms in an industry, the more difficult it is for them to engage in price-fixing agreements. It is much easier to convince two competitors to enter into such an agreement than it is to convince ten.

Another obvious way for firms to decrease competition among themselves is to buy up one another or in some other way join together to produce a smaller number of firms in the market. During the late 1800s, some firms were able to eliminate competition almost completely by entering into a formal arrangement known as a **trust**—a device that for all practical purposes converted a group of firms into a single monopoly. For example, during the 1880s and 1890s, John D. Rockefeller organized more than 40 oil companies into the Standard Oil Trust, which nearly monopolized the entire crude and refined oil market in the United States. In response to the public outcry over the monopolization that was taking place in the oil industry and other industries, both state governments and the federal government began enacting antitrust laws. In all, five major antitrust laws were enacted by the federal government during the period 1890 to 1950. Let us briefly examine each of these laws.

Sherman Antitrust Act (1890)

The Sherman Antitrust Act was the first significant law against monopolies passed in this country. This law prohibited "every contract, combination in the form of a trust or otherwise, or conspiracy" that limited competition. In short, this law made it illegal to monopolize or even to attempt to monopolize trade. For those who violated the law, the penalties of imprisonment and/or fines were clearly prescribed.

Unfortunately, the language of the Sherman Act was vague, and it was not clear which specific acts constituted violation of the law. Furthermore, since the act did not establish any government agency for enforcing its provisions, it was poorly administered in its early years.

Clayton Antitrust Act (1914)

In order to clarify the intent of the Sherman Antitrust Act, Congress passed the Clayton Antitrust Act in 1914. This act explicitly prohibited the following four specific practices if their "effect was to substantially lessen competition or tend to create a monopoly": (1) price discrimination (selling the same good to different buyers at different prices); (2) exclusive dealing arrangements (requiring a buyer to agree not to purchase goods from competitors); (3) interlocking directorates (a practice in which the same person serves on the board of directors of two or more competing companies); and (4) the acquisition of the stock of one company by competing companies.

Federal Trade Commission Act (1914)

To make sure that the Clayton Antitrust Act was properly enforced, Congress passed the Federal Trade Commission Act in the same year. This act created the Federal Trade Commission (FTC) to administer the Clayton Act and to investigate, hold hearings, and issue cease and desist orders in cases of "unfair methods of competition" and "unfair acts or practices." The Federal Trade Commission Act was later amended to extend protection to consumers as well as competitors. By broadening the FTC's power, the government made it a major force in policing deceptive advertising practices.

Robinson-Patman Act (1936)

The Rohinson-Patman Act was passed in response to complaints by small retailers that large chain stores and mass distributors were getting quantity discounts from suppliers that enabled them to undersell the small retailers. This law made it illegal for the suppliers to sell "at unreasonably low prices" when such practices reduced competition. In addition, it prohibited them from giving rebates and discounts to large buyers unless the rebates and discounts were available to all.

Cellar-Kefauver Antimerger Act (1950)

Whereas the Clayton Act prohibited one firm from acquiring shares of stock of another if this lessened competition, it said nothing about purchasing outright the assets of another firm. As a result, a number of companies got around the intent of the Clayton Act by purchasing competing firms' assets. To curtail this practice and to strengthen the prohibition against firms joining together to control too large a part of the market, Congress passed the Celler-Kefauver Antimerger Act. This act, which was an amendment to the Clayton Act, specifically prohibited firms from purchasing either the assets or stock of other firms where "the effect of such acquisition may be substantially to lessen competition, or to tend to create a monopoly." Together with the other antitrust legislation, the Celler-Kefauver Act tried to curb monopolistic practices and to promote competition.

Chapter Highlights

- A business firm is an organization that brings together the factors of production for the purpose of producing goods and services.
- Businesses are characterized by specialization and the division of labor, as well as by a certain amount of risk.
- Firms that produce identical or similar products are said to be in the same industry. Many major companies produce products in more than one industry.
- The three basic forms of business organization are (1) the individual proprietorship; (2) the partnership; and (3) the corporation.
- Advantages of the individual proprietorship are (1) it is

easy and relatively inexpensive to start up; (2) the owner gets all the profits; and (3) the owner is the sole decision maker. Disadvantages are (1) unlimited liability; (2) limited ability to raise financial capital; and (3) limited life.

- Advantages and disadvantages of the partnership as a form of business organization are essentially the same as those for an individual proprietorship, except on a different scale.

- A corporation is a form of business organization that is collectively owned by a number of individuals called stockholders, and that has the legal status of a single fictitious individual.

- Corporations raise money by selling stocks and bonds. There are two basic kinds of stock: preferred stock and common stock. Common stock may yield higher income than preferred stock in the long run.

- Advantages of the corporation as a form of business organization are (1) limited liability; (2) ability to raise large sums of money; and (3) unlimited life. Disadvantages are (1) separation of ownership and management; and (2) double taxation.

- The four basic categories of market structure are (1) pure competition; (2) monopoly;   (3) oligopoly; and (4) monopolistic competition.

- There are few actual examples of either pure competition or monopoly in the American economy. Most firms operate under market structures of either oligopoly or monopolistic competition.

- Oligopoly is characterized by (1) a few sellers; (2) substantial barriers to entry; (3) standardized or differentiated products: and (4) substantial nonprice competition.   Monopolistic competition is characterized by (1) many sellers; (2) differentiated products; (3) nonprice competition; and (4) relatively easy entry and exit.

- The promotion and maintenance of competition have long been important goals of government in the United States. During the period 1890 to 1950, five major antitrust laws were enacted by the federal government in order to eliminate business practices developed to limit competition.

Important Terms

Match each of the following terms with the correct definition:

monopolistic competition   economies of scale
oligopoly   pure competition
monopoly   antitrust laws

1. Laws designed to promote and maintain competition by prohibiting practices that tend to lead to the creation of monopoly power.

2. The increased efficiency resulting from specialization and the division of labor that makes possible the production of a large volume of output at a lower cost per unit than a small volume of output.

3. A market structure characterized by a few sellers, substantial barriers to entry, standardized or differentiated products, and substantial non-price competition.

4. A market structure characterized by a single seller, a product for which there are no close substitutes, and strong barriers to entry that prevent potential competitors from entering into the market.

5. A market structure characterized by many sellers, standardized products, easy entry and exit, and no artificial restrictions on the free movement of prices and wages up and down.

6. A market structure characterized by many sellers, differentiated products, nonprice competition, and relatively easy entry and exit.

Review Questions

1. What is meant by economies of scale? Give an example of how economies of scale work.

2. What are the four characteristics of pure competition? Does pure competition exist?

3. What problems would exist in a purely competitive economy?

4. Describe four characteristics of monopoly. What are the two key factors that determine the market power of a single seller?

5. Identify four characteristics of oligopoly. What is meant by "mutual interdependence"? Describe nonprice competition.

6. What are the four characteristics of monopolistic competition? In what ways is monopolistic competition similar to oligopoly? In what ways is it similar to pure competition?

7. Why is the promotion and maintenance of competition such an important goal of the American government?

8. How have firms tried to reduce competition among themselves?

9. Describe the five major antitrust laws That were enacted between 1890 and 1950.

Discussion Questions

1. Why does the government enact and enforce antitrust laws and other measures designed to prevent monopoly power? What do you think would happen if the government repealed all antitrust laws and abandoned all efforts to control monopoly power?

CHAPTER TEN

Labor Economics and Labor Relations

Labor unions are an important and a controversial force in the United States. They improve the economic status and working conditions of many Americans, and sometimes participate in work stoppages that inconvenience many other Americans. They play an important role in American politics and have a substantial influence on the nation's economy. In this chapter we will examine the history of American labor unions, the role that unions and collective bargaining play in today's economy, and the factors that determine wages in the American economy. Let's begin by examining union history.

The History of American Unionism

The history of union activity in the United States dates back almost as far as the history of the nation itself. As early as 1636, a group of fishermen in what is now Maine organized a protest against having their wages withheld. And in 1741, bakers in New York City called a strike to protest a municipal regulation on the price of bread. It was not until the closing years of the eighteenth century, however, that unions as we know them today appeared on the American scene. We will begin our study of union history with a look at these unions.

The First Unions

The first labor unions—or *societies* as they were called at the time—were formed around 1790 in response to changing economic conditions. Prior to this time, many of the essential products that could not be made in the home, such as shoes, were produced by local craftspeople who hired a small number of local workers to help them complete certain jobs. Employers and employees were often good friends, and since production was on a custom-work basis, prices could be manipulated so that both the employer and the employees earned a good income.

By the late 1700s, however, improved transportation facilities and reduced transportation costs helped to change the relationship between employer and employee. Gradually, markets in different regions came into competition with one another as shoes and other commodities from some regions began to appear in other regions many miles away. As local employers faced increasing competition from outside areas, they were forced to become more cost conscious. Since labor was the major source of production costs, employers were forced to restrain wage increases and in some cases to actually cut wages. This conflict between employer and employee interests set the stage for the organization of the first unions.

These first unions were local organizations of skilled craftsmen such as shoemakers, tailors, and printers. They sought higher wages, improved working conditions, and a shorter workday. Employers resisted the demands of these early unions; and in some instances, the unions engaged in strikes against the employers. However, the success of these early unions was very limited.

The economic hard times and high unemployment that accompanied what historians call the Panic of 1819 brought an end to most of these early unions. As economic conditions improved, new unions were formed, but many of them lasted only until the next economic downturn. The period 1837-1852, which some historians describe as the "long depression," wasn't very conducive to sustained union growth, but the terrible working conditions that existed in many places of employment motivated workers to continue their struggle. Workers often had to work 72-hour workweeks (six 12-hour days) for very small wages, and employers often relied on children as a source of cheap labor. The increased industrialization during the 1840s and 1850s did enable unions to make some small gains. The most significant development during this period was the gradual decline in the length of the average working day to 10 or 11 hours in most factories.

The Knights of Labor

Following the Civil War, the nation experienced phenomenal industrial growth. As the railroad lines from the east and west merged to form a transcontinental transportation system, a national market came into being. This industrial growth was accompanied by growth in union membership, and by increased efforts to combine local unions across the country into national organizations. One of the first labor organizations to be organized on a national level was the Noble Order of the Knights of Labor. Founded in 1869 as a secret society by seven Philadelphia tailors, the organization originally was characterized by an elaborate system of rituals, secret handshakes, and passwords. Ten years later, however, the secrecy was dropped, and the Knights became a national labor organization with the goal of bringing together into one giant organization workers of all types—both skilled and unskilled.

Membership in the Knights of Labor, which had grown from 9,000 in 1879 to 100,000 in 1885, suddenly increased sevenfold to a peak of 700,000 members in 1886, following an important strike victory against a major railroad company. However, the success of the Knights was short lived. A series of unsuccessful strikes, internal squabbling, and inept leadership led to a rapid decline in membership after 1886. By 1893, membership had fallen to 75,000, and by the early 1900s, the organization was virtually extinct.

The American Federation of Labor

In 1886, the same year that the Knights of Labor reached its peak, a group of national unions held a meeting in Columbus, Ohio. Each of these unions was a *craft union*, a union composed of workers in a particular trade or craft, such as carpenters, electricians, or plumbers. The purpose of their meeting was to form a new labor organization, which was called the American Federation of Labor. This organization was itself not a union, but a collection of unions under central leadership that was to promote and coordinate the overall labor movement. Each member union was to make all of its own internal decisions, with the new organization serving to maintain general harmony. Samuel Gompers, an official of the cigar-makers' union, was elected president of the AFL, and he held that post continuously, except for one year, until his death in 1924.

The early history of the AFL is largely a history of the efforts of Samuel Gompers, who more than any other individual is responsible for the success of the American labor movement. Born in London, Gompers' formal education ended when he was 10; and when he was 13, he and his family migrated to the United States. The following year, Gompers became involved with union work, and thereafter devoted his entire life to the union movement. For the first few years, Gompers was the only full-time officer of the AFL, and at first his office was a room in his apartment. The AFL was so poor that even the purchase of a used typewriter involved a major financial decision.

From such modest beginnings, the AFL grew into a giant federation, and its success can be attributed primarily to Gompers' determination to promote a specific type of unionism. Gompers believed that the failure of earlier labor organizations resulted from too much emphasis on social and political reform, and he was determined to lead the AFL in a new direction. Instead of trying to bring about reform through direct involvement in party politics, as earlier labor organizations had done, Gompers advocated "economic unionism"—a practical policy of seeking basic improvements in wages and working conditions by bargaining directly with employers. Through Gompers' leadership, the AFL and its member unions were able to achieve higher wages, shorter hours, and a better working environment for their members.

Antiunion Policies

From the time of the formation of the first unions in the late 1700s until the 1930s, there were no federal or state laws governing union activities. Without legal protection, unions faced a losing battle in their attempts to organize American workers. Employers resisted unions every step of the way, and the nation's courts provided employers with the legal power they needed to block unionization through the conspiracy doctrine and court injunctions.

The Conspiracy Doctrine Since there were no state or federal laws governing union activities, judges made their decisions on the basis of common law. *Common law*, which was a concept inherited from the British, consists of the accumulation of judicial decisions over time that have the force of law in the absence of specific statutes enacted by legislatures. Common law may be thought of as law by tradition. An example of common law occurred in 1806 when a Philadelphia court ruled that a group of workers, who had banded together in an effort to obtain higher pay, were guilty of a criminal conspiracy. The court based its decision on the common law doctrine that it is illegal for two or more people to conspire to commit an illegal act. The implication of this ruling was that the organization of workers for the purpose of obtaining higher wages was a violation of property rights, and thus illegal. Many other courts handed down similar rulings against unions, and the *conspiracy doctrine* posed a major obstacle to union organization for many years.

The Court Injunction When later court decisions made the conspiracy doctrine ineffective as a legal barrier to unionization, the courts began to issue injunctions. An *injunction* is a court order issued by a judge requiring a party to do, or cease doing, specific activities. For example, a judge might issue an injunction ordering striking workers to return to work. Failure to obey an injunction can result in a jail sentence. The injunction became the standard remedy for unauthorized union practices. If an employer wanted to stop a specific union activity, he or she would ask a judge to issue an injunction against it. If the judge complied with the request, the activity became illegal and union members who failed to obey the injunction could go to jail.

Other Antiunion Activities In addition to the court injunction, employers used a number of other devices to combat the efforts of employees to form unions. Some hired *labor spies* to infiltrate unions and provide the employers with names of workers who were union members or union sympathizers. These workers were then fired, and their names were added to an industry-wide list of "union activists" that was circulated among employers. This made it difficult, if not impossible, for these workers to find jobs elsewhere. Some employers also forced employees to sign agreements known as *yellow-dog* *contracts.* Such contracts required the employees to promise, as a condition of employment, not to join a union. In addition, some imposed *lockouts*—the temporary closing of plants by employers—to persuade workers to abandon their union efforts.

Pro-labor Legislation and Mass Unionization

After nearly a century and a half of government hostility toward unions, the fortunes of organized labor underwent a dramatic reversal during the 1930s. During that decade, the United States Congress passed a series of laws that were designed to reverse past government policies and encourage the growth of unions. Workers were guaranteed the right to organize and engage in union activities, and employers were prohibited from engaging in certain practices that had long been used to oppose unionism. Two of the most important laws passed during this period are the Norris-LaGuardia Anti-Injunction Act (1932) and the National Labor Relations Act (1935). Both will be discussed in the next section.

This pro-union legislation set the stage for unprecedented growth in union membership in the United States. Millions of previously unorganized workers in the automobile, steel, and other mass-production industries suddenly became interested in joining unions.

The Congress of Industrial Organizations

Most of the new unions were industrial unions. An *industrial union* is a union composed of workers from a particular industry regardless of the kind of jobs they hold. Examples of industrial unions include unions of coal miners, steel workers, or autoworkers. Unlike craft unions, industrial unions included many unskilled workers. Because of their composition, these new industrial unions posed a problem for the AFL, which had a long history of admitting only skilled craftsmen. A controversy arose within the AFL leadership over the admission of industrial unions. Finally, in 1938 the industrial unions banded together and formed a rival organization called the *Congress of Industrial Organizations (CIO)*. These two giant organizations competed for union members for many years with both experiencing substantial growth. In 1955, however, the two giants merged into a single organization known as the *American Federation of Labor—Congress of Industrial Organizations (AFL—CIO)*.

The Structure of Organized Labor

The structure of organized labor in the United States today involves three levels of organization—the local union, the national union, and the federation.

Local Unions The most basic level of organization is the local union. Some local unions have only a few dozen members, while others have thousands of members. A local craft union would consist of all the plumbers, or all the electricians, in a specific community. A local *industrial union* would usually consist of all the production workers in a given factory. There are approximately 70,000 local unions in the United States. The local union enrolls members, collects dues, holds meetings to discuss problems, and negotiates contracts.

National Unions The next level of organization is the national or international union. (If a union has some local branches in Canada, it is considered to be an international union.) Most local unions are branches of national unions, and they must pay a portion of their dues to the national union. The national union determines the broad policies within which the locals must operate and provides assistance in the organization of new locals. The staff of the national union usually includes expert lawyers and negotiators, who often assist local officials during contract talks with employers.

The Federation The third level of organization is the federation. Most national unions are affiliated with the AFL-CIO, which is a giant federation of American unions. The AFL-CIO depends on the national unions for funds, and its primary role is to promote the cause of all unionized workers by lobbying for pro-labor legislation at the state and federal levels and by soliciting public support for organized labor. Although most national unions are affiliated with the AFL-CIO, a few important national unions—including the Teamsters, the International Longshoremen, and the United Mine Workers—are *independent unions* that do not belong to the AFL-CIO.

Collective Bargaining

The primary way in which unions attempt to improve the status   of their members is through collective bargaining. *Collective bargaining* is the process by which a union negotiates with an employer (management) in an attempt to reach a mutually acceptable agreement with regard to wages, hours, and other terms and conditions of employment. The union negotiates collectively on behalf of all union members, regardless of the length of time they've been on the job, their financial status, or their individual personalities.   Through collective bargaining, the workers gain power. Whereas management is not likely to listen if one worker tries to bargain alone, it is very likely to pay attention when workers bargain as a group. In this section, we want to examine the various aspects of collective bargaining. We will examine the legal framework under which collective bargaining takes place, union security arrangements, major bargaining issues, and methods of settling labor-management disputes. Let's begin with an examination of the legal framework of collective bargaining.

The Legal Framework

Like any other process, effective and orderly collective bargaining requires a set of rules and procedures that both parties must follow during the negotiations The legal framework of collective bargaining is based on four major labor-relations laws that were enacted by the federal government during the period 1932-1959. Let us examine the major provisions of each of these laws.

Norris-LaGuardia Anti-Injunction Act (1932) The Norris-LaGuardia Act, the first piece of pro-labor legislation passed by Congress, was enacted at a time when the fortunes of unions were at their lowest point. It marked a significant change in public policy—from strong repression to strong encouragement of union activity. This law greatly restricted the power of the courts to issue injunctions against union activities, and it made yellow-dog contracts illegal.

The National Labor Relations Act (1935) This law, also known as the *Wagner Act,* is the cornerstone of modern labor-relations law. It guaranteed workers the right to organize unions and engage in collective bargaining, and it required employers to bargain in good faith with unions. This law also made it illegal for employers to interfere with legitimate union activities or discriminate against workers who form unions or engage in union activities.   In addition, the act established the *National Labor Relations Board (NLRB).* The Board's job was to enforce the act and to conduct and supervise free elections among a company's employees to determine which union, if any, shall represent the workers.

Labor-Management Relations Act (1947), This law, which is usually called the *Taft-Hartley Act,* amended the National Labor Relations Act. It came at a time when anti-union sentiment was strong, and one of its most important provisions was to prohibit mandatory union membership as a precondition for employment. Prior to this law, many unions forced employers to hire only union members. When this law took affect, both union and nonunion workers could be hired for a job.

Another important provision of the act gave power to the President to temporarily halt strikes that threaten to "imperil the national health or safety." The President has the power to order workers back to work for an 80-day "cooling-off period" in the case of such strikes, to give management and labor the opportunity to reconsider their positions and to resolve their differences under calmer circumstances. A long-lasting national trucking strike could fall under this category. If such crucial items as food and medicine were unable to reach their destinations, life-threatening situations could result. In addition, factories that depend on trucks to deliver their raw materials and to haul their finished products to customers might be forced to lay off their employees until the strike was over. Under such circumstances, the President might use the provisions of the Taft-Hartley Act to order the workers back to work.

Even strikes of a less crucial nature can lead to serious problems for the nation if they last long enough. In 1959, a national steel strike that had lasted for 116 days came to an end only when the President used the powers of the Taft-Hartley Act to order the strikers back to work.

The Labor-Management Reporting and Disclosure Act (1959), better known as the *Landrum-Griffin Act*, regulated union activities even further. Specifically, the law required all union officers to submit detailed financial reports to the Secretary of Labor and to hold periodic secret-ballot elections of union officers.

Union Security Arrangements

When a group of employees wishes to form a union, the group submits a petition (signed by at least 30 percent of the employees) to the National Labor Relations Board, requesting a representation election. The NLRB will then conduct a secret-ballot election. If a majority of the employees vote for the union, the NLRB will certify the union as the exclusive bargaining agent for all the employees. This means that the union must represent all employees equally, and any gains made by the union will go to all the employees, including those who are not union members. Because nonunion members receive the benefits of the union, too, some workers choose not to join and, thus, avoid paying union dues. Most unions are against this practice and attempt to negotiate a union security arrangement with the employer. A *union security arrangement* is an agreement between the union and the employer that requires employees to join the union or, at least, pay union dues.

Under the *closed-shop* arrangement, the employer agrees to hire only union members. This means a potential employee must join the union before he or she can get a job. The closed shop was common in the United States during the late 1930s and early 1940s. However, the Taft-Hartley Act of 1947 made the closed shop illegal. Despite the legal ban, arrangements very similar to the closed shop still exist today. For example, many building contractors hire most or all of their construction workers through union hiring halls. In practice, this means that workers must join the union in order to get a job.

Under the *union shop,* employers can hire nonunion workers. However, the employees are required to join the union within a specified time period (usually 30 to 60 days) as a condition of continued employment. The union shop is the most common form of union security arrangement today, although many states have passed *right-*

to-work laws, which make mandatory union membership illegal.

Under an *agency-shop* arrangement, employees are not required to join the union, but they are required to pay union dues. Agency shops exist primarily in states where the union shop has been outlawed. This arrangement represents a compromise between those who argue that workers should not have to join the union against their will and those who say that workers should have to pay for any benefits of union representation they receive. States can make the agency shop illegal if their "right-to-work" laws specifically prohibit the collection of fees as a condition of employment.

Major Bargaining Issues

The primary purpose of collective bargaining from the union's point of view is to improve the economic status and working conditions of the employees. The union tries to negotiate the most favorable contract possible; and there are many issues that come up during the negotiations. Let's briefly examine some of the most important bargaining issues.

Wages and Fringe Benefits Perhaps the most important issue from the standpoint of both the union and management is that of wages and fringe benefits. Fringe benefits include such things as paid holidays and vacations, sick pay, retirement programs, and employer-financed insurance coverage. Because wages and fringe benefits are, in effect, income to employees and costs to employers, there is a natural conflict of interests. Unions push hard for higher wages and improved fringe benefits, and employers push just as hard to keep worker compensation as low as possible.

There are many wage-related issues. In addition to the question of basic hourly wages, there is the question of differential pay for workers with different skill levels and different lengths of service with the company. For example, should skilled workers get a bigger pay increase than unskilled workers? And, if so, how much more should they get? Similarly, how much more should employees with ten years of service to the company earn than employees with only five years of service? There is also the question of overtime pay. Federal law requires employers to pay workers time and one half for any work over 40 hours per week. Unions, however, often attempt to negotiate overtime pay rates above those established by law. For example, a union may attempt to negotiate a provision that would require the employer to pay double time for work on Saturdays and triple time for work on Sundays and holidays.

Job Security Another very important issue is job security. High wages are of no value to workers if they lose their jobs, so unions push hard to negotiate contract provisions that will provide the maximum job security for their members. A typical collective bargaining contract will include provisions stipulating the conditions under which an employer legally can fire employees, as well as guidelines for determining which employees will be laid off during periods of declining employment.

A major goal of unions is to obtain contract provisions that guarantee seniority rights. *Seniority rights* grant certain privileges to employees on the basis of length of service with the company Those who have the most seniority (who have been with the company the longest) are given preferential treatment over those with less seniority. For example, most contracts state that when layoffs are necessary, those with the most seniority shall be laid off last, and those employees with the least seniority must be the first to go. Seniority rights provide a great deal of job security for employees who have held their jobs for several years. Seniority is also often an important factor in determining which employees will be promoted to higher paying jobs.

Working Conditions Improved working conditions are an important goal of most unions. There are many topics that fall under this category. Shorter hours, longer rest periods, safer working conditions, and well-defined job descriptions are just a few of the issues involving working conditions that are regularly negotiated by unions.

Grievance Procedures No matter how careful the union and employer are in negotiating and writing a collective bargaining contract, there will almost always be later disagreements over its interpretation.   Such disagreements often take the form of *grievances*, which are formal complaints accusing one of the parties of violating the collective bargaining agreement. Because grievances are common, it is important that the provisions of the contract include a good grievance procedure, which is used to settle disagreements over the implementation of the contract without strikes.

A typical *grievance procedure* will call for a series of meetings, at different levels of authority, between union and management representatives. If a grievance cannot be satisfactorily resolved at these meetings, it will usually move on to binding arbitration. *Binding arbitration* involves submitting the grievance to a neutral third party, acceptable to both the union and the employer, who will listen to the arguments of both parties and   then issue a decision.   This decision is binding on both the union and the employer in that both parties agree in advance to accept the decision as the final settlement of the grievance.

Settling Labor-Management Disputes
Collective bargaining is a power relationship in

which both sides make threats to back up their demands. The union's major weapons are the boycott and the strike. A *boycott* is a campaign by workers to discourage people from buying the employer's product in an effort to put economic pressure on him or her. In the late 1960s, for example, farm workers called for a nationwide boycott of grapes to pressure grape growers to make concessions to workers. A *strike* is a mutual agreement by the employees to stop working until their demands are met. During a strike, workers usually also engage in *picketing,* which involves standing or walking in front of the employer's place of business with signs that spell out the workers' complaints against the employer. Picketing can sometimes prove embarrassing to the employer, and it can also discourage non-striking workers from entering the place of employment.

The employer's major weapon is the lockout, which is just the opposite of the strike. In a *lockout,* the employer closes down the place of employment, thus depriving workers of their jobs, in an effort to put pressure on them to accept the employer's contract demands. In actual practice, the lockout is not used nearly as frequently as the strike.

Because strikes make the news, and peaceful settlements do not, there is an exaggerated notion of the amount of work time lost each year because of strikes. In actuality, studies have shown that since 1935 the amount of work time lost each year from strikes has averaged less than one percent of total work time. This is far less than the amount lost because of the common cold. Yet those strikes that do occur are costly to both employer and employees, and every effort is usually made to resolve disputes peacefully before resorting to a strike. Two procedures often used are mediation and advisory arbitration.

Mediation When negotiations break down between a union and an employer, sometimes a strike can be avoided by the use of *mediation*. This process, which is also sometimes called *conciliation*, is a means by which a third party, the mediator, tries to resolve the differences between the two parties. The mediator tries to keep the parties talking and may suggest compromises that might lead to a peaceful resolution of the dispute. However, unlike an arbitrator, a mediator does not make a specific recommendation for settling the dispute. The federal government, most states, and some large cities, provide mediation and conciliation services.

Advisory Arbitration Advisory arbitration, which is sometimes used when collective bargaining talks break down, should not be confused with the binding grievance arbitration discussed earlier. In grievance arbitration, both parties agree in advance to accept the arbitrator's decision with regard to a specific grievance. However, usually the stakes are too high in the negotiation of an entire collective bargaining contract for either party to agree to a binding settlement. Instead, they agree to *advisory arbitration*, which is a procedure giving either or both parties the right to reject an arbitrator's decision.

Wage Determination

There are many different occupations and labor markets in the United States, and each has its own unique characteristics. For our purposes, however, let's group all occupations into two categories—those that involve primarily unskilled and semiskilled workers, and those that involve primarily skilled and professional workers.

Unskilled and Semiskilled Workers—Unskilled and semiskilled workers are people who have little or no special work skills. They include maids, janitors, low-level factory production workers, and so forth. Most unskilled and semiskilled workers usually attempt to find employment in or near their home community Thus, there are literally thousands of local labor markets for such workers, and the supply and demand conditions will vary from one area to another. However, the demand for such workers is usually low relative to the supply. And with the increasing use of modern labor-saving technology, this gap between the supply and demand for such workers is likely to widen even farther.

Because of supply and demand conditions, unskilled and semiskilled workers often have difficulty finding employment, and their pay is usually low relative to that of other groups. They have almost no individual bargaining power with employers because they can be easily replaced. For this reason, such employees often benefit greatly from unionization. Whereas an employer can easily replace one or a few individual workers, it is not so easy to replace a thousand unionized workers who have banded together to call a strike.

Skilled and Professional Workers—Skilled workers include such groups as carpenters, plumbers, electricians, typists, and computer programmers; whereas professional workers include doctors, lawyers, entertainers, professional athletes, and so forth. Both skilled and professional workers have special skills and training, and they can be replaced only by other workers with similar attributes. As is the case for any group, the wages and salaries of skilled and professional workers are determined by supply and demand. And because the demand is often strong relative to the supply, such workers frequently experience high earnings compared to other groups of employees.

In the case of some skilled workers, such as electricians and plumbers, the supply may be kept artificially low by unions. To become a plumber or an electrician, workers usually must obtain special training through apprenticeship programs that are at least partially controlled by craft unions. Some critics argue that these craft unions deliberately restrict the supply of such labor, and keep wages artificially high, by limiting the number of apprentices accepted into these training programs. However, union supporters argue that some restriction is necessary to protect the job security of those who have already gone through the apprenticeship programs. Moreover, craft unions are not the only organizations accused of restricting entry into their occupations. Some critics charge that the American Bar Association and the American Medical Association act like unions and attempt to restrict the supply of lawyers and doctors.

In the case of some professional employees, there will always be a relatively small supply. It's not possible to mass-produce highly talented entertainers and professional athletes. Although there are millions of people who would love to enter these fields, most of them do not have the talent necessary to achieve stardom. Thus, the demand for such "stars" will always be high relative to the supply, and those who make it to the top will be rewarded highly both financially and otherwise.

The Effects of Minimum Wage Laws

Minimum wage laws set a lower limit on the wage that can be paid to most workers. The first national minimum wage law was enacted by Congress in 1938 and established a minimum wage of 25 cents per hour. This law has been amended periodically over the years, and the minimum wage has gradually been adjusted upward in an effort to keep pace with inflation. However, since politics play a major role in the feasibility of adjusting the minimum wage rate upwards, there have been periods when the rate remained stuck for many years.

In 1997, the minimum wage was increased to $5.15 per hour and it stayed at that level for a decade. Finally, in

2007, the rate was increased to $5.85 per hour, with provisions for increases to $6.55 in 2008 and $7.25 in 2009, where it still remains as of 2012.

The federal minimum wage does not cover all workers in all occupations. Examples of workers usually not covered by the federal law include domestic workers, fishermen, baby sitters, and seasonal workers. Those not covered by the federal law come under the state minimum in states that have state minimum wage laws. Some state minimums are higher than the federal minimum, and some are even lower. In 2011, the State of Washington had a minimum wage of $8.67, whereas the minimum wage in Georgia was only $5.15 per hour.

Most workers in the United States earn wages above the minimum wage and, as a result, are not directly affected by the minimum wage law. However, a substantial number of younger and older workers, who work at unskilled and often part-time jobs, are paid only the minimum wage. Thus, whenever the minimum wage goes up, these workers get an automatic pay raise that they would not get if it were not for the minimum wage law.

Minimum-wage laws have long been a source of controversy among economists and others. Some argue that minimum-wage laws do more harm than good by reducing employment opportunities. They argue that many teenagers, who are unable to find jobs at the current minimum wage, could find employment at a lower wage. Their reasoning is based on the belief that employers would find it more profitable to hire teenagers if they were allowed to pay less than the minimum wage. Others contend that these workers would be exploited if it were not for the minimum wage.

Chapter Highlights

- Organized activity among workers in the United States was recorded as early as 1636, but unions as we know them today first appeared during the period 1790 to 1820. These first unions were formed in response to changing economic conditions that caused a conflict to develop between employer and employees.

- The strong industrial growth that followed the Civil War led to growth in union membership and increased efforts to combine local unions into national organizations. The Knights of Labor was founded in 1869, and by 1886 it had 700,000 members. However, a series of unsuccessful strikes, internal squabbling, and inept leadership led to a rapid decline after 1886.

- The American Federation of Labor (AFL) was founded in 1886 by Samuel Gompers, who served as president of the AFL from 1886 until his death in 1924 except for one year. Gompers emphasized "economic unionism" instead of the "political unionism" that had characterized earlier federations. The AFL attempted to make basic gains in wages and working conditions by bargaining directly with employers.

- Prior to the 1930s, there were no statutory laws governing union activities or collective bargaining. And without legal protection, labor unions faced opposition from both employers and the courts in their attempts to organize workers. The courts used both the conspiracy doctrine and injunctions in their battle against unions, and employers used a number of antiunion weapons including labor spies, yellow-dog contracts, and lockouts.

- Following the enactment of prolabor legislation in the 1930s, many new unions were formed. Most of the new unions were industrial unions, representing workers in the mass-production industries. A controversy arose within the AFL leadership over the admission of industrial unions and finally, in 1938, the industrial unions banded together and formed a rival federation called the Congress of Industrial Organizations (CIO).

- The structure of organized labor in the United States involves three levels of organization: the local union, the national union, and the federation. The local union enrolls members, collects dues, holds meetings to discuss problems, and negotiates contracts. The national union determines broad policies within which the local union must operate, provides assistance in the organization of new locals, and assists local officials during contract talks. The federation promotes the cause of all unionized workers by lobbying for prolabor legislation and soliciting public support for organized labor.

- Collective bargaining is the process by which unions negotiate with management in an attempt to reach a mutually acceptable agreement with regard to wages, hours, and other terms and conditions of employment.

- The legal framework of collective bargaining is based on four labor-relations laws. They are: Norris-LaGuardia Anti-Injunction Act (1932); National Labor Relations Act (1935); Labor-

Management Relations Act (1947); and Labor-Management Reporting and Disclosure Act (1959).

- A union security arrangement is an agreement between the union and the employer that requires employees to join the union or, at least, pay union dues. Examples of union security arrangements include the closed shop, the union shop, and the agency shop.

- Wages and fringe benefits, job security, working conditions, and grievance procedures are some of the most important collective bargaining issues.

- Mediation and advisory arbitration are often used in an effort to settle labor-management disputes and avoid a work stoppage. The union's major weapons for pressuring management to agree to its terms are the strike and the boycott. A lockout is a work stoppage called by management.

- Unskilled and semiskilled workers often have difficulty finding employment, and their pay is usually low relative to other groups. Since they have almost no individual bargaining power, unionization is often especially beneficial to such workers.

- Skilled and professional workers have special skills and training and can be replaced only by other workers with similar skills and training. Because the demand is often very strong relative to the supply, such workers frequently experience high earnings compared to other groups of employees.

- Minimum wage laws set a lower limit on the wage

that can be paid to most workers. Such laws are controversial because some critics believe they do more harm than good by reducing employment opportunities.

Important Terms

Match each of the following terms with the correct definition:

yellow-dog contract

craft union

collective bargaining

conspiracy doctrine

advisory arbitration

court injunction

minimum wage laws

labor spy

right-to-work laws

industrial union

strike

grievance procedure

seniority rights

binding arbitration

mediation

lockout

closed shop

union shop

agency shop

boycott

picketing

1. A union composed of workers in a particular trade or craft.

2. The common law doctrine that the organization of workers for the purpose of obtaining higher wages was a violation of property right and, thus, illegal.

3. A union composed of workers from a particular industry.

4. An arrangement under which employers are free to hire nonunion workers, but the new employees are required to join the union within a specified time period as a condition of continued employment.

5. A person hired by management to infiltrate unions

and provide management with the names of union members and supporters.

6. State law that makes it illegal to require workers to join a union as a condition of employment.

7. Standing or walking in front of an employer's place of business with signs that spell out the worker's complaints against the employer.

8. A process under which grievances are submitted to a neutral third party acceptable to both the union and management who issues a decision that is binding on both parties.

9. The temporary closing of the place of employment by management in an effort to pressure unions to agree to management's terms.

10. An arrangement where employees are not required to join the union but they are required to pay union dues.

11. Laws that set a lower limit on the wage that can be paid to most workers.

12. A campaign by workers to discourage people from buying the employer's product in an effort to put economic pressure on the employer.

13. Rights that give certain privileges to employees on the basis of length of service with the employer.

14. The process by which a union negotiates with management in an attempt to reach a mutually acceptable agreement with regard to wages, hours,

and other terms and conditions of employment.

15. A court order issued by a judge requiring a party to do or to cease doing specific activities.

16. An arrangement under which employers agree to hire only union members.

17. A procedure for settling disagreements over the implementation of the collective bargaining contract without resorting to strikes.

18. A process in which a neutral third party's recommended settlement for a labor-management dispute can be refused by either party.

19. A mutual agreement by employees to stop working until their demands are met.

20. A process under which a neutral third party tries to keep the union and management talking in an effort to reach a peaceful settlement to a labor-management dispute.

21. An agreement under which employees promise not to join a union as a condition of employment.

Review Questions

1. .When were the first unions formed in the United States? Why did unions come into existence at that particular time?

2. How successful was the Knights of Labor?

3. Who was the man who founded the American Federation of Labor? When was it formed?

4. Give examples of anti-union weapons commonly used in an effort to keep unions from succeeding.

5. What do the initials, CIO, stand for? When was the CIO formed?

6. What are the three levels of union organization in the United States?

7. Name the four major labor relations laws that govern collective bargaining in the United States.

8. What is a union-security arrangement? Give examples of such arrangements.

9. Define mediation and arbitration. What is the difference between the two?

10. What types of workers tend to benefit most from union representation?

Discussion Questions

1. Why was it so difficult for unions to organize American workers prior to the 1930s?

2. Do you think it is fair to require workers to join a union as a condition of employment? Why or why not?

3. Suppose unions and collective bargaining were made illegal in the United States. How do you think disagreements between employers and employees would be settled in the absence of collective bargaining?

CHAPTER ELEVEN

The Laws of Supply and Demand

It has been said that most basic economic questions could be answered with three simple words. These words are, "supply and demand." There is much truth to this statement. Take the following questions, for example: (1) Why are the prices of gold, silver, and diamonds so high while the prices of some other commodities, such as salt and flour, are relatively low? (2) Why are the incomes of professional athletes, movie and TV stars, and certain other workers so high while the incomes of unskilled workers are very low? (3) Why do interest rates and stock prices fluctuate up and down so much? Each of these questions could be correctly answered with the words "supply and demand."

Of course, knowing that the answer to a particular question is "supply and demand" is not very helpful unless you understand what these words mean. Let's examine the meaning of these words, and why they are so important to the understanding of economics.

Demand 需求
The word "demand" has a different meaning in economics than in everyday life. Many people use the word, demand, to give a command or ultimatum. For

example, a union negotiator might say, "We demand higher wages and better working conditions." In economics, however, the word "demand" refers to the ability and willingness of people to buy things.

The Law of Demand 需求定律

The law of demand is a simple concept. According to this economic law, *as the price of an item rises, and other factors remain unchanged, the quantity demanded by buyers will fall; as the price of an item falls, and other things remain unchanged, the quantity demanded by buyers will rise.* The law of demand is little more than common sense. It says simply that people will buy more of an item if the price is low than they will if the price is high.

There are a couple of reasons why the law of demand holds true. First of all, as the price of an item declines, people can buy more of it out of a given income, and it becomes more attractive to buyers relative to other items they might spend their money on. For example, if the price of beef falls, while the price of pork remains the same, not only will people be able to buy more beef out of a given income, but also some people will substitute beef for pork because they consider beef a greater bargain.

Secondly, there is a concept in economics known as *the law of diminishing marginal utility.* According to this law, as an individual obtains more and more units of an item, during a specified time period, he or she will obtain less and less additional utility (or satisfaction) from each additional unit. For example, suppose you are very hungry and you stop at a hotdog stand for lunch. The first hotdog will give you a great deal of satisfaction, and if forced to do so, you would pay a fairly high price for it. The second hotdog will probably give you a little less satisfaction than the first; and the third one will give you still less satisfaction. In other words, the more hotdogs you consume in a fixed time period, the less utility (or satisfaction) you will get from each additional hotdog. Thus, since you get less and less additional satisfaction from each unit of most items as you obtain more and more units, you will buy increasing quantities only at decreasing prices.

Supply 供给

Like the word "demand" the word "supply" also has a very specific meaning in economics. It refers to the ability and willingness of sellers to make things available for sale.

The Law of Supply 供给定律

According to the law of supply, *as the price of an item rises, and other factors remain unchanged, the quantity supplied by suppliers will rise; as the price of an item falls, and other factors remain unchanged, the quantity supplied by suppliers will fall.* The law of supply, like the law of demand, is little more than common sense. It should come as no surprise to any reader that suppliers are willing to supply larger quantities of their goods and services at higher prices than at low prices.

供给, 需求及市场
Supply, Demand, and Markets

Supply and demand together make a market. A market is *the arrangement through which potential buyers and sellers come together to exchange goods and services.* A market exists whenever and wherever the decisions of buyers and sellers interact through the laws of supply and demand. A market can be a specific place, such as a local farmers' market where sellers and buyers come together to exchange goods. However, markets usually involve a much larger geographic area, and may extend over an entire nation or even the whole world.

The markets for professional athletes and coaches are examples of labor markets that are national in scope. 范围 Professional athletes and coaches transfer to new jobs in

other sections of the country on a regular basis. The same is
true of most professions. Also, most products produced in
the United States are sold in national markets.

Examples of world markets are the markets for
gold, silver, and crude oil. In these markets, buyers and
sellers from all over the world interact with one another
through the laws of supply and demand.

Supply and Demand Determine Prices

Unless there is government interference with the
forces of supply and demand, or other artificial barriers to
the free operation of markets, supply and demand
determine the prices of almost everything. As a first step
toward understanding how supply and demand determine
prices, let's look at the hypothetical demand schedule for
corn that is presented in Table 11-1A.

Table 11-1A
Demand Schedule for Corn
(hypothetical data)

Price ($ per bu.)	Quantity Demanded (Million bu. per mo.)
5	200
4	250
3	300
2	350
1	400

Before looking at the data in the table, it is
important to make a distinction between the terms, **demand**
and **quantity demanded**. Although these terms sound

almost identical, there is an important difference between them that is crucial to the proper understanding of supply and demand analysis. The term, demand, refers to *the whole schedule of quantities that will be bought at different possible prices*. If we refer to a specific quantity that will be bought at a specific price, we use the term, quantity demanded. In other words, in our hypothetical example, presented in Table 11-1A, the quantity of corn demanded at a price of $5 per bushel is 200 million bushels per month. The quantity demanded at $4 per bushel is 250 million bushels per month. At a price of $3 per bushel, 300 million bushels will be purchased, and so forth. Again, the term, quantity demanded, refers to a specific quantity that will be purchased at a specific price. The term, demand, always refers to the whole schedule of possible price and quantity combinations.

If you take a close look at Table 11-1A, you will observe the law of demand at work. The lower the price, the larger the quantity demanded. Likewise, as the price rises, the quantity demanded becomes smaller and smaller.

A hypothetical supply schedule for corn is presented in Table 11-2A. Again the term, "supply," refers to the whole schedule of quantities that will be supplied at various possible prices, and the term, quantity supplied, refers to a specific quantity that will be supplied at a specific price. Note the law of supply at work in this table. At the low price of $1 per bushel, farmers will be willing to supply only 200 million bushels per month.

However, as the price rises to $2 per bushel, farmers will supply 250 million bushels per month and, the higher the price, the larger the quantity supplied. Although this table contains only hypothetical data, it is very realistic to expect that producers will supply larger quantities of their product at higher prices than at lower prices.

Table 11-2A
Supply Schedule for Corn
(hypothetical data)

Price ($ per bu.)	Quantity Supplied (Million bu. per mo.)
5	400
4	350
3	300
2	250
1	200

In Table 11-3A, the supply and demand schedules are put together to determine the equilibrium price. The **equilibrium price** is *that price at which the quantity demanded is exactly equal to the quantity supplied.* In our hypothetical example, the equilibrium price of corn is $3 per bushel. At a price of $3 per bushel, the quantity that will be bought is 300 million bushels per month, and the quantity that will be offered for sale is also 300 million bushels per month. There is neither a surplus nor a shortage at this price.

At any price other than $3 per bushel, there will be either a surplus or a shortage. For example, at a price of $4 per bushel, suppliers will want to sell 350 million bushels per month while only 250 million bushels will be purchased. At a price of $2 per bushel purchasers will want to buy 350 million bushels per month while suppliers will be willing to sell only 250 million bushels. At prices which are too high for equilibrium, the existence of a surplus will tend to force prices down. At prices below the equilibrium level, the resulting shortage will tend to cause prices to rise as buyers compete with each other for the short supply. Therefore, market   forces will tend to move the price toward the equilibrium level of $3 per bushel, the price at which the quantity demanded is exactly equal to the quantity supplied.

Table 11-3A
Supply and Demand Schedules for Corn
(hypothetical data)

Price ($ per bu.)	Quantity Demanded (Million bu.per mo.)	Quantity Supplied (Million bu.per mo.)	
5 (Price too high for	200	(Surplus will	400
4 equilibrium.)	250	exist.)	350
3 (Equilibrium price.)	300	(Neither a surplus nor a shortage.)	300
2 (Price too low for	350	(Shortage will	250
1 equilibrium.)	400	exist.)	200

TRANSITION NOTE: The "bare basics" of how supply and

demand determine prices have been presented in this short introduction for those teachers who do not want to work with graphics. The schedules used above are reproduced below in order to introduce supply and demand curves for those who wish a more comprehensive analysis of supply and demand.

Supply and Demand Curves

The data from the hypothetical demand schedule in Table 11-1B are plotted in the diagram in Figure 11-1 to produce a demand curve. Price is measured on the vertical axis, and quantity is measured on the horizontal axis of the demand model. For simplicity, the supply and demand curves are drawn as straight lines although they usually have some curvature to them.

Table 11-1B
Demand Schedule for Corn
(hypothetical data)

Price (per bu.)	Quantity Demanded (Million bu. per mo.)
$5.00	200
4.00	250
3.00	300
2.00	350
1.00	400

You will note that the demand curve slopes downward to the right, indicating that larger quantities will be demanded at lower prices and smaller quantities at higher prices. For example, at the high price of $5 per bushel only 200 million bushels per month will be demanded. However, at a low price of $1 per bushel, 400 million bushels will be demanded per month.

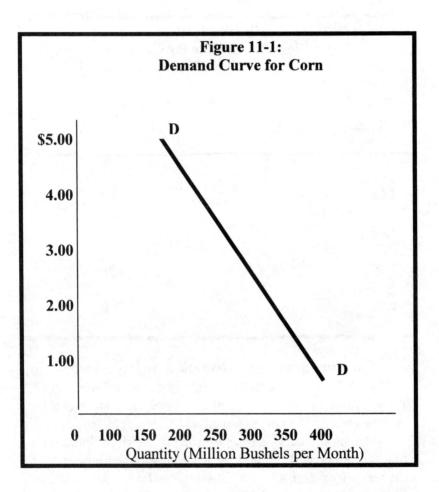

Figure 11-1:
Demand Curve for Corn

The specific amounts that will be purchased at the various possible prices in this hypothetical demand curve may or may not be realistic. However, there is no doubt that larger quantities of corn would be purchased at low prices than at high prices. The principle of the downward-sloping demand curve holds true for almost all items.

Table 11-2B Supply Schedule for Corn (hypothetical data)	
Price (per bu.)	**Quantity Supplied (Million bu. per mo.)**
$5.00	400
4.00	350
3.00	300
2.00	250
1.00	200

The data from the hypothetical supply schedule in Table 11-2B are presented as a supply curve in Figure 11-2. Again, price is measured on the vertical axis, and quantity is measured on the horizontal axis.

The supply curve slopes upward to the right, indicating that suppliers will be willing to supply larger amounts at higher prices and smaller amounts at lower prices. For example, at a price of $5 per bushel, 400 million bushels per month will be supplied, and at the low price of $1 per bushel suppliers would be willing to supply only 200 million bushels per month. Again, the specific quantity and price combinations listed in this hypothetical example may or may not be realistic. However, the fact that the quantity supplied will increase as the price rises is very realistic.

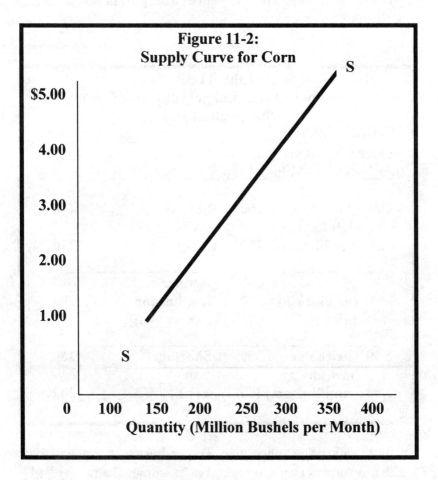

Figure 11-2:
Supply Curve for Corn

In Table 11-3B, the supply and demand schedules are put together to determine the equilibrium price. The **equilibrium price** is *that price at which the quantity demanded is exactly equal to the quantity supplied.* In our hypothetical example, the equilibrium price of corn is $3 per bushel. At a price of $3 per bushel, the quantity that will be bought is 300 million bushels per month, and the quantity that will be offered for sale is also 300 million bushels per month. There is neither a surplus nor a shortage at this price.

Table 11-3B
Supply and Demand Schedules for Corn
(hypothetical data)

Price (per bu.)	Quantity Demanded (Million bu.per mo.)		Quantity Supplied (Million bu.per mo.)
$5.00	(Price too high for	200 (Surplus will	400
4.00	equilibrium.) 250	exist.)	350
3.00	(Equilibrium price.) 300	(Neither a surplus nor a shortage.)	300
2.00	(Price too low for	350 (Shortage will	250
1.00	equilibrium.) 400	exist.)	200

At any price other than $3 per bushel, there will be either a surplus or a shortage. For example, at a price of $4 per bushel, suppliers will want to sell 350 million bushels per month while only 250 million bushels will be purchased. At a price of $2 per bushel purchasers will want to buy 350 million bushels per month while suppliers will be willing to sell only 250 million bushels. At prices that are too high for equilibrium, the existence of a surplus will tend to force prices down. At prices below the equilibrium level, the resulting shortage will tend to cause prices to rise as buyers compete with each other for the short supply. Therefore, market forces will tend to move the price toward the equilibrium level of $3 per bushel, the price at which the quantity demanded is exactly equal to the quantity supplied.

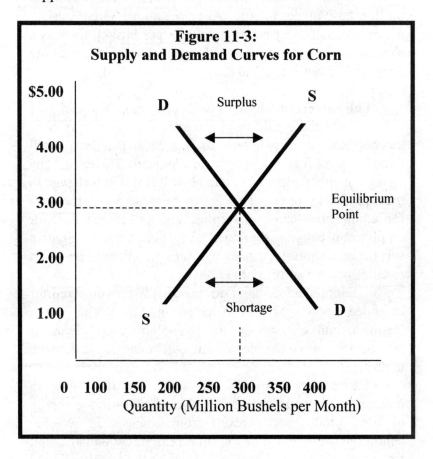

Figure 11-3:
Supply and Demand Curves for Corn

In Figure 11-3 the data from Table 11-3B are presented in the form of supply and demand curves. You will again note that the demand curve slopes downward to the right, indicating that increased quantities will be purchased as the price declines. The supply curve, on the other hand, slopes upward to the right, indicating that smaller and smaller quantities will be supplied as the price falls. The one unique point on the diagram where the two curves intersect is the *equilibrium point.* The *equilibrium price* is $3 per bushel, and the *equilibrium quantity* is 300 million bushels per month. At prices above $3 per bushel, a surplus exists. At prices below $3 per bushel, there is a shortage. Only at the price of $3 per bushel is the quantity demanded exactly equal to the quantity supplied.

The Effects of Changes in Supply and Demand

Once the equilibrium price for a good or service is reached, the price will tend to remain at that level until there is a change in supply or demand. However, any change in either supply or demand will result in a change in the equilibrium price. This is true because prices too high for equilibrium cause a surplus, and prices too low for equilibrium cause a shortage. Any time there is either a surplus or a shortage, prices will tend to adjust in an effort to eliminate the surplus or shortage.

Supply and demand do not usually remain fixed for extended periods of time. Changes in tastes, changes in incomes, and changes in the availability and prices of related items are examples of things that can cause demand to change.

Changes in supply can result from changes in production methods and costs. Also, changes in the supply of food products can result from changes in weather conditions. Too much or too little rain, insect damage, and frosts can all result in major changes in the supply of food items.

An increase in demand will cause the price of a product to rise, whereas a decrease in demand will cause a decline in price. Changes in supply, on the other hand, have just the opposite effect on price. An increase in the supply of an item will cause the price to fall while a decrease in supply will cause the price of the item to rise. In other words, prices tend to be forced up by increases in demand and/or decreases in supply, both of which will result in shortages if prices do not adjust upward.

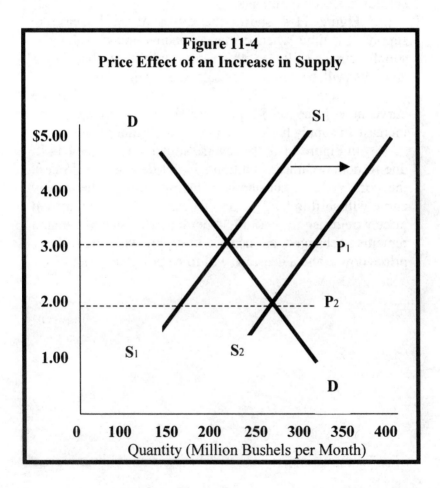

Figure 11-4
Price Effect of an Increase in Supply

Likewise, prices tend to be forced down by decreases in demand and/or increases in supply, both of which usually lead to surpluses. Thus, price changes are often easily explained by simple supply and demand factors. If there is a shortage of an item at current prices, then prices will tend to rise until the shortage is eliminated. If there is a surplus of an item, prices will fall until the surplus has been eliminated.

Figure 11-4 shows the effect of an increase in supply at a time when demand remains unchanged. The supply curve shifts to the right, indicating that larger amounts will be offered for sale at all prices than before. The new supply curve S_2 intersects the unchanged demand curve at a price of $2 per bushel instead of $3. The increase in supply has reduced the equilibrium price.

In Figure 11-5, the reverse situation is presented. If, due to poor weather conditions, insect damage, or disease, the corn yield is substantially below normal, the supply curve will shift to the left. In this example, the equilibrium price would rise from $3 to $4 per bushel. Thus, if demand remains unchanged, an increase in supply will tend to force prices down, and a decrease will force prices up.

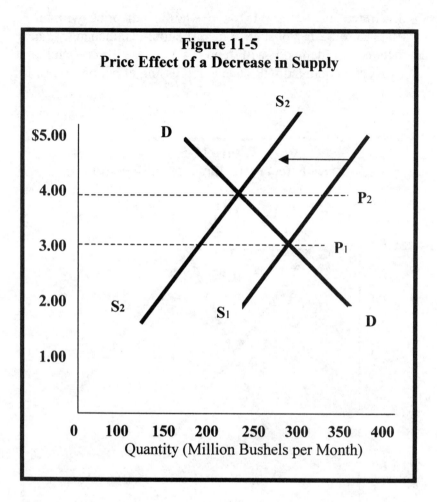

Figure 11-5
Price Effect of a Decrease in Supply

In Figures 11-6 and 11-7, changes in demand are illustrated. If, as a result of increased exports or other factors, total purchases of corn at all prices tend to rise, this will cause a shifting to the right of the demand curve as illustrated by the curve D2 in Figure 11-6. The result will be a rise in the equilibrium price from $3 to $5 per bushel. If, on the other hand, there is a decrease in demand as illustrated by Figure 11-7, the equilibrium price will fall from $3 to $2 per bushel. Thus, if supply is unchanged, an increase in demand will tend to increase prices and a decrease in demand will have a depressing effect on prices.

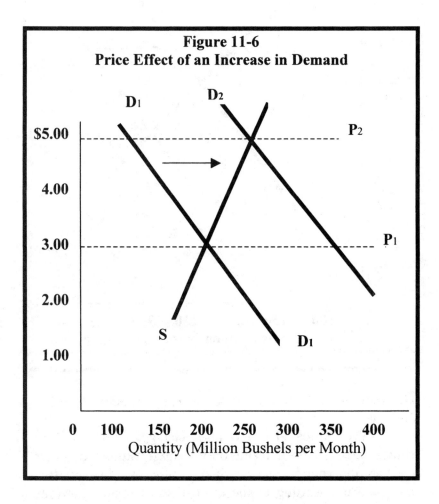

Figure 11-6
Price Effect of an Increase in Demand

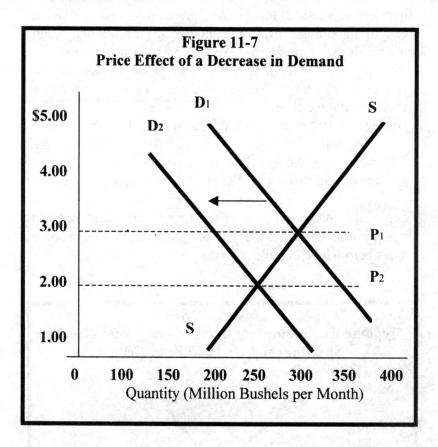

Figure 11-7
Price Effect of a Decrease in Demand

Government Interference with the Laws of Supply and Demand

The forces of supply and demand will determine market prices and eliminate both shortages and surpluses if they are allowed to operate freely. However, sometimes the government intervenes and establishes prices that are either above or below the prices set by the free market. This intervention takes the form of either price ceilings or price floors.

Price Ceilings--Price ceilings are government-imposed regulations that prevent prices from rising above a certain maximum level. During periods of rapidly rising prices, the government has sometimes attempted to halt the price increases by making it illegal for prices to rise above a certain level that it has established. In order to better understand the effects of a price ceiling, let's use an example. During the 1970s, the price of gasoline rose at an alarming rate. When the price reached $1 per gallon, many people demanded that the government impose a price ceiling in order to halt further rises. The government refused to impose a price ceiling, preferring to allow the forces of supply and demand to interact and establish prices. Prices continued to rise, ultimately reaching $1.50 per gallon or higher in some areas before leveling off.

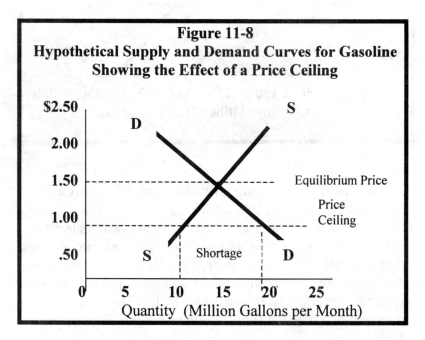

Figure 11-8
Hypothetical Supply and Demand Curves for Gasoline
Showing the Effect of a Price Ceiling

Now let's suppose the government had imposed a price ceiling of $1 per gallon. How would such a ceiling have affected buyers and sellers of gasoline? Since the forces of supply and demand ultimately established an equilibrium price of $1.50, a legally imposed maximum price of $1 would have led to critical shortages. The quantity of gasoline that people would have wanted to buy at a price of $1 per gallon would have greatly exceeded the quantity available for sale at that price. Thus, the nation would have experienced a critical gasoline shortage.

The effect of a price ceiling is shown graphically in Figure 11-8. Since there would not have been nearly enough gasoline to meet the demand of consumers at a price of $1 per gallon, it would have been necessary for the government to establish some sort of artificial rationing program in an effort to distribute the scarce gasoline equitably. In fact, the government did have a standby rationing plan. Rationing coupons were printed and, had the government decided to ration gasoline, each motorist's weekly allotment would have depended on the number of coupons issued to that motorist by the government.

Since the government decided not to impose a price ceiling on gasoline, no such artificial rationing program was necessary. Instead, the free market was allowed to do the rationing through the forces of supply and demand. Consumers reacted to the rising prices by buying smaller, more fuel-efficient cars and by driving fewer miles. Thus, at a price of $1.50 per gallon, the quantity of gasoline demanded by consumers was less than it would have been at $1 per gallon. Also, the quantity supplied at $1.50 per gallon was larger than it would have been at $1 per gallon. The net effect was that, at $1.50 per gallon, the quantity of gasoline demanded was approximately equal to the quantity supplied at that price.

Most economists oppose price ceilings and government rationing under normal circumstances.

Instead, they prefer to allow the market to do the rationing through the forces of supply and demand. Because gasoline prices were allowed to rise to the equilibrium level during the 1970s, market forces did the rationing so there was no need for a government-rationing program.

Price Floors--Price floors are just the opposite of price ceilings. With price floors, the government imposes regulations that prevent prices from falling below a certain minimum level. The government has often established price floors for agricultural products to prevent the prices of these products from falling below the cost of production. In this way, the government guarantees farmers a certain minimum price.

Suppose that, if the forces of supply and demand were allowed to operate freely, they would establish an equilibrium price for corn of $3 per bushel. However, suppose the government establishes a legal price floor of $4 per bushel. At this price, the quantity of corn supplied exceeds the quantity demanded, resulting in a surplus. Such a situation is depicted in Figure 11-9.

Thus, if the government maintains a price floor of $4 per bushel, it will have to devise some plan for dealing with the surplus of corn. Over the years, the government has used a number of plans to deal with agricultural surpluses resulting from price floors. In all plans, however, either the government buys up the surplus, or it encourages farmers to reduce the quantity supplied by planting fewer acres.

Figure 11-9
Hypothetical Supply and Demand Curves for Corn
Showing the Effect of a Price Floor

Elasticity of Supply and Demand

As you already know, a change in the price of a product will cause the quantity demanded and the quantity supplied to change. However, the amount of change in quantity demanded and quantity supplied from a given percentage change in price can vary enormously depending upon the product in question. For example, if the price of a box of table salt doubles from 50 cents to $1, the quantity demanded will probably change only slightly. However, the doubling of the price of some products would result in enormous reductions in sales. The resulting change in quantity demanded from a given change in price depends on a concept known as the elasticity of demand. Likewise, the change in quantity supplied resulting from a given change in price will depend on the elasticity of supply.

Elasticity of demand *is a measure of the responsiveness of quantity demanded to a change in price.* If a change in the price of an item will have a very big effect on the quantity demanded, we say the demand is very elastic. On the other hand, if a change in the price of an item will have little effect on the quantity demanded, we say the demand is very inelastic.

The elasticity of demand for an item depends on several factors, the most important of which is the degree to which the item is a necessity. The demand for a life-maintaining medication is very inelastic. If the buyer must have the medication in order to live, he or she will probably continue to buy the same amount no matter how high the price goes. On the other hand, luxury items typically have a very elastic demand. Other factors that help to determine elasticity of demand are the cost of the item relative to consumers' total expenditures, and the availability and cost of good substitutes for the item.

Elasticity of supply is *a measure of the responsiveness of quantity supplied to a change in price.* If a change in price has a very big effect on the quantity supplied, the supply is very elastic. However, if a change in price has very little effect on the quantity supplied, the supply is very inelastic.

The elasticity of supply for an item depends largely on the time period under consideration. A large increase in the price of corn, for example, will probably cause farmers to produce substantially more corn during the next growing season. Thus, the supply of corn is quite elastic. However, suppose there is a significant increase in the price of apples. Will apple growers increase production substantially during the following season? No. Apple producers may plant more apple trees, but it will be several years before the new trees will be mature enough to bear fruit. Thus, in the short run, the supply of apples is very inelastic.

Chapter Highlights

- The words "supply" and "demand" are two of the most important words in economics. A sound understanding of the principles of supply and demand will help you to understand both specific economic issues and the operation of the entire economic system.

- It is important to make a distinction between the terms "demand" and "quantity demanded." "Demand" refers to the whole schedule of possible prices and quantities demanded. "Quantity demanded refers to a specific quantity demanded at a specific price.

- "Supply" refers to the whole schedule of possible prices and quantities supplied. "Quantity supplied" refers to a specific quantity supplied at a specific price.

- Supply and demand together create markets and establish prices within these markets. A market is the organized action through which potential buyers and sellers come together to exchange goods and services. a Market exists whenever and wherever the decisions of buyers and sellers interact through the forces of supply and demand to determine prices.

- The equilibrium price is that price at which the quantity demanded is exactly equal to the quantity supplied. When the equilibrium price has been reached, the market price will tend to stay at that level until some external force causes a change in demand

and/or supply.

- When allowed to operate freely, the price system tends to eliminate both shortages and surpluses through the forces of supply and demand. If the government interferes with the price system through the use of price ceilings or price floors, then the government will have to establish policies for coping with the resulting shortages and/or surpluses.

- An increase in demand will cause the price of a product to rise; whereas a decrease in demand will cause a decline in prices. Changes in supply have just the opposite effect on price. An increase in the supply of an item will cause the price to fall, and a decrease in supply will cause the price of the item to rise.

- The resulting change in quantity demanded from a given change in price depends on the elasticity of demand. Likewise, the change in quantity supplied resulting from a given change in price will depend on the elasticity of supply of the item.

Important Terms

Match each of the following terms with the correct definition:

demand	supply
quantity demanded	quantity supplied
law of demand	law of supply
demand schedule	supply schedule
equilibrium price	market
elasticity of demand	elasticity of supply
price ceiling	price floor

1. A listing showing the various amounts of an item that sellers are willing to sell at various possible prices.

2. A law stating that as the price of an item rises and other things remain unchanged, the quantity demanded by buyers will fall; as the price of an item falls and other things remain unchanged, the quantity demanded by buyers will rise.

3. A listing showing the various amounts of an item that buyers are willing and able to buy at various possible prices during some stated time period.

4. A law stating that as the price of an item rises and other things remain unchanged, the quantity supplied by sellers will rise; as the price of an item falls and other things remain unchanged, the quantity supplied by sellers will fall.

5. The arrangement through which potential buyers and sellers come together to exchange goods and services.

6. The ability and willingness of people to buy things.

7. The ability and willingness of sellers to make things available for sale.

8. The price at which the quantity demanded is exactly equal to the quantity supplied.

9. A government-imposed upper price limit that prevents market forces from establishing a price above this limit.

10. A government imposed lower price limit that prevents market forces from establishing a price below this limit.

11. A specific quantity that will be demanded at a specific price.

12. A specific quantity that will be supplied at a specific price.

13. A measure of the responsiveness of quantity demanded to a change in price.

14. A measure of the responsiveness of quantity supplied to a change in price.

Review Questions

1. How is the word "demand" used in economics?

2. State the law of demand.

3. What is the difference between demand and quantity demanded?

4. How is the word "supply" used in economics?

5. State the law of supply.

6. Describe the difference between supply and quantity supplied.

7. What is a market?

8. How do supply and demand determine prices?

9. What is an equilibrium price? How is it achieved?

10. What happens when prices are too high for equilibrium?

11. What happens when prices are too low for equilibrium?

12. What is a price ceiling? A price floor?

13. What is meant by elasticity of demand and elasticity of supply?

Discussion Questions
1. Under what circumstances do you think the government might be justified in imposing price controls on the American economy? What problems would be created by price controls?

CHAPTER TWELVE

The Economics of the Firm

The primary reason that most firms are in business is to make a profit, and most firms try to earn as much profit as possible. In order to maximize profits, a firm must adjust its level of production until it reaches that level of output where profits are as high as possible. The amount of profit that a firm can make is determined by two key factors: production costs and revenues. In this chapter, we will examine both of these concepts, which are equally important in determining a firm's profit-maximizing level of output.

Five Important Cost Concepts

Costs can be classified in a number of ways. For purposes of determining how costs affect output, we need to be able to observe how costs change as output changes. In this section, we will examine the following five important cost concepts: fixed costs, variable costs, total cost, average total cost, and marginal cost.

Fixed Costs

Fixed costs are those costs that do not vary with changes in output. Fixed costs, sometimes called "overhead costs," include such things as rent, interest on borrowed money, insurance premiums, and property taxes. Fixed costs are the same whether a firm is operating at full capacity, half capacity, or zero capacity. Even if a firm produces nothing at all during a given day, week, or month, it still must pay its rent, insurance, and other fixed costs.

    Paul Henderson operates a small firm that manufactures picnic tables. We'll use Paul's firm throughout this chapter as an example to illustrate the various costs that all firms incur. Paul's production costs are presented in Table 12-1. Note that Paul's fixed costs (column 2) are $100 per day no matter how many tables he produces. He must pay the $100 of fixed cost whether he produces one, five, or ten tables per day. He must also pay it even if he doesn't produce any tables at all.

TABLE 12-1
COST DATA FOR THE PRODUCTION OF PAUL'S PICNIC TABLES

Output Tables per day (1)	Total Fixed Costs (2)	Total Variable Costs (3)	Total Costs (4)	Average Total Costs (5)	Marginal Costs (6)
0	$100.00	0	$100.00		
1	100.00	$120.00	220.00	$220.00	$120.00
2	100.00	220.00	320.00	160.00	100.00
3	100.00	300.00	400.00	133.33	80.00
4	100.00	360.00	460.00	115.00	60.00
5	100.00	425.00	525.00	105.00	65.00
6	100.00	540.00	640.00	106.67	115.00
7	100.00	700.00	800.00	114.29	160.00
8	100.00	880.00	980.00	122.50	180.00
9	100.00	1,080.00	1,180.00	131.11	200.00
10	100.00	1,300.00	1,400.00	140.00	220.00

Variable Costs

Variable costs are those costs that change as the level of output changes. Variable costs rise as output increases, and fall as output decreases. Variable costs include such things as labor, raw materials, and power to operate machines.

Column 3 in Table 12-1 shows how Paul Henderson's variable costs change with the level of output. When Paul produces only one picnic table per day, his variable costs are $120. However, these costs rise to $220 when he produces two tables per day, $425 when he produces five picnic tables per day, and $1,300 when he produces ten tables per day. They would continue to rise even further if Paul increased his output beyond ten tables per day.

Note, though, that these costs do not rise by the same amount each time. They rise by $100 when Paul increases his output from one to two tables, by $80 when he increases his output from two to three tables, and by only $60 when output is increased from three to four tables. In contrast, they rise by $220 when daily output is increased from nine tables to ten. This variation is the result of how efficiently all resources are being used. When resources are being used most efficiently, the increase in variable costs is at its lowest point. Your understanding of this variation will be important when we examine marginal costs.

Note, also, that when Paul does not produce any picnic tables, he does not have any variable costs. Variable costs depend on the level of output, and any time a firm closes down temporarily and produces nothing, it will have no variable costs. This is because the firm's owner will not have to pay such costs as workers' salaries and the cost of power to run idle machinery.

Total Cost

Total cost is the sum of fixed and variable costs at each level of output. Paul Henderson's total cost at each level of production is shown in column 4 of Table 12-1. You can see that when Paul produces one table per day his total cost is $220. This is calculated by adding the $100 of fixed cost to the $120 of variable cost at that output. Notice, though, that Paul's total cost is $100 even when he does not produce any tables at all. Since Paul has no variable costs when he has an output level of zero, the entire $100 is fixed cost. This fixed cost remains constant regardless of the level of output. Thus, each time Paul increases his production by one picnic table per day, his total cost will increase by only the amount of the additional variable cost of producing one more unit.

Average Total Cost

Average total cost is calculated by dividing the total cost at each output level by the number of units being produced. Average total cost declines as output is increased up to the point where it reaches its minimum level, and then it begins to rise and continues to rise as output is increased beyond that point. Note in Table 12-1 that Paul Henderson's average total cost declines from $220 when he is producing only one table per day to a minimum of $105 at an output of five tables per day. However, increases in production beyond the minimum cost level of five tables per day will result in higher and higher average total costs. If Paul produces ten tables per day, his average total cost will be $140 per table.

Marginal Cost

Marginal cost is the additional cost of producing one more unit of output. As you learned above, variable costs do not change by the same amount each time output is increased. The same holds true for marginal cost. It is calculated by computing the increase in total cost that results from increasing production by one additional unit. Let's look again at Table 12-1 to further examine this concept.

Paul Henderson's marginal cost schedule is presented in column 6 of this table. When Paul goes from zero production to the production of one table per day, his total cost per day rises from $100 to $220. Thus, Paul's marginal cost of producing one picnic table per day is $120 ($220-$100). If Paul increases production from one table per day to two tables per day, his total cost will rise from $220 to $320. Therefore, the marginal cost of producing the second picnic table is $100 ($320-$220). And each time Paul increases production by one more picnic table per day, the marginal cost of that table is determined by calculating the increase in total cost that results from producing the additional table.

If you examine the table closely, however, you will notice that, like average total cost, marginal cost decreases to a certain point and then rises again. In this case, the lowest marginal cost is $60, and that occurs when Paul produces four picnic tables daily. This variation in marginal cost is used to determine the level of output that will yield the maximum profit for a firm. We will examine this relationship later in this chapter. Because of the relationship between marginal cost and profit maximizing, make sure you understand how marginal cost is calculated before reading on.

Law of Diminishing Returns

You have just learned that Paul Henderson's average total cost and marginal cost both decrease until they reach a minimum level. They then begin to rise and continue to rise as Paul produces more and more tables per day. The minimum average total cost of $105 is reached at

TABLE 12-2
PRODUCTION SCHEDULE
FOR PAUL'S PICNIC TABLES

Number of of Workers	Total Product (Number of Tables Produced per Day)	Marginal Product (Additional Tables Produced per Day)	Stages of Increasing and Diminishing Returns
0	0	0	
1	1	1	Increasing
2	2 ½	1 ½	Returns
3	5	2 ½	
4	7	2	
5	8 ½	1 ½	Diminishing
6	9 ½	1	Returns
7	10	½	

an output level of five picnic tables per day. As Paul increases production beyond that level, his average total cost will become larger and larger. Paul's costs behave in this way because of an economic principle known as **the law of diminishing returns**. This law states that increasing the quantity of one factor of production while quantities of the other factors of production remain fixed will result in smaller and smaller increases in total output.

The size of Paul's small manufacturing plant is fixed for the present, and he has a fixed number of tools and machines in the plant with which to turn lumber into picnic tables. However, Paul can increase or decrease the amount of labor he uses. Thus, labor is Paul's variable productive resource. Table 12-2 shows what happens when Paul adds additional workers to his fixed-size plant in order to increase output. If Paul uses only one worker, himself, he alone will have to perform all the tasks of producing a table—saw the lumber, assemble the table, paint it, and so forth. As a result, he will be able to produce only one picnic table per day. This would be a very inefficient use of Paul's plant because much of its capacity would be unused. If Paul uses two workers, himself and one employee, each worker can specialize in certain tasks; and the two of them will be able to produce two and one-half tables per day. If Paul uses three workers, they can be still more efficient and produce five tables per day.

As Paul increases production from one table per day to five tables per day, he is experiencing what economists call **increasing returns** from the additional labor used. That is, each additional unit of labor causes the total product to rise by a greater amount than was caused by the previous unit. In other words, the additional units of labor enable Paul to make more efficient use of his fixed-size plant. These increasing returns can be seen in column 3 of Table 12-2, which shows the increased output, or **marginal product**, resulting from each additional worker. Note that the marginal product of the first worker is one picnic table per day, the marginal product of the second worker is one and one-half tables per day, and the marginal product of the third worker is two and one-half tables per day. As long as the marginal product is rising, Paul's firm is experiencing increasing returns.

Note that the marginal product is at its maximum (two and one-half tables per day) when three workers are used, and when five tables are produced per day. This is the level at which Paul's small plant was designed to operate, and thus it is the most-efficient level of production. Paul can use additional workers and produce more tables per day; but if he does, he will experience **diminishing returns**. In other words, each additional worker will add less and less additional output. For example, the marginal product of the fourth worker is two tables per day as compared to two and one-half for the third worker. And the marginal product of the seventh worker is only one-half table per day.

When Paul operates his plant at its most-efficient level, using three workers to produce five picnic tables per day, his cost per table will be at its lowest level. However, as he attempts to increase production beyond that point by adding more units of labor, his cost per table will increase because of the law of diminishing returns.

Like Paul Henderson's manufacturing plant, all business firms experience diminishing returns if they continue to increase the quantity of one productive resource while the quantities of other productive resources remain fixed. For example, if a shoe store has only one salesperson, that salesperson may be unable to wait on all the customers that come into the store, thus resulting in some loss of sales. By adding a second salesperson, the store can increase its total sales. If the store has sufficient customers, it might be able to increase sales still further by adding a third sales clerk, but the chances are that this third salesperson will not add as much to total sales as the second one did. And a fourth salesperson would not increase sales at all if the three clerks are capable of serving all the customers that enter the store. The shoe store is experiencing diminishing returns as it increases the quantity of labor beyond the level at which this store of fixed size was designed to operate.

Diminishing returns can also occur when one of the

other productive resources is varied while the quantity of labor remains fixed. For example, suppose Tom Anderson owns and operates a 500-acre corn farm. Tom has a fixed amount of farm equipment, and he uses no hired workers. If Tom increases his acreage of land (natural resources) from 500 acres to 600 acres, he can increase his production by making more efficient use of his time and machinery. However, if Tom increases his acreage to 700 acres, he will have difficulty getting all the work done with his fixed equipment and labor. As a result, the addition of the second 100 acres will result in less increase in total corn production than did the first 100 additional acres. Thus, Tom is experiencing diminishing returns. If Tom adds still more acres of land, he will experience little or no increase in production because his fixed equipment and labor will not allow him to handle the additional land. Similarly, if Tom increases the quantity of machinery (capital goods) while his labor and acreage of land remain fixed, he will soon experience diminishing returns because he already has adequate machinery to farm the five hundred acres of land.

However, we cannot yet conclude that Tom's most profitable level of output is 600 acres. Similarly, we cannot yet conclude that Paul Henderson's most profitable level of output is five tables per day just because that is his least-cost level of production. In order to determine a firm's most profitable level of production, you also need revenue data.

Revenue

Revenue is, for example, the money that Paul Henderson gets for his picnic tables. If a firm's revenue is greater than its costs, it earns a profit. If costs exceed revenue, the firm suffers a loss. Let's examine three revenue concepts: revenue per unit, total revenue, and marginal revenue.

Revenue Per Unit

The **revenue per unit** of any product is simply the selling price. For some firms, the revenue per unit may remain constant no matter how much is sold. For example, if the market price of corn is $3 per bushel, a farmer will receive that price whether he sells 10 bushels or 10,000 bushels. However, some firms can sell different amounts at different prices. For example, a firm might find that at a price of $100 it could sell 600 units of a product per month; but if it lowered the price to $90, it could sell 700 units per month.

Firms operating in a market structure of, or approximating, pure competition are faced with a constant selling price no matter how much they sell. If they tried to raise this price, they would be left with most of their goods unsold. Thus, if the farmer in the example just mentioned was asking $3.50 for a bushel of corn, he or she probably couldn't sell any corn at all. In contrast, firms operating under market structures of monopoly, oligopoly, and monopolistic competition, have varying degrees of control over their selling prices. For example, an automobile firm that can sell a given number of cars at a price of $20,000 each, can raise or lower its price and still sell cars. It might sell fewer cars at $21,000 than at $20,000, but it could still sell some cars at the higher price.

Total Revenue

Total revenue is the selling price of an item times the quantity sold. For example, if a farmer sells 10,000 bushels of corn at a price of $3 per bushel, his or her total revenue is $30,000. Since firms operating under monopoly and oligopoly have some control over their prices, they must calculate the potential total revenue at various price and quantity combinations. For example, if a firm finds that it can sell 600 units at a price of $100, its total revenue will be $60,000 ($100 x 600 units). If it establishes a price of $90 per unit and can sell 700 units, its total revenue will be $63,000 ($90 x 700 units). In this case, should the firm set the price at $90 per unit since it will receive more total revenue at that price? Not necessarily. The most profitable price and output combination depends on both revenue and cost data, which we will see later.

Marginal Revenue

Marginal revenue is the additional revenue that results from producing and selling one more unit of output. It is calculated by computing the increase in total revenue that results from the production and sale of this additional unit. Like marginal cost, marginal revenue is a very important concept because it too is used to determine the level of output that will yield the maximum profit for a firm.

For firms operating under pure competition, marginal revenue is the same as price. This is because the price of each additional unit of output is the same as that for all the other units of output.   When a farmer, who is selling corn at the market price of $3 per bushel, decides to sell one more bushel of corn, his or her marginal revenue will be $3, the same as the selling price. However, for firms operating in markets characterized by monopoly, oligopoly, and monopolistic competition, marginal revenue and price are not equal. When such a firm lowers its price to sell more units of its product, it will have to lower the price on all units sold, including those units that it was selling at a higher price. For our discussion, we are using an example in which marginal revenue and price are equal. Keep in mind, however, that in market structures other than pure competition, marginal revenue will be less than the price.

The Profit-Maximizing Level of Output

Paul Henderson wants to make as much profit as possible with his picnic tables. It is reasonable to assume that most business firms want to maximize their profits. How do they accomplish this objective? They accomplish it by continuing to expand production so long as the revenue brought in by each additional unit of output exceeds the costs of producing that additional unit. If the production of one more unit will add more to Paul's revenue than to his costs, it is profitable for him to produce that unit. However, when Paul reaches the point where the production of one more picnic table will add more to his costs than to his revenue, he should not expand production any further. He has reached his profit-maximizing level of output, and any additional production beyond that point will result in a reduction in his total profit.

As you have already learned, the additional cost of producing one more unit of an item is the marginal cost. The additional revenue resulting from the production and sale of one more unit is the marginal revenue. Therefore, in order to maximize profit, a firm will continue to expand production so long as marginal revenue exceeds marginal cost.

In Table 12-3, selected portions of Paul Henderson's cost, revenue, and profit data are presented so that we can see how Paul determines his profit-maximizing level of output. Paul is able to sell all the picnic tables he produces at a price $175 each, so he has no reason to lower his price. On the other hand, Paul knows that if he raises his price by very much, people may buy elsewhere, and he will not be able to sell all of his tables. Thus, Paul's price is fixed at $175 per table no matter how many tables he produces per day.

Since Paul's price remains constant at $175 per table no matter how many tables he produces, his marginal revenue will be equal to the price. Every time he produces and sells one more table he will add $175 to his total revenue. Thus, Paul's marginal revenue is $175 at all levels of production. This is shown in column 7 of Table 12-3.

Unlike marginal revenue, marginal cost is not the same at each level of output. Paul's marginal cost starts at $120 with the production of one table per day, and then declines until it reaches a minimum of $60 at an output of four tables per day. Beyond that point, marginal cost increases with each additional table produced. Remember that marginal cost is simply the increase in total cost that results from the production of one more table. The fact that marginal cost declines up to a certain level of production and then begins to increase, is explained by the law of diminishing returns.

As you will recall from our discussion of average total cost, when Paul is producing only one or two tables per day he is not using his plant very efficiently Therefore, as he expands production, the additional cost of producing each extra table will decline at first. But, as Paul adds more and more units of labor, while the size of his plant and the number of tools and machines remain constant, he will get less and less extra production from each additional unit of labor. Thus, the cost of producing each additional table will rise.

At what level of output should Paul operate in order to maximize his profit? You can easily find the answer to this question by looking at the last column of Table 12-3. As you can see from studying this profit or loss column, Paul will earn a maximum total profit of $425 if he produces seven picnic tables per day. This is more profit than he could earn at any other level of output. At an output of seven tables per day, Paul's total revenue will be $1,225 per day, and his total cost will be $800 per day. As you already know, total profit is the difference between total revenue and total cost.

Table 12-3
COST, REVENUE, AND PROFIT DATA
FOR PAUL'S PICNIC TABLES

Output per day	TC	MC	ATC	Price	TR	MR	Profit or Loss
0	$100				0		-$100
1	220	$120	$220.00	$175	$175	$175	-45
2	320	100	160.00	175	350	175	+30
3	400	80	133.33	175	525	175	+125
4	460	60	115.00	175	700	175	+240
5	525	65	105.00	175	875	175	+350
6	640	115	106.67	175	1,050	175	+410
7	800	160	114.29	175	1,225	175	+425
8	980	180	122.50	175	1,400	175	+420
9	1,180	200	131.11	175	1,575	175	+395
10	1,400	220	140.00	175	1,750	175	+350

TC = Total Cost
MC = Marginal Cost
ATC = Average Total Cost
TR = Total Revenue
MR = Marginal Revenue

Suppose that Table 12-3 did not present either profit and loss data, or total revenue and total cost data. Could we still determine Paul's maximum-profit level of output? The answer to this question is yes. As long as we knew the marginal revenue and marginal cost for each level of output we could determine the maximum-profit level of output without any of the other data. Let's examine the relationship between marginal revenue and marginal cost at four different levels of output in Table 12-3.

We will begin by observing the cost and revenue data at an output of five tables per day. Note that at this level, the marginal cost of producing the fifth table is only $65 while the marginal revenue of the fifth table is $175. Therefore, Paul adds $110 more to his total revenue than he adds to his total cost when he produces the fifth unit. This means that his profit at five tables per day is $110 higher than at four tables per day.

Now let us examine the marginal cost and the marginal revenue of producing the sixth table. Note that the marginal cost of producing the sixth table is $115 while the marginal revenue of the sixth table is $175. Thus, Paul adds $60 more to his total revenue than he adds to his total cost when he produces the sixth table. His total profit, therefore, is $60 higher for six tables than for five tables.

Let's see what happens when Paul increases production from six tables to seven tables per day. The additional cost (marginal cost) of the seventh table is $160, while the additional revenue (marginal revenue) of that table is $175. Thus, by producing the seventh table, Paul adds $15 more to total revenue than he adds to total cost, and increases his profit from $410 to $425. This is Paul's maximum profit.

Just to make sure that Paul couldn't increase his profit still more by producing eight tables per day, let's see what happens to total cost and total revenue when production is expanded to that level. The marginal cost of the eighth table is $180, while the marginal revenue is only $175. Thus, when Paul produces the eighth table, he adds $5 more to total cost than he adds to total revenue. As a result, Paul's total profit declines by $5 from $425 to $420.

Note that Paul's profit-maximizing level of output is not his least-cost level of output. Paul's average total cost is at its lowest level at an output of five tables per day. Although Paul could earn a profit by operating at that level, it would not be his maximum profit. By using marginal cost and marginal revenue to determine the most profitable level of output, Paul is able to earn considerably more profit than he would if he operated at the point where his average total cost is at a minimum.

Can you see why the concepts of marginal cost and marginal revenue are so important in economic analysis? Do you have a clear understanding of how marginal cost and marginal revenue are related to total cost and total revenue? If you don't, study the data in Table 12-3 until you understand these relationships. To test your understanding of the concepts, suppose that due to increased competition Paul suddenly finds that he must lower the price of his tables from $175 to $150 per table. If Paul's price and marginal revenue were $150 instead of $175, would his maximum-profit level of output still be seven tables per day? If not, what would it be?

Equating Marginal Cost and Marginal Revenue

The marginal cost and marginal revenue concepts, which are so crucial to sound decision-making, are not widely understood. It is probable that many businesses would be unable to answer the question, "Do you maximize profit by operating at that level where marginal cost equals marginal revenue?" They would not know the terminology, but their business behavior would probably tend to have the effect of following the marginal cost equal marginal revenue rule if they used rational thinking in making production decisions.

Marginal cost is simply the additional cost of producing one more unit, and marginal revenue is the additional revenue received by producing and selling one more unit. Anytime a business can add more to revenue than it adds to cost by producing one more unit of a product, it is profitable to do so. For example, if producing one more unit of a product will add $1,000 to total cost, but the additional item will add $1,200 to total revenue, profit will go up by $200.

It is in a firm's best interest to continue to expand production as long as marginal revenue is higher than marginal cost. However, once the firm reaches the level of production where marginal cost is equal to marginal revenue, any further expansion will not add to profit. Suppose that the production of one more unit of a product will add $1,000 to cost and only $900 to revenue. It would not be profitable to produce this additional unit. On the contrary, total profit would be reduced by $100 as a result of producing this unit.

When a rational business firm considers expanding production, it will consider whether or not expanded production will increase profit. If profit will not go up as a result of expansion, it is not good business sense to expand. Even if an entrepreneur does not know the meaning of the terms marginal cost and marginal revenue, he or she will be following the marginal cost equal marginal revenue rule by asking whether or not an expansion will add to profit.

Profit Maximization Under Other Market Structures

Paul Henderson operates under a market structure very similar to that of pure competition. Since there are many other producers of picnic tables, and since there are no significant barriers to prevent additional firms from entering the market, Paul has little or no control over the price of his product. However, as you have already learned, most firms in the United States operate under market structures other than pure competition.

How do firms operating under monopoly, oligopoly, and monopolistic competition maximize their profits? They do so in the same way that Paul Henderson does, by expanding production up to, but not beyond, the point where marginal cost equals marginal revenue. There is an important difference, however. As you learned earlier, under market structures other than pure competition, marginal revenue is not equal to price. A monopolistic firm has some control over its price and output. If it lowers its price, it will be able to sell more of its product; and if it raises its price, it will sell less. But when a monopolistic firm lowers its price in order to sell more units, it will have to do so on all units, including those that were selling for a higher price. For this reason, the marginal revenue of a monopolistic firm will be lower than its price.

When monopolists attempt to maximize profits, the results will be much less desirable from the standpoint of society than when a firm operating under pure competition seeks to do so. Because monopolists often restrict output in order to obtain higher prices, they produce less and receive higher prices than firms operating under pure competition. The same is true, but to a lesser extent, in the cases of oligopoly and monopolistic competition.

Other Cost Concepts

In our discussion so far, we have delayed the introduction of certain other important cost concepts. Let us examine these other concepts.

Explicit and Implicit Costs

Production costs can be classified on the basis of whether they are explicit costs or implicit costs. **Explicit costs** are those costs that involve an actual payment of money to "outsiders" who supply labor, raw materials, fuel, the use of buildings and equipment, and so forth to the firm. Wages and salaries, rent, insurance premiums, utility bills, and payment for raw materials are all examples of explicit costs.

In addition to costs that involve a direct cash payment (explicit costs), most firms have other costs in which a regular direct cash outlay is not involved. For example, if a firm owns its own building, it does not have to make a monthly rent payment. Yet there is a cost in this case, too. If the firm did not use the building for its own operations, it could rent the building to another firm and receive a monthly rental payment. As you learned in Chapter 1, this type of cost is called opportunity cost. If the building could be rented for $1,000 per month, the firm's opportunity cost of using the building for its own business operations is that amount.

The opportunity costs resulting from a firm's use of resources that it owns are called **implicit costs**. The opportunity cost of managerial labor contributed to a business is an implicit cost. Since Paul Henderson contributes his time and managerial skills to his business, he must include as part of his production costs an amount equal to what he could earn if he were employed by another firm. Also, the opportunity cost of funds invested in a business must be included as implicit costs. If a person has $100,000 of his or her own money invested in a business, he or she must include as an implicit cost an amount equal to what could have been earned if the $100,000 had been invested elsewhere. Even if the money just set in the bank, there would be an implicit cost involved. If it were placed in a bank account, the $100,000 would earn some interest.

Short-Run and Long-Run Costs

Economists usually distinguish between the "short run" and the "long run" when analyzing production costs.

The **short run** is a time period too short to allow a firm to alter the size of its plant, yet long enough to allow the firm to change the level at which the fixed plant is used. There is no definite time period affixed to the term "short run." Rather, short run is determined more by a firm's ability to make major changes in the size of its plant than by the calendar. All our analysis of Paul Henderson's firm in this chapter involved the short run. Paul was able to vary the amount of labor used, but he was not able to alter the size of his plant. Because a firm's plant is fixed in the short run, it can expand output only by adding more units of variable inputs, such as labor. And as the firm adds more and more units of variable inputs to a fixed-size plant, it is able to get less and less additional output from these additional inputs. As you have already learned, this tendency for output to taper off is called the law of diminishing returns.

In contrast, the **long run** is a time period long enough to allow a firm to vary all of its productive resources, including the size of its plant. In the long run, everything is variable. For example, in the long run, Paul Henderson would be able to double or triple the size of his plant, or make any other adjustment in plant size that would enable him to reduce production costs. Because it is based on the assumption of a fixed-size plant, the law of diminishing returns does not apply in the long run. However, two other important concepts that affect cost do exist in the long run. They are economies and diseconomies of scale. Let's examine each of these concepts briefly.

Economies of Scale. As you learned in an earlier chapter, economies of scale occur when a large volume of output can be produced at a lower cost per unit than can a small volume of output. As a firm expands its capacity over the long run, a number of factors will contribute to its economies of scale, including labor specialization, managerial specialization, and more efficient use of capital goods (machines, tools, and so forth).

As the number of workers hired increases, jobs can be divided and subdivided so that each worker becomes proficient at one or a few tasks. One of the greatest sources of economies of scale, however, is the increased efficiency with which capital goods can be utilized. In many industries, the most efficient machinery is available only in very large and expensive units, and efficient utilization of this equipment requires a high volume of production. For example, a machine that can produce ten times the output of a smaller machine will not cost nearly ten times as much.

Diseconomies of Scale. In some industries, it is possible for firms to grow so large that they experience **diseconomies of scale**. This means that costs per unit begin to rise as the firm becomes larger and larger. The major cause of diseconomies of scale appears to be the inability of management to control and coordinate all of a large firm's operations efficiently. In a giant firm, top management may be so far removed from the actual production operations of the plant that communication and coordination problems occur.

However, economists do not agree on the extent to which diseconomies of scale are a problem in the American economy. Some economists argue that the success and continued growth of giant corporations indicate that diseconomies of scale are not a serious problem for American firms. What most economists do agree on is that the costs of production are affected by plant size and scale of operation in both the short run and the long run. The ultimate goal should be to use our productive resources as efficiently as possible. The greater the efficiency, the lower the production cost, and, if there is adequate competition in the markets, the lower the price to consumers.

Chapter Highlights

- Firms maximize profits by adjusting output to the profit-maximizing level, which is determined primarily by production costs.

- Fixed costs are those costs that do not vary with changes in output. They include such things as rent, interest on borrowed money, insurance premiums, and property taxes.

- Variable costs are those costs that change as the level of output changes. They include such things as labor, raw materials, and power to operate machines.

- Total cost is the sum of fixed and variable costs at each level of output. Because fixed costs remain constant at all levels of output, any change in total cost can be attributed to a change in variable costs.

- Average total cost is calculated by dividing the total cost at each output level by the number of units being produced. Average total cost declines as output is increased up to the point where it reaches its minimum level, and then it begins to rise again as output is expanded beyond that point.

- Marginal cost is the cost of producing each additional unit of output. Like average total cost, marginal cost decreases to a certain point and then rises again.

- The behavior of marginal cost and average total cost as output is expanded can be explained by the law of diminishing returns. This law states that increasing the quantity of one productive resource, while quantities of the other productive resources remain fixed, will result in smaller and smaller increases in total output.

- The money a firm receives for the products it sells is its revenue. The revenue per unit is simply the selling price. The total revenue is the selling price times the quantity sold. Marginal revenue is the additional revenue that results from producing and selling one more unit of output.

- A firm maximizes its profit by continuing to expand production so long as marginal revenue exceeds marginal cost.

- Explicit costs are those costs that involve an actual payment of money. Implicit costs are the opportunity costs resulting from a firm's use of resources that it owns.

- The short run is a time period too short to allow a firm to alter the size of its plant, yet long enough to allow the firm to change the level at which the fixed plant is used. The long run is a time period that is long enough to allow a firm to vary all its productive resources, including the size of its plant. In the long run everything is variable.

- Economies of scale occur when a large volume of output can be produced at a lower cost per unit than a small volume. If firms grow too large, they may begin to experience diseconomies of scale.

Important Terms

Match each of the following terms with the correct definition:

economies of scale
variable costs
revenue per unit
explicit costs
diseconomies of scale
marginal cost
marginal revenue
implicit costs
revenue

law of diminishing returns
average total cost
long run
total revenue
total cost
fixed cost
short run

1. The cost is calculated by dividing the total cost at each output level by the number of units being produced.

2. A law stating that if one factor of production is increased while the others remain fixed, after a certain point each additional unit of the variable factor of production will result in smaller and smaller increases in total output.

3. A time period long enough to allow a firm to vary all of its factors of production, including the size of its plant.

4. The additional revenue that results from producing and selling one more unit of output.

5. Those costs that do not vary with changes in output.

6. Those costs that involve an actual payment of money.

7. Reduction in efficiency and increased cost per unit that sometimes result from a firm's becoming too large.

8. The opportunity costs resulting from a firm's use of resources that it owns.

9. The additional cost of producing one more unit of output.

10. The selling price times the quantity sold.

11. The increased efficiency resulting from specialization and the division of labor that makes possible the production of a large volume of output at a lower cost per unit than a small volume of output.

12. The money a firm receives for the products it sells.

13. The selling price of a product.

14. Those costs that change as the level of output changes.

15. The sum of fixed and variable costs.

16. A time period too short to allow a firm to alter the size of its plant yet long enough to allow the firm to change the level at which the fixed plant is used.

Review Questions

1. What must firms do in order to maximize profits?

2. Define the law of diminishing returns?

3. How does the law of diminishing returns explain the behavior of marginal cost and average total cost?

4. Give examples of variable costs.

5. Give examples of fixed costs.

6. What is the difference between the short run and the long run?

7. What is the difference between explicit costs and implicit costs? Give examples of both.

8. How is average total cost calculated?

9. Define marginal cost. How is it calculated?

10. What determines the marginal revenue of a firm at any given level of production?

Discussion Questions

1. Do you think most firms operate at a level that maximizes their profits? Why or why not?

2. Does it make any difference to consumers whether or not firms operate at the profit-maximizing level of output? Explain.

3. If you were operating your own business, would you automatically stop production if you began to operate at a loss? Why or why not?

CHAPTER THIRTEEN

Other Markets and Market Limitations

In order for production to take place, factors of production, which are also called productive resources, must be combined to form a production unit. Productive resources are bought and sold in resource markets. Let's first examine the basic factors of production, and then we will consider resource markets.

Factors of Production

There are three basic factors of production—natural resources, capital goods, and labor. In addition, many economists add a fourth factor of production, entrepreneurship, to the list.

Natural Resources

Natural Resources are things provided by nature such as land, air, water, forests, coal, iron ore, oil and other minerals. Natural resources are the basic materials an economy has to work with. They are the starting point of all production, and they represent the most basic limitation on the productive capacity of an economy. No matter how much skilled labor and technological knowledge an economy has, it cannot create goods if it lacks natural resources.

Capital Goods
Capital goods are human-made resources that are used for the production of other goods and services. Factories, machines, tools, railroads, trucks, and business buildings are all example of capital goods. Without capital goods, natural resources would not be very useful. For example, timber is a natural resource. No matter how much timber a nation has, however, it is of little use unless capital goods are available to turn it into lumber, firewood, or other usable products. In this instance, possible capital goods might include a simple axe, a chain saw, or a giant sawmill.

Capital goods must be distinguished from consumer goods. Consumer goods—which are not a factor of production—are finished products sold to consumers for their own personal use. They include such things as food, clothing, and television sets. In contrast, capital goods are things that are used in the production of consumer goods and services, as well as in the production of additional capital goods. A factory that manufactures TV sets is a capital good. Some things can be either consumer goods, or capital goods, depending on how they are used. For example, an automobile purchased for personal use is a consumer good. However, automobiles purchased for use as taxis, or for other business purposes, are capital goods.

Labor
Labor, sometimes called human resources, is any form of human effort exerted in production. It includes all kinds of work. The work of a janitor, teacher, lawyer, engineer, and the governor of your state are all example of labor. Labor is essential to production, since natural resources and capital goods are of no value unless they can be put to use.

Entrepreneurship
The three factors of production described above must be combined and organized before production can take place. This is where entrepreneurship, the fourth factor of production, enters the picture. Entrepreneurship may be defined as the function of combining and organizing natural resources, capital goods, and labor; assuming the risks of business failure; and providing the creativity and managerial skills necessary for production to take place. An entrepreneur is a person who carries out these tasks in the hope of making financial gains from the endeavor.

Resource Markets
Resource markets are similar to product markets. However, in product markets, households are the buyers and businesses are the sellers. By contrast, in resource markets, the buyer/seller relationship is just the opposite. In resource markets, businesses are the buyers and households are the sellers.

Households sell their labor, and any other productive resources they might own, to businesses. With the money they earn from selling resources to businesses, household buy products from businesses.

Businesses use money, received from selling their products to households, to partially pay wages to households for their labor. In a crude and very simplified way, we can say that workers trade some of their labor to businesses for the products produced by businesses.

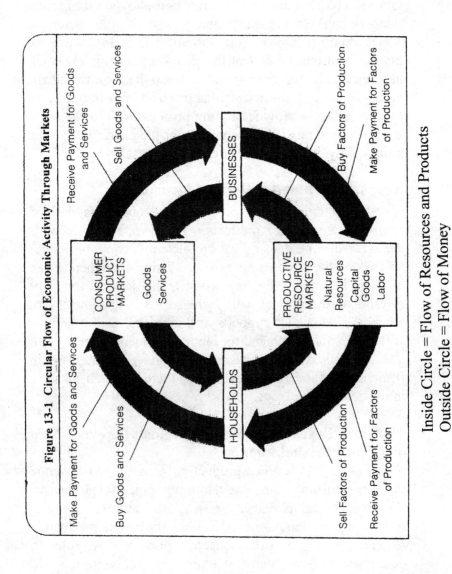

Figure 13-1 Circular Flow of Economic Activity Through Markets

Inside Circle = Flow of Resources and Products
Outside Circle = Flow of Money

The flow chart in Figure 13-1 shows the flow of resources and products on the inside circle. Goods and services flow from businesses through the product markets to households. Labor flows from households, through the resource markets, to businesses.

Another way to look at the flow is by looking at the top half and bottom half of the charts separately. By using this approach, we can see in the top half of the chart, money flowing from households to businesses in exchange for the products provided by the businesses. On the other hand, by looking at just the bottom of the chart, we can see money flowing from businesses to the households.

Resource Demand is Derived Demand

The demand for productive resources is derived from the demand for products. The demand for labor is derived from the demand for products, which require labor as part of the production process. Any time there is an increase in demand for any product, the demand for labor to produce the product will increase. By the same token, when the demand for goods and services declines, there will be a reduced demand for labor, and unemployment will rise. That is why it is necessary to have an increase in demand for goods and services for there to be an increase in the demand for labor.

Marginal Revenue Product, Marginal Resource Cost and Profit Maximization

Marginal revenue product is the additional revenue that results from adding one additional unit of a productive resource. Marginal resource cost is the additional cost that results from adding one additional unit of a productive resource. These two concepts play a key role in determining how many workers, or other productive resources, a firm will choose to employ.

How does a firm decide how many units of a productive resource, such as labor, to hire? For example, suppose a small firm has 83 employees. Now suppose a potential new worker comes along and applies for a job. Should the firm employ the new worker and raise its labor force from 83 workers to 84 workers? That depends on how much the new employee will add to total revenue as compared to how much he will add to total cost.

Let's suppose that the additional cost of employing the worker, including fringe benefits and other costs, will be $100 per day. If the employee will add less than $100 per day to revenue, then it will not be profitable to employ him. However, if the new worker will add $150 per day to revenue, compared to the $100 per day of additional labor cost, the firm will make a profit of $50 from employing the new unit of labor.

Whether it is another unit of labor, or another unit of another productive resource, employers will be guided by how much additional revenue will be gained compared to the additional cost. A firm will maximize profits by expanding employment up to the point where marginal revenue product equals marginal resource cost. It is profitable to hire additional units of a productive resource so long as you are adding more to revenue that you are adding to cost. But once the point is reached where marginal revenue product equals marginal resource cost, it will not be profitable for the firm to employ more units of the productive resource.

Land and the Concept of Economic Rent

Land is defined by economists as all natural resources—everything given by nature. It includes all mineral deposits, trees in the natural forests, and natural streams and lakes. Land can be improved by adding capital goods. For example, drainage, irrigation, and fencing can be added to the land. However, once that is done, the resource becomes partly land and partly capital goods.

The supply of land in the world is perfectly inelastic because there is a fixed quantity. No matter how high, or low, the price of land, the total quantity of land will remain the same. Although there can be increases and decreases in the supply of land for sale in a specific market, there cannot be an increase in the supply of land in the entire world.

Land has unique characteristics, as compared to labor and capital goods. An increase in the demand for labor can cause wages to increase. At the higher wage, a larger quantity of labor will be available. The same is true of capital goods. If there is an increase in demand for bulldozers and other earth moving equipment, the price of the equipment will rise, and at the higher price a larger quantity will be available. Thus, supply and demand interact in the markets for labor and capital goods, and this interaction can result in an increase in the supply.

On a world basis, an increase in the demand for land will certainly increase the price of land, but the price increase cannot result in the production of more land. Therefore, demand is the primary determinant of the price of land. With a perfectly inelastic supply for any commodity, increases in demand will cause the price to rise, but will not result in a larger quantity of the commodity.

The price paid for the use of land and other natural resources is called economic rent. If the supply for land is perfectly inelastic, the supply curve is vertical. An increase in demand will result in a higher price for land, but the quantity of land will remain unchanged.

In the case of residential homes, an increase in demand will increase both the price and the quantity supplied. The supplies of non-land resources are responsive to rising prices. Therefore, the rising price performs an incentive function. If buyers signal their desire for an increase in quantity of houses, by bidding the price up, the higher prices will motivate builders to build more houses.

This is not true of land. Rent serves no incentive function because the total supply of land is fixed. If the rent for land is $100,000 per acre, $10,000 per acre, or $0.00 per acre, the same quantity of land will be available to society. In other words, rent for land could be eliminated without affecting the productive capacity of the economy. That is why economists consider rent to be a surplus. It is a payment, which is not necessary to ensure that the land will be available to the economy as a whole.

This raises the question of why rent should be paid to landowners. Henry George, an American economist, whose provocative book, *Progress and Poverty*, published in 1879, led a single-tax movement, which gained considerable public support in the late 1800s. The thesis of the book, and the movement, was that economic rent might be completely taxed away without reducing the available supply of land or the productive capacity of the economy as a whole. Henry George argued that many land owners were receiving extremely high incomes, not through efforts of their own, but simply because they happened to hold strategically located land whose value soared because of the growth of the population and the advancing geographic frontier.

As the transcontinental railroad was built, connecting the western and eastern regions of the United States, many people became super rich because they owned land in the pathway of the western expansion. Most of these landowners could not have known where the first cross-country railway would be located when they settled their land. Yet they became rich while their neighbors, a few miles to the south or to the north, envied their good fortune.

The same thing happened in more recent history with the construction of the interstate highway system. Farmers who happened to own land in the path of the highways saw the value of their land soar. Similarly, landowners in Florida, whose land just happened to be on or near the site where Walt Disney decided to build Disney World, also became rich. Although there are professional land speculators who do take risks in an effort to buy land that might greatly increase in value, most of the landowners whose land turns to gold because of economic growth are just lucky because they happened to own land in the path of economic expansion.

Henry George believed that the phenomenal gains in the value of land, which were the primary result of the actions of others, should belong to society as a whole, and he proposed taxing heavily what he considered to be the "unearned" gains in land rent. The single-tax movement advocated getting rid of most other taxes and relying heavily on a tax on land rent for the nation's revenue needs. He argued that, unlike most taxes, the land tax would not have a negative impact on the economy.

Loanable Funds Market and Interest
The loanable funds market refers to the set of markets in which people borrow and lend money. Money is not an economic resource, and it is incapable of producing goods and services. However, money can be used to acquire capital goods, such as factory buildings, machines and tools, which do contribute to the production of goods and services. When individuals, businesses, or units of government, borrow money, they are buying the use of money for a given period of time. The money will eventually have to be repaid, and during the period in which the money is being used, payment must be made for the use of the money.

The price paid for the use of money is called interest. Interest is usually stated as a percentage of the amount of money borrowed. For example, $1,000 borrowed for one year at a ten percent interest rate will cost $100 for the use of the money during the year. If the money is borrowed at a seven percent interest rate, the amount of the interest payment for the year will be $70.

The Demand for Loanable Funds

Businesses, households, and government make up most of the demand for loanable funds. Businesses borrow money primarily for the purpose of purchasing capital goods. Rarely do businesses have cash with which to pay for a major expansion, or the building of a new manufacturing plant, so they have to borrow the money. .

Households demand loanable funds when they purchase such things as automobiles and major appliances. Although most households cannot spend a great deal more than their total lifetime earnings, they can live partially on borrowed money, at least for short periods of time.

Federal, state, and local governments are major borrowers. In recent times the federal government, and some state and local governments, have spent a great deal more on government programs than the amount of revenue available to them. When a unit of government spends more than its incoming revenue, it has to borrow to pay for the difference, and this borrowing contributes to government debt.

Since the 1980s, our federal government has been engaging in some of the most irresponsible spending policies in the nation's history. As mentioned in an earlier chapter, it took 200 years, and the deficit spending of all the presidents from George Washington through Jimmy Carter combined, for the nation to accumulate the first $1 trillion in debt. It then took only five yeas for the national debt to double to $2 trillion, and the debt quadrupled to $4 trillion during the 12 years that Ronald Reagan and George H.W. Bush occupied the White House.

Government competes with businesses and households for the limited supply of loanable funds so, when the government demands a disproportionate share of the total loanable funds, they tend to crowd out other borrowers and force interest rates up.

Potential Supply of Loanable Funds

Although many households may spend most, or all, of their current year's income during the current year, not all households do so. In any given year, households as a group will spend less than their total earnings, the difference being personal saving. The personal saving of households as a group is, therefore, one component of the supply of loanable funds.

Since businesses do not distribute all of their profits to stockholders, they are a major sources of loanable funds. In prosperous years, businesses save substantial amounts in the form of undistributed profits which can become a part of the supply of loanable funds.

A third potential source of loanable funds is newly created money resulting from commercial bank lending. As you learned in Chapter Seven, the most important function of the Federal Reserve System is controlling the nation's money supply. The Fed can, through deposit expansion by the banking system as a whole, increase or decrease the nation's money supply. Monetary policy tools available to the Fed include, changing reserve requirements, changing key interest rates, and open-market operations.

It is important to note that the savings of households and businesses are only potential sources of supply for loanable funds because the households and businesses may not always be willing to make these funds available to borrowers. Since money serves as a store of value, households may choose to hold their savings in idle cash or put it in a place where it cannot be loaned out. Furthermore, just because the Fed is trying to expand the money supply, there is no guarantee that banks will actually make new loans. One of the legacies of the financial meltdown of 2008, and the accompanying hard economic times, was a reluctance, on the part of banks, to actually make new loans. Some banks and other financial institutions chose to just sit on large amounts of idle cash.

Determinants of Interest Rates

Although the supply and demand of loanable funds play a role in determining interest rates, the interest rate is actually an administered price which is deliberately influenced by the government. The federal government has two powerful reasons for regulating interest rates. First of all, the government is a major borrower, and the interest cost to the government on its borrowed funds is a big budget item. Secondly, interest rates play a key role in the performance of the economy. During periods of recession, the government can encourage economic growth by keeping interest rates low, which also helps the federal budget.

Market Limitations

As you learned in Chapter Two, the price system is the basic coordination and communication system of a market economy. Through the price system, producers and consumers transmit valuable information to each other that helps keep the economy in balance. This information helps producers decide whether to increase or decrease production of various products. It also helps employees decide which careers to choose. Messages are communicated between buyers and sellers in the product markets, and messages are communicated between employers and employees in the resource markets.

For the market system to function efficiently, there must be a lot of competition so that the various participants are unable to take advantage of each other. As you learned, some markets have adequate competition to operate efficiently, but others do not have sufficient competition to provide for the best interests of everyone. This lack of competition is one of the reasons that government intervention in the markets is necessary. Two special types of markets--the market for public goods and the markets where activities have substantial external effects on third parties--also require government intervention. Let's look at these two special types of markets.

Public Goods
Public goods are such things as highways, flood control, national defense and police and fire protection, that are collectively consumed by the population. The market, if left to itself, does not supply these items, or only supplies them inadequately. Public goods have the unique characteristic that they cannot be withheld from members of the public if they refuse to pay. For example, national defense and police protection are available to everyone, whether they pay for them or not.

For an enterprise to be profitable, the business owner must be able to charge for access to the product and to withhold the product from anyone who does not pay. If left totally to the market, very little national defense or police and fire protection would be produced. Therefore, it is necessary for the government to produce public goods and pay for them by taxing the citizens.

Externalities
For the market system to work correctly, all of the costs of an activity must be reflected in the price. No firm will produce a product unless it can sell it for more than

total production costs. If you cannot produce a product at a cost as low as your competitors, you will not produce it.

But what if you found a way to make other third parties pay for part of the production cost. If that could be done, your price would only have to be higher than the cost that you pay, even though others are also paying a cost for your activity.   Many activities generate economic side effects that harm third parties not directly involved in the activity. Pollution is a prime example.

Suppose a firm wants to start up a production unit in which a large part of the cost is finding a cheap way to dispose of wastewater.   After considering many other expensive alternatives, the firm decides that the cheapest way to dispose of the wastewater is to dig a ditch to a nearby river and just allow the wastewater to flow into the river. Downriver a few miles from the site, a community uses treated water from the river for its water supply. The treatment of the river water is expensive, but necessary. After the firm upstream has been dumping its wastewater into the river for a period of time, the community downriver finds that the cost of treating its water supply rises substantially. It can only conclude that the water is dirtier than before, but it may not know why.

This was a very common problem in the United States prior to the establishment of the Environmental Protection Agency. Large amounts of waste materials were being dumped into the nations rivers and lakes, simply because that was the cheapest way to dispose of the wastes. In our example, if the firm is ordered to stop polluting the river and find another way to dispose of its wastewater, it may discover that, if it has to pay the full cost of disposal, the costs will be so high that it will no longer be profitable to operate the plant.

Let's look at another example involving external costs. Suppose that the small retirement town of Pleasant View is located in a peaceful valley surrounded by hills that are covered with beautiful pine trees. The developer who established Pleasant View had grandiose dreams of building expensive homes on the hillsides that would look down on the valley below.

The valley lots were developed first, and the buyers of these homes expected that the long-term development plan would be followed. They thought that they would always be surrounded by the beautiful forested hills. Because of their vision of what the area would look like when all building was completed, these early buyers paid premium prices for their homes, with the expectation that the values would only go up, as had been the case for all residential real estate for many decades. None of these homebuyers could have possibly foreseen the great housing bubble and the ultimate crash in home prices.

As a result of the 2008 financial meltdown and the Great Recession, the over-extended developer went bankrupt, and the hillside property surrounding the valley was put on the market. After months of unsuccessful attempts to sell the property to another developer, the banks who had foreclosed on the property, decided to liquidate the land at public auction. To the horror of the residents of Pleasant View, the highest bidder, and thus the new owner of the hillside property, was a large lumber company that planned to cut the pine trees down and turn them into lumber.

The market system, left alone without government intervention, had brought about the above sequence of events. Before the real estate crash, the forces of supply and demand had pushed the value of the land surrounding the valley so high that it was far too expensive for a profitable logging operation. The lumber companies had to go to remote areas where the demand for land, relative to the supply, was so low that land prices were low enough to make logging a profitable operation.

However, after the housing collapse, there was almost no demand for land to be used for real estate development. That is why, when the land was auctioned off, nobody was interested in buying it for development purposes. But, because the land sold for such a low price, the lumber company thought it could make just as much profit from logging this land as they could logging land in remote areas.

This is a case where the markets have failed to bring about what is best for the public in general. The reason is that the lumber company is not paying for all the costs of the logging operation. As the beautiful trees begin to disappear from the hillsides, life in Pleasant View will become less pleasant. Many of the residents may want to sell their homes and move elsewhere, but most will not be able to sell without taking big losses. The removal of the trees will contribute to soil erosion and possibly mudslides. Some homeowners may consider suing the lumber company for their losses. If they are successful, in winning compensation, the lumber company may find its costs rising so much that it will wish it had bought land in a remote area instead of a populated area.

The key point here is that the cost of the lumber company turning the trees into lumber is a lot more that the money it paid for the land. The introduction of logging to the community will place heavy external costs on the residents of the area, for which they may not be compensated. This is why government intervention into the economy is often necessary. If the local government had zoned the land around Pleasant View for residential use only, the lumber company would have had no interest in buying the property, and the residents of Pleasant View would not have had their lives turned upside down.

Chapter Highlights

- In order for production to take place, factors of production, which are also called productive resources, must be combined to form a production unit. Productive resources are bought and sold in resource markets.

- There are three basic factors of production—natural resources, capital goods, and labor. Many economists also add a fourth factor, entrepreneurship, to the list.

- Resource markets are similar to product markets. However, in product markets, households are the buyers and businesses are the sellers. In resource markets, businesses are the buyers and households are the sellers.

- Marginal revenue product is the additional revenue that results from adding one additional unit of a productive resource. Marginal resource cost is the additional cost that results from adding one additional unit of a productive resource. A firm will maximize profits by expanding employment up to the point where marginal revenue product equals marginal resource cost. But, once the point is reached where marginal revenue product equals marginal resource cost, it will not be profitable for the firm to employ more units of the productive resource.

- Land is defined by economists as all natural resources. It includes mineral deposits, trees in the natural forests, and natural streams and lakes. The supply of land in the world is perfectly inelastic because there is a fixed quantity. No matter how high, or low, the price of land, the total quantity of land will remain the same. The price for the use of land and other natural resources is called economic rent. Because the rent for land does not result in the creation of more land, economists consider economic rent to be a surplus. In the late 1800s, American economist, Henry George, led the single tax movements which advocated eliminating all other taxes and placing a heavy tax on land.

- The loanable funds market consists of a set of markets in which people borrow and lend money. Businesses, households, and government make up most of the demand for loanable funds. The potential supply of loanable funds includes household saving, business saving, and money that has been newly created money by the banking system. Interest rates are influenced by the supply and demand of loanable funds, but the actual interest rate is ultimately set by the Fed.

- Public goods are such things as highways, flood control, national defense, and police and fire protection. These public goods cannot be withheld from the public for lack of payment. Therefore, it is necessary for the government to produce public goods and pay for them by taxing the citizens.

- For the market system to work correctly, all of the costs of an activity must be reflected in the price. Unfortunately, many activities generate economic side effects that harm third parties, not directly involved in the activity. Costs that affect third parties, who are not involved in the production activity are called external costs. Because of externalities, the government may have to intervene.

Important Terms
Match each of the following terms with the correct definition:

resource markets   marginal resource cost
natural resources   economic rent
capital goods   loanable funds market
labor   interest
entrepreneurship   public goods
marginal revenue product   externalities

1. Things provided by nature.

2. Human-made resources that are used for the production of other goods and services.

3. Any form of human effort exerted in production.

4. The function of combining and organizing factors of production, assuming the risks of business failure, and providing the creativity and managerial skills necessary for production to take place.

5. Markets where productive resources are bought and sold.

6. The additional revenue that results from adding one additional unit of a productive resource.

7. The additional cost that results from adding one additional unit of a productive resource.

8. The price paid for the use of land and other natural resources.

9. The set of markets in which people borrow and lend money.

10. The price paid for the use of money.

11. Goods that are collectively consumed by the population, and cannot be withheld from members of the public if they refuse to pay.

12. Costs that affect third parties, who are not involved in the production activity.

Review Questions

1. What are the basic things needed for economic production to take place?

2. Define entrepreneurship. Why can production not take place without it?

3. Who are the buyers and sellers in product markets? Resource markets?

4. How does a firm know how many units of a productive resource to use in order to maximize profits?

5. Who was Henry George? What kind of reform was he proposing?

6. How are interest rates determined?

7. What are public goods? What unique characteristic do they have?

8.   Who pays for external costs?

Discussion Questions
1.   How do product markets and resource markets interact with each other?

2.   Who was Henry George?   What was he trying to accomplish? Do you agree with his goal?

3.   What are external costs?   What are the environmental implications of external costs?

CHAPTER FOURTEEN

The Financial Meltdown and The Great Recession

The Financial Meltdown

In mid-September 2008, the world was stunned when, in a matter of days, the world financial system melted down, causing massive financial losses and global panic. How could the world financial system, and the economies of almost all nations deteriorate so much, so fast? This is the question that everyone was asking.

Prior to 2008, there was little indication to the average person that anything was wrong with the financial system. Some economists had been warning about irresponsible government policies for years and at least a few of them warned that, if we continued with the reckless policies, a day of reckoning would eventually come. But probably very few economists thought it would come so soon or be so severe.

There were at least a few hints of trouble more than a year before the actual Wall Street meltdown. On July 19, 2007, Federal Reserve Chairman, Ben Bernanke told the United States Senate's Banking Committee that there might be as much as $100 billion in losses associated with subprime mortgages. This may have raised some concerns in the minds of members of Congress, but average citizens never knew about the warning.

On August 22, 2007, Countrywide Financial Corporation, the biggest U.S. mortgage lender, sold $2 billion of preferred stock to Bank of America in order to bolster its finances. This raised a lot of eyebrows in the financial industry, and some began to wonder if any other large banks were in trouble. The anxiety in the banking community was greatly heightened when on January 11, 2008, Bank of America agreed to buy Countrywide for approximately $4 billion.

A month later, it became clear that Countrywide was not just an isolated case when Bear Stearns became insolvent and was purchased by JP Morgan Chase for 7 percent of its market value in a sale brokered by the Fed and the U.S. Treasury Department. Just 4 months later, IndyMac Bancorp, Inc., the second-biggest independent U.S. mortgage lender, was seized by federal regulators after a run by depositors depleted its cash.

On September 7, 2008 the U.S. government seized control of Fannie Mae and Freddie Mac, the largest U.S. mortgage-finance companies. On September 15, Lehman Brothers Holdings, Inc. filed the largest bankruptcy in history, and on the same day, Bank of America agreed to acquire Merrill Lynch for about $50 billion. The following day, September 16, American International Group, Inc. accepted an $85 billion loan from the Federal Reserve to avert the worst financial collapse in history, and the government took over the company.

As one bank after another hemorrhaged in the United States in mid-September, banks in other countries, around the world, were also failing. The world's financial system was collapsing, and there was little anyone could do to halt the momentum. The unthinkable was happening.

On September 21, 2008 Goldman Sachs Group and Morgan Stanley received approval to become commercial banks regulated by the Fed in order to widen their sources of funding. On September 26, Washington Mutual, Inc.

was seized by federal regulators and its assets were sold to JPMorgan Chase. This was the biggest United States bank failure in history.

During September, October, and November, 2008, there was so much bad economic news, that even the most vocal Pollyannas were having trouble seeing a silver lining in the dark cloud that had descended upon the world. As the election passed and President Barack Obama was inaugurated on January 20, the mood throughout America was very different from what it would have been in the absence of the avalanche of bad economic news.

Repeal of the Glass-Steagall Act

Although much of the financial system collapse occurred over a relatively short period of time, the factors that led to the collapse had been several years in the making. Many economists believe that one of the biggest factors in the collapse was the deregulation of banks, which resulted from the enactment of the Gramm-Leach-Bliley Act in 1999.

This law repealed part of the 1933 Glass-Steagall Act, which was passed during the Great Depression in an effort to prevent a repeat of the banking crisis of the 1930s. The Glass Steagall Act had placed strict regulations on the banking industry, and some argued that removing those regulations was very risky. North Dakota Senator Byron Dorgan warned at the time, "I think we will look back in 10 years' time and say we should not have done this, but we did because we forgot the lessons of the past."

The Gramm-Leach-Bliley Act was signed into law by President Bill Clinton on November 12, 1999. The final version of the bill was passed by the Senate 90-8 and by the House 362-57. Although the legislation was sponsored by the Republicans, and initially received stiff opposition from Congressional Democrats, the final version was overwhelmingly supported by both parties. Therefore, if this legislation was one of the primary causes of the Wall Street meltdown, members of Congress from both parties, and Democratic President Bill Clinton all share in the blame.

The repeal of the Glass-Steagall Act in 1999 sealed the economic fate of the nation and the world. This inexcusably, irresponsible act by our government doomed us to repeat history because it activated a time bomb that would continue to tick until it exploded. Senator Dorgan's warning that we would look back in 10 years' time and say "we should not have done this," was right on target.

The Glass-Steagall Act, enacted during the Great Depression for the explicit purpose of preventing financial institutions from engaging in reckless behavior that could lead to another financial meltdown, had served the nation well for decades. However, after years of lobbying, which included the spending of billions of dollars, the financial industry managed to free itself from the protective constraints of the law by getting it repealed.

What did the financial industry get for all that money it paid to politicians? It got a few years to wallow in greed. Since the cat was taken away, the Wall Street mice were free to play, but the party was short-lived. When the time bomb went off in 2008, the Wall Street mice were the first to feel the blast, but soon the whole financial world would come tumbling down.

The Subprime Mortgage Crisis

The triggering mechanism for the ultimate financial collapse was the subprime mortgage crisis, and the bursting of the housing bubble. In order to understand how this unfolded, it is necessary first to talk about how home mortgage loans were transformed into mortgage-backed securites by Wall Street investment firms.

Historically, banks would make mortgage loans only to people who had a substantial down payment, a good credit record, and adequate income to repay the loan.

There was little risk to the banks in making such loans. Most people would repay the loans as scheduled and, if a few people defaulted, the bank would simply foreclose on the property and sell it for at least enough to pay off the loan balance. When a bank loaned a maximum of 80 percent of the appraised value of a home, and home values were either stable or rising, there was little likelihood that the bank could loose any money even if the borrower defaulted.

The safety and good yields on mortgages made it attractive for Wall Street investment firms to buy large numbers of mortgages, bundle them together in large packages, and then sell shares of the mortgage backed securities to investors. Demand for these mortgage backed securities became so high in the early 2000s that banks sought to make more and more mortgage loans so they could sell them to the Wall Street investment firms at a good profit. At one point in 2003, the demand was so high that everyone who met the qualifications for a conventional mortgage loan was able to get one. But, even then, the demand for mortgage-backed securities was not met. It was at this point that the seeds of the 2008 meltdown began to be sowed. And it was at this time that adequate government regulations could have prevented the misery that the whole world now finds itself in.

Since everyone who met the qualifications for mortgage loans were able to get such loans, the only way to make more mortgage loans was to lower the mortgage qualification requirements so that more people would qualify for such loans. These circumstances gave birth to the subprime mortgage loan. Subprime mortgage loans are made to people who do not qualify for the standard conventional mortgage that usually required a 20 percent down payment, a good credit history, and a good income. By their very nature, subprime mortgage loans are more risky than conventional mortgage loans, so the interest rate is higher for such loans.

The first subprime loans called SIVA loans required borrowers only to "state" their income—not prove it. However, the borrower did have to verify that they had money in the bank. The next modification in loan qualifications resulted in NIVA loans which meant that borrowers still had to verify assets but didn't even have to "state" their incomes. With these loans, the lender was no longer interested what the borrower did for a living or how much he or she earned. These relaxed rules made a lot more people eligible for mortgage loans, but they still did not satisfy the huge appetite of global investors who wanted to invest in mortgage backed securities.

Finally, the eligibility requirements were almost eliminated, and people were able to get no income, no asset verification (NINA) mortgage loans. All you needed was to have a credit score to get a NINA loan. You didn't have to have any income or any assets. Also, you did not have to have a good credit score. You just had to have a score above a minimal level set by the lenders.

By 2006, more than 20 percent of all mortgage loans in the United States were subprime. The banks and mortgage companies sought borrowers from middle-class families who had accumulated too much debt to qualify for a conventional mortgage loan as well as low-income families who were seeking their share of the American dream through home ownership. In 2007, 11 percent of all subprime loans were made to first-time home buyers. The other 89 percent went to borrowers who chose to refinance their homes in order to get some additional equity out with which to pay off credit card debt, pay for health care, or meet other needs.

Many of the subprime loans were made at relatively low teaser rates for the first two or three years. However, the rates were adjustable, and when it came time to reset them, they usually went up substantially, causing monthly payments for many buyers to rise so high that they could no longer make those payments. This is when foreclosure rates began to soar. Apparently, many realtors and lenders used the hard-sell approach to encourage people to buy homes that they could not afford. With little or no down payment, and artificially low interest rates initially, a lot of people were fooled into believing they could afford unaffordable homes. When the interest rates were reset and the borrowers discovered that they were in over their heads, many simply walked away and allowed the mortgage owners to foreclose on them.

The housing bubble masked the subprime problem as long as prices continued to rise. Up until 2006, the housing market was booming. It was easy to get loans, so a lot of people bought homes. This increased demand caused housing prices to increase. These rising prices attracted speculative buyers who hoped to buy homes, keep them for a short period, and then sell them at a profit. The speculative demand, added to the demand of those who were obtaining easy loans and buying homes to live in, sent home prices even higher.

Because of the rising prices, the ultimate consequences of the "bad" loans was delayed. As a result of the easy lending practices, and the rising value of homes, people who had trouble making payments just took out second loans to make ends meet. But the belief that housing prices would continue to rise indefinitely was based on wishful thinking, not solid economics. Prices finally rose so high that families found homes no longer affordable.

A chain of interactions, similar to those of the housing bubble, but in the opposite direction, began to appear. Default rates and foreclosures escalated. This put even more empty homes on the market. With the oversupply of houses and the lack of demand, home prices began to drop. As panic began to set in, prices plummeted lower and lower. In late 2006 and early 2007 home prices took a real nosedive, and that is when Wall Street began to panic.

Why were banks willing to issue such risky loans? In the past, banks were very careful when making mortgage loans, especially those local banks that held the loans on their books until the loan was totally repaid. Many small community banks have rarely sold mortgages to outside investors. They focus on doing business with local customers who deposit money in the banks and borrow money from the banks. When they make a 20-year mortgage loan to a local resident, they want to make absolutely sure that the borrower will be able to repay the loan. That is why a sizeable down payment and proof of sufficient income to repay the loan, are required. Such banks would be irresponsible if they used depositors' money to make risky loans. It is because of such sound lending practices that there were almost no bank failures from the enactment of FDIC during the Great Depression until very recent years.

That all changed with the deregulation of the banking industry, beginning with the repeal of the Glass-Steagall Act in 1999. With the rules relaxed, many of the banks that issued mortgage loans did not keep them. They almost immediately sold the mortgages to Wall Street investment firms. Since the banks did not keep the mortgages, it did not matter all that much to them whether or not the loans were ever repaid. They made their money upfront by making the loans and then selling the mortgages. No matter how risky a loan was over the long run, there was little risk to the bank that made the loan and then promptly sold the mortgage.

Wall Street firms had been packaging bundles of mortgages, and selling shares to investors for many years, with no major problems. Credit rating agencies like Standard and Poor's and Moody's had usually given the mortgage-backed securities the top AAA rating, the same as they gave to United States government bonds. The problem came when these mortgage bundles began to include a few subprime mortgages, along with the conventional mortgages. Nobody seemed to notice at first, and gradually more and more subprime mortgages were included in the packages. However, once the default and foreclosure rates began to build up momentum, investors started to discover that they had "toxic" assets on their books. We were about to reap the harvest from the seeds that were sown when the mortgage qualification guidelines were relaxed and subprime loans began to be made.

It is important to note that the subprime mortgage crisis was only the mechanism that triggered the financial meltdown. It was not sufficient, in and of itself, to bring down the whole financial system. It was essentially just the first domino to fall. Irresponsible behavior on the part of the government, businesses, and consumers had made the whole system vulnerable in many ways. Consumers had been living beyond their means for years, just like the government, and corporate mismanagement had put many businesses on very shaky financial ground. Once the meltdown had been triggered, the panic and plummeting confidence of both consumers and investors kept it going.

The Great Recession

The recession, which has been dubbed "The Great Recession," because of its severity, began in December 2007. If the meltdown had not occurred, the recession would probably have been just another normal downturn in the business cycle, which would have been similar to other post World War II recessions in terms of length and severity. But the fallout from the meltdown ensured that the 2007 recession would be more like the Great Depression of the 1930s than any other recession since then.

In both the early 1930s, and in the years following the 2008 meltdown, consumer confidence and spending plummeted. Those who lost their jobs didn't have money to spend, and those who had money were afraid to spend it. A worldwide panic set in, changing the mindset of almost everyone. Instead of continuing the spending binge, individuals and institutions were forced to tighten their belts in an effort to pay down debt.

The reason that the Great Depression was so deep and lasted for so long, is that the economic system broke down and, without appropriate actions by the government to fix it, the economy stayed broken. Roosevelt's public works projects helped the economy by creating jobs, and generating paychecks that would result in the creation of still more jobs. But the government and the American people were not willing to spend enough to bring the economy totally out of the depression. It was the enormous spending that resulted from America's entry into World War II, following the attack on Pearl Harbor, that finally ended the Great Depression.

It is important that we understand clearly that World War II did not rescue America from the Great Depression. It was the spending on the war, not the war, itself, that ended the depression. If the United States had been willing to spend as much as was spent on the war, on domestic projects like building schools, libraries, and roads, the depression could have ended, and prosperity could have been restored to the nation, without a single bullet being fired.

The state of the American economy, in the wake of the 2008 meltdown, was similar to what it was in the early days of the Great Depression. Consumer spending declined sharply, and each month brought a new round of layoffs. As more and more workers lost their jobs, consumer spending was further reduced. And, as consumer spending fell, even more workers were laid off. The recession was technically declared to have ended in June 2009, because the declining economic growth had finally bottomed out, and the GDP had risen for two consecutive quarters.

However, the technical end of the recession did not mean that hard economic times were over. On the contrary, many economists were predicting that the economy would soon enter a new recession and that it might take years for the economy to return to full prosperity.

Three years after the 2008 financial meltdown, the unemployment rate was still extremely high. The official unemployment statistics for August 2011 showed the unemployment rate holding steady at 9.1 percent. According to the Labor Department, 14 million American workers were officially counted as unemployed in August. An additional 8.8 million workers, who wanted to work full time, had only part-time employment. And 1.6 million "discouraged workers"—people who wanted jobs but were not actively seeking work because they did not think any jobs were available--were not counted as unemployed. If we add the three groups together, there were 19.5 million American workers, who wanted to work, who were partially or fully unemployed in August 2011.

Another disturbing measure of just how much Americans had been hurt by the meltdown and recession was the status of home ownership. When the housing bubble burst, real estate prices plummeted. In some areas, a house valued at $300,000 in 2006, dropped in value to $150,000 or, in some cases, to $100,000. This meant massive losses of wealth and put millions in jeopardy of losing their homes to foreclosure. In 2010, a record 1 million homes in the United States were lost to foreclosure, and experts were predicting that 1.2 million homes would be foreclosed on in 2011.

The foreclosures were only the tip of the iceberg, in terms of how many people were in jeopardy of possibly losing their homes. The term, "homes under water," became a part of everyone's vocabulary after the housing bust. It referred to homes on which more money was owed than the house was worth. As the value of houses plummeted, the amount of the mortgages did not change. For example, let's suppose that a family purchased a $500,000 home in 2006 at the peak of the housing bubble. If they took out a traditional home loan, they would have been required to have a down payment of 20 percent, or $100,000, and they could have gotten a mortgage loan of $400,000. In 2006, the family had $100,000 in equity in the home. They could probably have resold the house, at that time, for at least as much as they paid for it, and paid off the mortgage, and still had most of their original down payment. .

But when the housing bubble burst, the value of their home went into a rapid decline. By 2011, the value of the house had dropped by 50 percent, making it worth only $250,000, in a market where it is very difficult to sell any house. If they had just made the minimum mortgage payments, during the five years they owned the house, most of the money would have gone for interest, with the actual principal of the loan declining only a little. Even if they had paid more than the minimum payments, and had managed to reduce the mortgage down to $390,000, they would still owe $140,000 more than the $250,000 current market value of the home. Even if they could sell the home for $250,000 in 2011, they would have to come up with $140,000 of additional money just to pay off the mortgage, and they would lose most of their $100,000 down payment.

In 2011, an estimated 15.7 million homeowners owed more on their homes than the homes were worth. Nationally, approximately 25 percent of all homeowners with mortgages were under water. But some regions of the country were hit much harder than others. In Tampa, Florida, 60 percent of the homes with mortgages were under water. In Phoenix, Arizona, 68 percent were under water. And, Las Vegas, Nevada had the dubious honor of having the highest rate of homes, with more money owed on them than they were worth. An astonishing 85 percent of all homes with mortgages in Las Vegas were under water..

The multitude of problems, that led to the financial meltdown and the severe recession, had been accumulating for nearly three decades. The United States government and the American people lived beyond their means during the entire period. The huge tax cuts, which were not matched by corresponding spending cuts, under both President Ronald Reagan and President George W. Bush, contributed heavily to the $15 trillion national debt that exists today. A similar build up in consumer debt during the same period made consumers extremely vulnerable to any financial crisis.

During the Great Depression, President Hoover refused to take any action to relieve the suffering or help the economy. For more than three years, as the Great Depression became deeper and deeper, and the suffering of millions became more and more dire, Hoover sat on his hands and adamantly opposed any government action to help the economy. His political ideology was so opposed to government involvement in the economy that he would not budge on his principles, even for the good of the people and the country. He was going to stand by his principles come hell or high water.

It might be difficult for contemporary Americans to imagine this kind of stubborn behavior by government officials, if we had not observed irresponsible politicians, who shared the same ideology as President Hoover, leading the nation to the verge of national default in the summer of 2011. They refused to enact legislation that could have put many Americans back to work on the basis that it was inappropriate for the government to become so involved in the economy. Their goal was allegedly to reduce budget deficits and the national debt. They did not seem to understand that one of the greatest current contributors to the deficit was the high unemployment.

During recessions, when large numbers of workers lose their jobs, federal income tax revenue falls off sharply because the unemployed do not have income on which to pay taxes. At the very same time, government spending on programs such as unemployment compensation increases. The combination of more government spending, and reduced income-tax revenue, causes the budget deficit to rise. The best way to decrease the deficit is by growing the economy and creating new jobs. Yet, the legislative package finally agreed to during that 2011 showdown had a negative impact on the budget because it would tend to increase unemployment. The deficits are a terrible problem that we must work to reduce. But a large component of our current deficits is the high unemployment rate. If we solve our unemployment problem, we will have made a lot of progress in lowering the deficits.

Putting America Back to Work
The basic American infrastructure (roads, bridges, railroads, airports, power grids, etc.) is in a terrible state of disrepair, and improvements in the near future are essential to our remaining competitive in the rapidly changing global economy. At the same time, the nation faces the most critical unemployment problem since the Great Depression of the 1930s. Millions of Americans are out of work and unable to adequately provide for themselves and their families, solely because they are unable to find work.

We need to put the unemployed to work rebuilding our distressed infrastructure. Once the unemployed workers return to work, government spending for such programs as unemployment compensation will decline, and tax revenue will increase. At the same time, the newly employed workers will begin spending their earnings in the marketplace, creating increased demand that will lead to still more jobs throughout the economy.

The work would all be done by the private sector. Competitive bids would be taken from private contractors who would employ their own workers. This is no different from the way government has always funded roads, bridges, and other public projects.

Where do we get the money to pay for upgrading the infrastructure? Most economists would argue, that, given the current state of the economy, a tax increase on the lower and middle classes would reduce consumer spending by this group of taxpayers and, thus, be counterproductive. However, raising taxes on millionaires and billionaires would not have a detrimental effect on consumer spending. The rich usually do not reduce the quality of their lifestyles in response to tax increases. They have enough income that they can afford to buy most of the things they want, with or without a tax increase. They will probably complain about a tax increase, but they are not likely to change their spending habits

Those who oppose taxing the rich, to raise revenue for the economy as a whole, often accuse those who advocate such a tax increase of engaging in class warfare. But this claim is the ultimate in hypocrisy. The hard, cold truth is that class warfare has been going on ever since the United States was founded, and the rich are winning that war. The rich are not opposed to redistribution of income from the lower and middle classes to the very rich, as has been happening for the past three decades. They are only opposed to having to pay higher taxes that might result in a reversal of some of that redistribution.

In his book, *"Aftershock,"* noted labor economist, Robert B. Reich points out that, during the late 1970s, the richest 1 percent of Americans took in less than 9 percent of the nation's total income. By 2007, Reich reports that the richest 1 percent took in 23.5 percent of total national income. Reich says, "It is no mere coincidence that the last time income was this concentrated was in 1928."

Reich believes that the substantial redistribution of income from the bottom 80 percent of the population to the richest 1 percent is a major factor in the Great Recession. He points out that the rich don't spend nearly as large a portion of their income as the rest of us. Instead they invest their savings around the world, wherever they can reap the highest return. As a result, Reich says, "The rest of us, with a smaller share of the total, lack the purchasing power to keep the economy going full speed."

The only thing blocking efforts to put America back to work is a lack of political will on the part of conservative politicians. The conservatives are mimicking Herbert Hoover's lack of action during the 1930s. By opposing any tax increases, for any purpose they are prolonging the suffering of millions of unemployed Americans. Public opinion polls show that the majority of Americans want the government to take actions to reduce unemployment. Polls also show that the majority favors having the rich pay their fair share of taxes. But our nation does not govern by public opinion polls, and many politicians are a lot more interested in pushing their political ideology than they are in honoring the wishes of the majority of American voters.

Chapter Highlights

- In mid-September 2008, the world financial system melted down, causing massive financial losses and global panic.

- The triggering mechanism for the ultimate financial collapse was the subprime mortgage crisis and the bursting of the housing bubble.

- The demand for mortgage-backed securities became so high in the early 2000s that banks sought to make more and more mortgage loans so they could sell them to the Wall Street investment firms at a good profit.

- In order to meet Wall Street's increasing demand for mortgage loans, banks began to lower the mortgage qualification requirements so more people would qualify for loans. These loans with lower qualification requirements were called subprime mortgage loans.

- The eligibility requirements for subprime mortgage loans were lowered so much that many loans were made to borrowers who did not have the financial capability of repaying the loans.

- The Great Recession began in December 2007, and became much worse after the financial meltdown of 2008. Although the recession was technically declared to have ended in June 2009, hard economic times and high unemployment continued. Three years after the meltdown, the unemployment rate was still above 9 percent.

- Home prices plummeted after the housing bubble burst. The values of many homes declined by 50 percent or more and millions of homeowners found that their homes were worth less than they owed on the mortgage.

- By 2011, millions of Americans had lost their homes to foreclosure or were in jeopardy of losing them. More than a million foreclosures took place in 2011 alone.

Important Terms
Match each of the following terms with the correct definition:

financial meltdown   housing bubble
Glass-Steagall Act   Great Recession
subprime mortgage loan   Great Depression

1. The 2008 collapse of the world financial system.

2. Important legislation passed in the 1930s to regulate banks.

3. Mortgage loan with lower eligibility requirements than conventional loan.

4. Rapid rise in housing prices due to easy financing and speculators in the housing market.

5. Recession that began in December 2007 and became much more severe because of the financial meltdown.

6. Severe depression that followed the 1929 stock market crash and continued until World War II.

Review Questions
1. What led to the financial meltdown?

2. What was the triggering mechanism of the meltdown?

3. What role did the repeal of the Glass-Steagall Act play in the financial meltdown?

4. What is a subprime mortgage?

5. Why was there such a strong demand for mortgage loans?

6. What role did subprime mortgages play in the financial meltdown?

7. When did the Great Recession begin?

8. Why did the Great Depression of the 1930s last so long?

9. What is the American infrastructure? What role might it play in reducing unemployment ?

10. What does economist Robert Reich think is a major cause of the Great Recession?

Discussion Questions

1. Was the financial meltdown of 2008 inevitable? If not, what could have been done to prevent it?

2. Why is the Great Recession so much worse than most recessions? How is it comparable to the Great Depression of the 1930s?

3. Do you think it would be fair to increase taxes on millionaires and billionaires in order to generate revenue for putting America back to work rebuilding the infrastructure? Why or why not?

Appendix

Select Measures of Economic Performance

In order for policymakers to determine what actions need to be taken to improve the economy, at any given point in time, they need objective measures of how well the economy is currently performing. There are many measures of the economy's performance, but, among the most important measures, are the size and rate of growth of the Gross Domestic Product (GDP), the unemployment rate, the inflation rate, and the federal budget. This appendix provides historical data on these measures as well as some additional measures.

Table A-1
Gross Domestic Product, 1985-2010

Year	GDP (Billions of Current Dollars)	Real GDP (Billions of 2005 Dollars)	Percent Change in Real GDP
1985	4,217.5	6,849.3	4.1
1986	4,460.1	7,086.5	3.5
1987	4,736.4	7,313.3	3.2
1988	5,100.4	7,613.9	4.1
1989	5,482.1	7,885.9	3.6
1990	5,800.5	8,033.9	1.9
1991	5,992.1	8,015.1	-0.2
1992	6,342.3	8,287.1	3.4
1993	6,667.4	8,523.4	2.9
1994	7,085.2	8,870.7	4.1
1995	7,414.7	9,093.7	2.5
1996	7,838.5	9,433.9	3.7
1997	8,332.4	9,854.3	4.5
1998	8,793.5	10,283.5	4.4
1999	9,353.5	10,779.8	4.8
2000	9,951.5	11,226.0	4.1
2001	10,286.2	11,347.2	1.1
2002	10,642.3	11,553.0	1.8
2003	11,142.1	11,840.7	2.5
2004	11,867.8	12,263.8	3.6
2005	12,638.4	12,638.4	3.1
2006	13,398.9	12,976.2	2.7
2007	14,061.8	13,228.9	1.9
2008	14,369.1	13,228.8	.0
2009	14,119.0	12,860.6	-2.6
2010	14,660.2	13,248.7	2.9

SOURCE: Economic Report of the President, 2011

Table A-2
Civilian Unemployment Rate 1985-2010
(Percent)

Year	All Civilian Workers	Males	Females	Teenagers (Both Sexes 16-19 years old)
1985	7.2	7.0	7.6	18.9
1986	7.0	6.9	7.1	18.3
1987	6.2	6.2	6.2	16.9
1988	5.5	5.5	5.6	15.3
1989	5.3	5.2	5.4	15.0
1990	5.6	5.7	5.5	15.5
1991	6.8	7.2	6.4	18.7
1992	7.5	7.9	7.0	20.1
1993	6.9	7.2	6.6	19.0
1994	6.1	6.2	6.0	17.6
1995	5.6	5.6	5.6	17.3
1996	5.4	5.4	5.4	16.7
1997	4.9	4.9	5.0	16.0
1998	4.5	4.4	4.6	14.6
1999	4.2	4.1	4.3	13.9
2000	4.0	3.9	4.1	13.1
2001	4.7	4.8	4.7	14.7
2002	5.8	5.9	5.6	16.5
2003	6.0	6.3	5.7	17.5
2004	5.5	5.6	5.4	17.0
2005	5.1	5.1	5.1	16.6
2006	4.6	4.6	4.6	15.4
2007	4.6	4.7	4.5	15.7
2008	5.8	6.1	5.4	18.7
2009	9.3	10.3	8.1	24.3
2010	9.6	10.5	8.6	25.9

SOURCE: Economic Report of the President 2011

Table A-3
Inflation Rate (as measured by annual percent change in Consumer Price Index): 1970-2010

Year	Percent Change in CPI	Year	Percent Change in CPI
1970	5.7	1991	4.2
1971	4.4	1992	3.0
1972	3.2	1993	3.0
1973	6.2	1994	2.6
1974	11.0	1995	2.8
1975	9.1	1996	3.0
1976	5.8	1997	2.3
1977	6.5	1998	1.6
1978	7.6	1999	2.2
1979	11.3	2000	3.4
1980	13.5	2001	2.8
1981	10.3	2002	1.6
1982	6.2	2003	2.3
1983	3.2	2004	2.7
1984	4.3	2005	3.4
1985	3.6	2006	3.2
1986	1.9	2007	2.8
1987	3.6	2008	3.8
1988	4.1	2009	-.4
1989	4.8	2010	1.6
1990	5.4		

SOURCE: Economic Report of the President, 2011

Table A-4
Federal Receipts, Outlays, Surplus or Deficit, and Debt,
1985-2010 in Billions of Dollars

Fiscal Year	Total Receipts	Total Outlays	Surplus or Deficit(-)	Federal Debt (end of period)
1985	734.0	946.3	-212.3	1,817.4
1986	769.2	990.4	-221.2	2,120.5
1987	854.3	1,004.0	-149.7	2,346.0
1988	909.2	1,064.4	-155.2	2,601.1
1989	991.1	1,143.7	-152.6	2,867.8
1990	1,032.0	1,253.0	-221.0	3,206.3
1991	1,055.0	1,324.2	-269.2	3,598.2
1992	1,091.2	1,381.5	-290.3	4,001.8
1993	1,154.3	1,409.4	-255.1	4,351.0
1994	1,258.6	1,461.8	-203.2	4,351.0
1995	1,351.8	1,515.7	-164.0	4,920.6
1996	1,453.1	1,560.5	-107.4	5,181.5
1997	1,579.2	1,601.1	-21.9	5,369.2
1998	1,721.7	1,652.5	69.3	5,478.2
1999	1,827.5	1,701.8	125.6	5,605.5
2000	2,025.2	1,789.0	236.2	5,628.7
2001	1,991.1	1,862.8	128.2	5,769.9
2002	1,853.1	2,010.9	-157.8	6,198.4
2003	1,782.3	2,159.9	-377.6	6,760.0
2004	1,880.1	2,292.8	-412.7	7,354.7
2005	2,153.6	2,472.0	-318.3	7,905.3
2006	2,406.9	2,655.1	-248.2	8,451.4
2007	2,568.0	2,728.7	-160.7	8,950.7
2008	2,524.0	2,982.5	-458..6	9,986.1
2009	2,105.0	3,517.7	-1,412.7	11,875.9
2010	2,162.7	3,456.2	-1,293.5	13,528.8

SOURCE: Economic Report of the President, 2011

Table A-5
Percent of Persons Below Poverty Level: 1980-2009

Year	All Races	White	Black	Hispanic
1980	13.0	10.2	32.5	25.7
1985	14.0	11.4	31.3	29.0
1988	13.0	10.1	31.3	26.7
1989	12.8	10.0	30.7	26.2
1990	13.5	10.7	31.9	28.1
1991	14.2	11.3	32.7	28.7
1992	14.8	11.9	33.4	29.6
1993	15.1	12.2	33.1	30.6
1994	14.5	11.7	30.6	30.7
1995	13.8	11.2	29.3	30.3
1996	13.7	11.2	28.4	29.4
1997	13.3	11.0	26.5	27.1
1998	12.7	10.5	26.1	25.6
1999	11.9	9.8	23.6	22.7
2000	11.3	9.5	22.5	21.5
2001	11.7	9.9	22.7	21.4
2002	12.1	10.2	24.1	21.8
2003	12.5	10.5	24.4	22.5
2004	12.7	10.8	24.7	21.9
2005	12.6	10.6	24.9	21.8
2006	12.3	10.3	24.3	20.6
2007	12.5	10.5	24.5	21.5
2008	13.2	11.2	24.7	23.2
2009	14.3	12.3	25.8	25.3

SOURCE: Statistical Abstract of the United States, 2011

Table A-6
Poverty Thresholds by Size of Family Unit: 1980-2009
(In dollars per year)

Year	One-person Household	Two-person Household	Four-person Household
1980	4,190	5,363	8,414
1990	6,652	8,509	13,359
1995	7,763	9,933	15,569
2000	8,791	11,235	17,604
2005	9,973	12,755	19,971
2006	10,294	13,167	20,614
2007	10,590	13,540	21,203
2008	10,991	14,051	22,025
2009	10,956	13,991	21,954

SOURCE: Statistical Abstract of the United States, 2011

MINI-DICTIONARY
OF ECONOMIC TERMS AND CONCEPTS

ability-to-pay principle A principle of taxation based on the assumption that those most able to pay taxes should pay the most taxes.

absolute advantage the ability of one nation to produce a product with fewer resources than another nation.

adjustable-rate mortgage a type of mortgage loan in which the interest rate for the loan can rise or fall with interest rates in general throughout the period of the loan.

adjusted balance method a method of calculating finance charges in which creditors add finance charges only after subtracting all payments made during the payment period.

advisory arbitration a process in which a neutral third party's recommended settlement for a labor-management dispute can be refused by either party.

agency shop an arrangement under which employees are not required to join a union but are required to pay union dues.

aggregate demand the total of consumption spending plus investment spending plus government spending when exports equal imports.

annual percentage rate(APR) the percentage cost of credit per year.

annually balanced budget a budget policy under which the government would attempt to have a balanced budget each and every year.

antitrust law   law designed to promote and maintain competition by prohibiting practices that tend to lead to the creation of monopoly power.

assets   properties, possessions, and anything else of value that a person, organization, or institution owns.

automatic fiscal stabilizers   built-in features of the economy that tend to change automatically government spending and taxes in the desired direction during the various phases of the business cycle.

average daily balance method   a method of calculating finance charges in which creditors compute the outstanding balance each day during the billing period.

average total cost   the cost that is calculated by dividing the total cost at each output level by the number of units being produced.

B

balance of payments   an accounting record of all of a nation's monetary transactions with other countries.

balance of trade   the difference in the dollar value of exports and imports.

barter   a form of trade in which people directly trade goods and services for other types of goods and services without using money.

benefit principle   the principle that those who benefit from a government program should pay taxes to finance the program.

binding arbitration   a process under which grievances are submitted to a neutral third party, acceptable to both the union and management, who issues a decision that is binding on both parties.

Board of Governors   the central policy-making body of the Federal Reserve System.

bonds   certificates that are issued by a corporation (or by government) in exchange for borrowed money and that bind the corporation (or government) to pay a fixed sum of money when the bonds reach maturity.

boycott a campaign by workers to discourage people from buying an employer's product in an effort to put economic pressure on the employer.

budget a spending plan based on expected income.

budgeting using a spending plan based on expected income.

business cycles recurrent but irregular fluctuations in economic activity.

C

capital gain an increase in the value of an investment.

capital goods human-made productive resources (such as factories, tools, and machines) that are necessary for the production of other goods and services; one of the three factors of production.

capital loss a decrease in the value of an investment.

capitalism an economic system in which businesses are privately owned and operated for profit and where free markets coordinate most economic activity.

certificate of deposit(CD) the type of bank deposit that offers the highest yield but requires the depositor to leave the money on deposit for a specific time period.

classical economics the ideas that were formulated by Adam Smith in The Wealth of Nations and redefined by his followers.

closed shop an agreement under which employers hire only union members.

collateral something of value that a borrower pledges as assurance that a loan will be repaid.

collective bargaining the process by which a union negotiates with management in an attempt to reach a mutually acceptable agreement with regard to wages, hours, and other terms and conditions of employment.

collective goods and services   items that tend to benefit large numbers of people collectively and that would not be available to everyone if each individual had to provide them; also called public goods and services.

command economy   an economy in which the basic economic questions are answered by government officials, with individuals having little control over economic decisions; also called planned economy.

commercial banks   financial institutions that have been chartered by the federal government or a state government to receive deposits and make loans.

common stock   a type of corporate stock that gives stockholders voting privileges but no prior claim on dividends.

comparative advantage   a situation in which a country has a greater absolute advantage or less of an "absolute disadvantage" in the production of one of two products.

competition   the economic rivalry that controls a market economy.

consumer cooperative   a cooperative formed for the purpose of collectively buying consumer products in large quantities at low prices to enable its members to enjoy the savings.

consumer goods   finished products sold to consumers for their own personal use.

consumer price index   the measure most often used to determine the inflation rate.

consumer protection   the process of protecting consumers from unsafe products, unsafe working conditions, and an unsafe environment.

consumer sovereignty   the process of allowing the people to decide what shall be produced by voting with their dollars for the goods and services they want most.

consumption spending   the purchase of consumer goods and services by consumers for their own personal use.

cooperative a voluntary association of people formed for the purpose of providing economic benefits for its members; and apartment building or group of dwellings that is owned by a nonprofit corporation and managed by a board of directors elected by the residents.

corporate charter a legal document granted by a state government that gives a business the authority to operate as a corporation in that state.

corporate income taxes taxes based on the net profits of corporations.

corporation a form of business organization that is collectively owned by a number of individuals but has the legal status to act as a single fictitious person.

cost-push inflation inflation caused by rising production costs.

craft union a union composed of workers in a particular trade, such as carpenters, electricians, or plumbers.

credit the lending of money, either directly or indirectly, to enable a person to buy goods now but pay for them at a later date.

credit bureau a private business firm that collects credit information about consumers and sells this information to lenders for a fee.

credit cards plastic, wallet-size cards enabling a customer to charge purchases.

credit rating an estimate of the probability that a potential borrower will repay a loan with interest when due.

credit unions cooperative associations often organized among the employees of large companies or the members of large labor unions in order to offer high interest savings accounts and low-interest loans.

customs duties taxes on goods brought into the United States from other countries.

cyclical unemployment unemployment caused by insufficient aggregate demand.

cyclically balanced budget   a budget policy under which the government would attempt to balance its budget over the course of the business cycle.

D

demand   the ability and willingness of people to buy things.

demand curve   a graphical representation of a demand schedule.

demand deposits   checkbook money.

demand-pull inflation   inflation caused by too much aggregate demand.

demand schedule   a listing showing the various amounts of an item that buyers are willing and able to buy at various prices during some stated time period.

depreciation   the wear and tear of the nation's factories, tools, and machines that results from production.

depression   a prolonged period of little or no growth in the GDP accompanied by high unemployment.

devaluation   the lowering of a currency's value in relation to other currencies by government order.

discount rate   the rate of interest that Federal Reserve Banks charge banks and other financial institutions for loans.

diseconomies of scale   the reduction of efficiency and increased cost per unit that sometimes results from a firm becoming too large.

disposable personal income   the amount of money that individuals have available for spending after personal taxes are paid.

dividends   cash payments made to stockholders out of a corporation's profits.

durable consumer goods   consumer goods, such as appliances and furniture, that usually last for several years.

E

easy-money policy a policy of expanding the money supply and reducing interest rates.

economic efficiency the process of producing the maximum amount and proper combination of goods and services from the nation's limited productive resources.

economic goods things of value that can be seen, touched, and shown to others.

economic growth an increase in the economy's capacity to produce goods and services.

economic models simplified representations of the real world that help economists analyze complex problems.

economic services intangible things that have value but cannot be seen, touched, or shown to others.

economic system the organized set of procedures for answering the basic economic questions, What? How? For whom?

economics the study of how individuals and society choose to use limited resources in an effort to satisfy unlimited wants.

economies of scale the increased efficiency resulting from specialization and the division of labor that makes possible the production of a large volume of output.

elasticity of demand a measure of the responsiveness of quantity demanded to a change in price.

elasticity of supply a measure of the responsiveness of quantity supplied to a change in price.

embargo a total ban by the government on the import or export of a particular product.

entrepreneur a person who organizes, manages, and assumes the risks and responsibility for a business.

entrepreneurship the function of combining and organizing natural resources, capital goods, and labor; assuming the risks of business failure; and providing the creativity and managerial skills necessary for production to take place.

equilibrium GDP   that level of GDP at which the total supply of goods and services is exactly equal to the total demand.

equilibrium price   the price at which the quantity demanded is exactly equal to the quantity supplied.

estate taxes   taxes levied on the estates or property of people who have died.

excess reserves   the difference between actual reserves and required reserves.

excise taxes   taxes levied on the production or sale of specific goods or services.

explicit costs   those costs that involve an actual payment of money to "outsiders" who supply labor, raw materials, fuel, and so forth to a firm.

export   to sell a product to another nation.

F

factors of production   the basic resources needed for the production of goods and services; sometimes called productive resources.

Federal Advisory Council   the twelve commercial bankers who advise the Federal Reserve Board of Governors on banking policy.

Federal Deposit Insurance Corporation (FDIC)   a government agency established by Congress in 1933 to insure bank depositors against bank failures.

Federal Open Market Committee   Federal Reserve Committee made up of the Board of Governors and five presidents of Federal Reserve Banks that is responsible for directing the buying and selling of government securities in the open market (open-market operations).

Federal Reserve Banks   the twelve banks established by the Federal Reserve Act of 1913.

Federal Reserve System   the nation's central monetary authority, or "central bank."

fiat money money that is declared legal tender by government decree.

finance charge the exact total cost of credit expressed in dollars and cents.

fiscal policy the deliberate use of the government's spending and taxing powers to influence economic activity in order to establish desired economic objectives.

fixed costs costs (such as rent, insurance premiums, and property taxes) that do not vary with changes in output; sometimes called overhead costs.

fixed exchange rates an exchange rate system under which the price of one currency is fixed in terms of other currencies so that the rate does not change.

fixed-rate mortgage a type of mortgage loan in which the monthly payment and the interest rate remain at one level for the lifetime of the loan.

flexible exchange rates an exchange rate system under which the forces of supply and demand determine the value of a country's currency in terms of the value of other currencies.

foreign exchange foreign currencies

foreign exchange markets markets that deal in the buying and selling of foreign currencies.

foreign exchange rate the price of one currency in terms of another.

fractional reserve banking a banking system based on the provision that only a fraction of a bank's deposits must be held as reserves.

frictional unemployment unemployment that involves people who are temporarily between jobs.

full-employment balanced budget a budget policy under which the federal budget would be balanced when, and only when, the economy is operating at the full-employment level.

G

geographic monopoly   monopoly that occurs because of a seller's location.

gift taxes   taxes on gifts of money or other forms of wealth.

government monopoly   monopoly in which the government itself is the sole producer of a product and serves as the barrier to entry.

government securities   IOUs issued by the United States Treasury, various agencies of the federal government, and state and local governments.

government spending   the total spending by all levels of government.

grievance   formal complaint accusing either labor or management of violating a collective bargaining agreement.

grievance procedure   a procedure for settling disagreements over the implementation and administration of a collective bargaining contract without strikes.

gross domestic product(GDP)   the total dollar value of all goods and services produced in a year's time, within a country's borders, measured in terms of their market prices.

gross national product (GNP)   the total dollar value of all goods and services produced in a year's time by the residents of a country, both inside and outside the country's borders, measured in terms of their market prices.

H

human resources   see **labor**.

implicit costs   the opportunity costs resulting from a firm's use of resources that it owns.

import   to buy a product from another nation.

import quota   a government policy that places a precise legal limit on the number of units of a particular product that can be imported into a country during a specified time period.

income-earning assets assets that earn money for a bank or other institution.

income effect the ability to purchase more or less of an item with a given amount of money because of a change in the price.

independent union a union that does not belong to the AFL-CIO, the federation of American unions.

indirect business taxes a variety of sales taxes that go directly to the government.

individual income taxes taxes paid by individuals based on their income.

individual proprietorship a form of business organization that is owned by a single individual who makes all the business decisions, receives all the profits, and is responsible for any losses of the firm.

industrial union a union composed of workers from a particular industry, regardless of the kinds of jobs they hold.

industry a group of firms producing the same or similar products.

inflation a general rise in the price level or a decline in the purchasing power of money.

interest money paid to lenders for the use of borrowed funds; money paid to depositors for keeping money in a financial institution.

investment spending business spending for capital goods: factories, tools, and machines.

invisible-hand principle the concept that in a market economy, if individuals were allowed to pursue their own self-interests without interference by government, their actions would lead to what is best for society.

K
Keynesian economics a body of economic theory based on the ideas of John Maynard Keynes, who argued that the

government should play an active role in maintaining the proper level of aggregate demand.

L

labor   any form of human effort exerted in production; one of the three factors of production; also called human resources.

labor productivity   the amount of output produced by a given quantity of labor.

law of demand   a law stating that as the price of an item rises and other factors remain unchanged, the quantity demanded by buyers will fall; as the price of an item falls and other factors remain unchanged, the quantity demanded by buyers will rise.

law of diminishing marginal utility   a law stating that individuals receive less and less additional satisfaction from an item as they obtain more and more units of the item during a specific time period.

law of diminishing returns   a law stating that increasing the quantity of one factor of production while quantities of the other factors of production remain fixed will eventually result in smaller and smaller increases in total output.

law of supply   a law stating that as the price of an item rises and other factors remain unchanged, the quantity supplied by suppliers will rise; as the price of an item falls and other factors remain unchanged, the quantity supplied by suppliers will fall.

liabilities   the debts and obligations of an individual, an organization, or an institution.

legal tender   money that must be accepted for all debts, public and private.

liquidity   the ease with which an asset can be converted into cash quickly without loss of value.

lockout   the temporary suspension of workers' opportunity to work by an employer in an effort to pressure unions to agree to management's terms.

long run a time period long enough to allow a firm to vary all of its factors of production, including the size of its plant.

M

macroeconomics the study of the economy as a whole.

marginal cost the additional cost of producing one more unit of output.

marginal product increased output resulting from an additional unit of labor or other input.

marginal revenue the additional revenue that results from producing and selling one more unit of output.

market an arrangement through which potential buyers and sellers come together to exchange goods and services.

market economy an economy in which the basic economic questions are answered by households and businesses through a system of freely operating markets.

markets for consumer products markets in which households are the buyers and businesses are the sellers of consumer goods and services.

markets for productive resources markets in which businesses are the buyers and, to some extent, households are the sellers of productive resources.

mediation a process under which a neutral third party tries to keep the union and management talking in an effort to reach a peaceful settlement to a labor-management dispute.

member banks commercial banks that are members of the Federal Reserve System.

microeconomics the study of the individual parts of the economy.

minimum wage laws laws that set a lower limit on the wage that can be paid to most workers.

mixed economy an economy that has characteristics of both a command and a market economy.

monetarism a school of economic thought that takes the position that the money supply is a key factor in determining the health of the economy.

monetary policy the actions taken by the Federal Reserve System to control the nation's money supply and interest rates in order to achieve desired economic objectives.

money anything that is generally accepted and generally used as a medium of payment.

money market account a high-yielding bank deposit that requires a substantial minimum balance in order to obtain the higher yield.

money market mutual fund a form of mutual fund in which the investors' money is used to buy large certificates of deposit, high-yield government securities, and high-yield bonds of major corporations.

money supply the total amount of money in circulation.

monopolistic competition a market structure that is characterized by many sellers, differentiated products, nonprice competition, and relatively easy entry and exit.

monopoly a market structure characterized by a single seller, a product for which there are no close substitutes, and strong barriers to entry that prevent potential competitors from entering the market.

mortgage loan a long-term loan that will be paid in many installments and that gives the lender a claim (mortgage) against the borrower's home or other collateral.

mutual fund an investment company that pools the money of many investors and uses it to buy stocks and other securities.

mutual savings banks financial institutions totally owned by their depositors, with the purpose of pooling the savings of many small depositors so they can be profitably invested.

N

national banks   banks chartered by the federal government.

natural monopoly   a monopoly that is formed because competition is not practical such as public utilities.

natural resources   productive resources that are provided by nature such as land, air, water, forests, coal, iron ore, oil, and minerals; one of the three factors of production.

near-money   savings accounts and time deposits that are not payable on demand but that can easily be converted into currency.

negative income tax   a proposed alternative to current welfare programs under which people who earn less than a certain income would receive cash payments from the government.

nondurable consumer goods   consumer goods such as food and clothing that usually do not last very long.

nonprofit organization   an organization that provides a service and whose revenue is used to further the purposes of the organization.

O

oligopoly   a market structure characterized by a few sellers, substantial barriers to entry, standardized or differentiated products, and substantial nonprice competition.

open-market operations   the buying and selling by the Fed of government securities in the open market for purposes of influencing the availability and cost of loanable funds.

opportunity cost   the next best alternative use of a resource that is given up when a decision is made to use resources in a particular way.

overhead costs   see **fixed costs.**

P

partnership   a form of business organization that is collectively owned by two or more people who jointly make the business decisions, share the profits, and bear the financial responsibility for any losses.

peak   the highest phase of the business cycle characterized by prosperity and low unemployment.

personal economics   areas of economics that deal with consumer issues and topics.

personal income   the total income received by all persons in the nation before personal taxes are paid.

picketing   standing or walking in front of an employers' place of business with signs that spell out the workers' complaints against the employer.

planned economy   see command economy.

poverty level   that level of income at or below which the government officially classifies individuals as poor.

preferred stock   a type of corporate stock that gives the stockholder a prior claim on dividends but no voting privileges.

price ceiling   a government-imposed upper price limit that prevents market forces from establishing a price above this limit.

price floor   a government-imposed lower price limit that prevents market forces from establishing a price below this limit.

price system   the coordination and communication system of a market economy based on the principle that everything bought and sold has a price.

prime rate   the rate of interest that large banks charge their best business customers.

private sector   areas of economic activity in which economic decisions are made primarily by individual households and businesses.

producer cooperative   a voluntary association of producers of certain products that attempts to obtain higher prices than the members could get by selling individually.

productive resources See factors of production.

profit the money a business has left over after all costs are paid; also refers to the financial gain or benefit received by an individual or business as a result of work activity.

profit motive the desire to maximize financial gains.

progressive tax a tax that takes an increasing percentage of income as income rises.

property taxes taxes levied primarily on land and buildings.

proportional tax a tax that takes a constant percentage of income as income rises.

proxy signing over voting privileges to the current management of a corporation or to some other group.

public finance the study of government expenditures and revenues at all levels of government.

public goods and services See collective goods and services.

public sector areas of economic activity in which economic decisions are made primarily by the government.

pure competition a market structure characterized by many sellers, standardized products, easy entry and exit, and no artificial restrictions on the free movement of prices and wages up and down.

Q

quantity demanded a specific quantity that will be demanded at a specific price.

quantity supplied a specific quantity that will be supplied at a specific price.

R

rate of return the percentage of the total investment that a business gets back each year from an investment.

recession   the downward phase of the business cycle characterized by a decline in GDP and rising unemployment.

recovery   the upward phase of the business cycle characterized by decreasing unemployment and increasing business activity.

regressive tax   a tax that takes a decreasing percentage of income as income rises.

required reserves   the amount of reserves that a bank is required to hold as backing for money that has been deposited with it.

reserve requirement   a rule that stipulates the percentage of deposits that must be kept as reserves to back up those deposits.

revenue   the money a firm receives for the products it sells.

right-to-work laws   state laws that make it illegal to require workers to join a union as a condition of employment.

risk   the degree of probability that a financial investment will lose money.

S

sales taxes   taxes levied on the sale of a wide range of goods and services instead of just specific items.

savings and loan associations   financial institutions owned and operated by savers that historically made mostly long-term loans for the purpose of buying or building homes.

scarcity   the problem of limited resources and unlimited wants.

seasonal unemployment   temporary unemployment caused by seasonal factors.

seniority rights   certain rights given to employees on the basis of length of service with the company.

short run a time period too short to allow a firm to alter the size of its plant yet long enough to allow the firm to change the level at which the fixed plant is used.

Social Security taxes payroll taxes, half of which are paid by employers and half of which are paid by employees.

socialism an economic system in which most businesses are owned and operated by the government.

spillover costs the costs borne by other members of society as a result of an act by an individual or business firm.

standard of living the quality of life based on the amount of goods and services, leisure time, and so forth that a population has.

state banks banks chartered by state governments.

stock shares of ownership in a corporation.

stockbroker a person who serves as a go-between for buyers and sellers of stock.

stockholders people who own stock in a corporation.

strike a mutual agreement by employees to stop working until their demands are met.

structural unemployment unemployment caused by a mismatch between job seekers and job openings.

substitution effect the tendency for consumers to substitute lower priced items for more expensive items.

supply the ability and willingness of suppliers to make things available for sale.

supply curve a graphical representation of a supply schedule.

supply schedule a listing showing the various amounts of an item that sellers are willing to sell at various possible prices.

supply-side economics a body of economic ideas based on tax cuts that became a part of national economic policy during the early 1980s under President Ronald Reagan.

surplus a situation that results when the quantity supplied exceeds the quantity demanded.

T

tariff   a tax imposed by the government on imported products.

technological monopoly a monopoly that is formed as the result of patents.

tight-money policy   a policy of restricting the availability of credit and forcing interest rates up.

total cost the sum of fixed and variable costs at each level of output.

total revenue   the selling price of an item times the quantity sold.

trade deficit   a situation in which a country's imports exceed its exports.

trade surplus   a situation in which a country's exports exceed its imports.

traditional economy   an economy in which the basic economic questions are answered directly by the people involved, with the answers usually based on how things were done in the past.

transfer payments   all sources of income to individuals that do not represent current income earned by them for producing goods and services.

trough   the lowest phase of the business cycle characterized by high unemployment and decreased business activity.

trust   a device that for all practical purposes converts a group of firms into a single monopoly.

U

union security agreement   an arrangement between a union and an employer that requires employees to join a union or at least pay union dues.

union shop   an arrangement under which employers are free to hire nonunion workers but the new employees are required to join the union within a specified time period as a condition of continued employment.

unlimited liability   the potential for a business owner to incur and have to pay unlimited business debts.

V

variable costs   costs (such as labor, raw materials, and power to operate machines) that change as the level of output changes.

W

wage-push inflation   cost-push inflation that is caused by rising wages.

welfare programs   programs that attempt to alleviate poverty by providing direct assistance to the poor.

World Bank   the International Bank for Reconstruction and Development, which provides foreign aid to the less developed countries.

Y

yield   the return on an investment.

Index

A

ability-to-pay-principle of
taxation 49
absolute advantage ... 162, 163,
164, 173, 174, 175, 176,
339, 342
actual reserves 146, 150
aggregate demand 69
aggregate supply 69
American economy. 23, 25, 30,
31, 32, 34, 35, 37, 39, 43,
45, 46, 47, 49, 87, 152, 192,
193, 194, 210, 287
American Federation of Labor
(AFL).... 213, 214, 216, 217
annually balanced budget . 122,
123, 124
antitrust laws 203, 207
antiunion policies 214
arbitration, advisory... 225, 226
arbitration, binding 224
average total cost 266, 269,
270, 279, 281

B

balance of payments .. 172, 174,
177, 340
balance of trade 171, 172, 174,
177, 340
balancing the budget.. 122, 126
Bank of America 314
banking 7, 130, 146, 313
banks 134, 137, 138, 139, 140,
142, 143, 144, 145, 146,
150, 188
barriers to entry .. 35, 191, 195,
196, 198, 199, 201
barriers to trade.............. 7, 165

Bear Stearns 314
benefit principle of taxation 49
Bernanke, Ben 136, 313
Board of Governors, Federal
Reserve System ... 105, 136,
137, 138, 139, 140
boycott.............................. 233
budget deficits.... 88, 115, 116,
123, 124, 126, 128, 129,
171, 326
budget surpluses 116, 118, 124
budget, annually balanced. 122
Bureau of Engraving and
Printing................. 134, 143
Bureau of the Census 78
Bureau of the Mint............ 133
Bush, President George H. W.
120
Bush, President George W... 7,
118, 119, 120, 302, 325
business cycle..... 81, 117, 123,
129, 154, 340, 343
business firms... 178, 179, 180,
184, 187, 202, 274, 277
business organization 178, 180,
181, 183, 184, 187, 188,
189, 205, 206, 343, 349,
353

C

capital goods ... 20, 23, 43, 70,
71, 98, 162, 275, 286
capitalism 31, 52, 53
Carter, President Jimmy.... 115
Celler-Kefauver Antimerger
Act of 1950................. 205

central bank. 136, 139, 156, 347
changing key interest rates 150
changing reserve requirements; 149
checking accounts..... 135, 142, 144
Clayton Antitrust Act 204
Clinton, President Bill 120, 315
closed shop 221, 233
coins .. 130, 132, 133, 134, 144
collective bargaining 210, 218, 219, 222, 224, 226
command economies 24, 25
Commerce Department.. 58, 60
commercial banks..... 139, 140, 143
common stock 185, 186
comparative advantage in trade 163, 164, 173, 174, 176, 342
competition..... 35, 38, 90, 172, 191, 192, 200, 201, 202
Congress of Industrial Organization (CIO)216, 217
Congress, United States 4, 105, 112, 114, 119, 120, 137, 138, 158, 165, 204, 205, 216, 217, 219, 228, 231, 313, 315, 346
conspiracy doctrine.... 214, 215
consumer goods 20, 23, 43, 45, 64, 66, 70, 96, 294
consumer price index.... 96, 98, 107, 108, 342
consumer sovereignty.... 43, 44
consumer spending. 43, 63, 64, 65, 66, 69, 81, 87, 88, 97, 105
corporate charter........ 185, 343
corporate income tax . 123, 189
corporations 184, 187

cost-push inflation. 96, 98, 107
costs, production 85, 266, 268, 284, 285
court injunction 214, 215
craft unions............... 216, 228
credit 135, 191
credit cards 133, 135
credit unions..................... 191
cyclical unemployment . 81, 97
cyclically balanced budget 122, 123, 124, 125

D

debit cards 135
debt, national 88, 115, 117
deficits, federal budget..... 104, 114, 116, 117, 118, 120, 123, 124, 125, 126, 127, 171, 326
demand... 8, 97, 135, 144, 145, 237, 238, 239, 240, 243, 244, 245, 248, 249, 250, 254, 255, 256, 259
demand deposits 135, 144, 145
demand-pull inflation... 96, 97, 103, 104, 105, 150, 152
deposit multiplier 147, 148
depression 47, 48, 49, 85, 114, 153
differentiated products198, 201
diminishing returns, law of274
discount rate 149, 151, 155
discouraged workers 79, 92, 323
diseconomies of scale 286, 287
dividends 185
division of labor 179
Dorgan, Senator Byron...... 315
double taxation 187, 189

E

easy-money policy 149, 151
economic expansion.. 112, 116

economic goods............ 19, 34
economic growth 6, 17, 26, 69,
    71, 73, 75, 301, 304, 323,
    345
economic incentives........... 46
economic services.............. 19
economic systems............... 24
economics.................... 12, 113
economies of scale.... 179, 182,
    199, 286
economists...... 20, 65, 80, 110,
    153, 167, 168, 179, 285
Edsel automobile............... 44
elasticity of demand.......... 263
elasticity of supply............ 263
employment............. 110, 167
entrepreneurship..... 20, 21, 22,
    293, 295, 310, 312
Environmental Protection
    Agency...................... 306
equilibrium.... 68, 69, 243, 248
equilibrium GDP..... 69, 73, 74,
    346
excess reserves . 146, 147, 148,
    149, 150
exchange rates.................. 169
explicit costs.................... 284
exports............................ 171
externalities.................... 305

F

factors of production 20, 59,
    178, 271
Fannie Mae...................... 314
FDIC.............................. 320
Fed.... 136, 137, 138, 139, 140,
    141, 142, 143, 144, 145,
    148, 149, 150, 151, 152,
    153, 154, 155, 156, 157,
    158, 303, 310, 314, 353
Federal Advisory Council 137,
    138
federal budget... 104, 114, 117,

125
Federal Deposit Insurance
    Corporation (FDIC)...... 142
federal funds rate.............. 151
Federal Open Market
    Committee.... 137, 138, 151
Federal Reserve Act of 1913
    139
Federal Reserve Banks..... 134,
    137, 138, 139, 140, 142,
    143, 146, 150
Federal Reserve Board of
    Governors..... 105, 136, 346
Federal Reserve map........ 140
Federal Reserve Notes..... 134,
    143
Federal Reserve System. 7, 68,
    88, 104, 105, 108, 136, 137,
    139, 140, 141, 148, 154,
    155, 156, 157, 158, 303,
    340, 347, 351, 352
Federal Trade Commission Act
    204
fiat money...................... 135
financial institutions. 140, 142,
    150, 151
financial meltdown........... 313
fiscal policy 7, 87, 88, 92, 104,
    109, 110, 111, 112, 113,
    118, 127, 128, 129, 154,
    347
fixed costs................. 266, 267
fixed-exchange-rate system.....
    169
flexible-exchange-rate system
    170
foreign exchange 169, 174, 176,
    347
foreign exchange markets . 169
Freddie Mac,.................... 314
free-enterprise system......... 31
frictional unemployment.... 80,
    86, 89

full employment 69, 70, 80, 81, 89, 98, 112, 117, 123, 152
full-employment balanced budget 122, 125

G

George, Henry 300
Glass-Steagall Act 315

gold... 131, 132, 134, 169, 237, 240, 301
gold standard 134
Goldman Sachs.................. 314
Gompers, Samuel 213
government securities 138, 142, 151
government spending ... 63, 68, 69, 81, 87, 88, 97, 104, 112, 113, 115, 118, 123, 124, 126
Gramm-Leach-Bliley Act in 1999............................. 315
Great Depression of the 1930s 20, 47, 49, 85, 114, 153
Greenspan, Alan 136
grievance procedure .. 224, 233
gross domestic product (GDP) 56, 71, 73, 74, 348
gross national product (GNP) 73, 74, 348

H

Hoover, President Herbert. 325
housing bubble . 307, 316, 319, 323, 324, 328, 329, 330
human resources, ... 21, 294
hyperinflation" 95

I

import quotas.... 165, 174, 176, 348
imports.. 63, 72, 159, 165, 166, 167, 170, 171, 172, 174,

175, 176, 339, 340, 358
income distribution 102
income taxes...... 116, 118, 123
Increasing returns 273
individual income tax 123
individual proprietorship.. 180, 181, 183, 184, 205, 206, 349
industrial unions................ 216
industry 166
inflation 95, 96, 97, 98, 99, 100, 102, 104
inflation, cost-push 98
inflation, definition of 7, 95, 107, 109, 335
inflation, demand-pull 97
infrastructure 326
interest...................... 110, 170
international finance.......... 168
international trade 101, 160, 163, 165, 167, 168, 169, 172
investment 66, 67, 68
investment opportunities 67, 68
investment spending 63, 72, 73, 339, 349
invisible-hand principle 34, 36, 37, 191, 192

J

job security....................... 223
Johnson, President Lyndon 112
JP Morgan Chase 314

K

Kennedy, President John F. 112
Keynes, John Maynard..... 110, 111, 113
Keynesian economics 110, 113, 114, 119, 127, 128, 129, 349
Knights of Labor 212, 213

L

labor.. 8, 21, 71, 73, 77, 78, 79, 91, 96, 107, 210, 213, 216, 217, 219, 220, 221, 224, 230, 231, 235, 294, 295, 323
Labor Department.......... 77, 78
labor force, ... 47, 70, 71, 162
labor productivity ... 71, 73, 75, 350
labor spies.......................... 215
labor unions 35, 103, 193, 194, 210, 211
Labor, Department of ... 77, 78, 79, 96
land...................................... 299
Landrum-Griffin Act 220
law of demand ... 238, 239, 241
law of diminishing marginal utility. 238
law of diminishing returns 271, 274, 279, 286
law of supply 239, 241
legal tender 134, 135
Lehman Brothers Holdings, Inc. 314
limited liability 187
limited resources 12, 22, 43, 70
loanable funds market 301
lockout.............................. 233
long run 63, 124, 125, 126, 171, 186, 285, 286

M

macroeconomics.................. 26
marginal cost 266, 268, 270, 277, 278, 279, 281, 282, 283
marginal resource cost....... 297
marginal revenue 275, 277, 278, 279, 281, 282, 283
marginal revenue product .. 297
market economy 25, 26, 31, 34, 35, 37, 38, 45, 51, 53, 54, 191, 202, 304
market structures 178, 192, 194, 206, 277, 283, 284
maximize profits 34, 266, 284, 287, 291, 298, 309, 312
mediation.................... 225, 233
meltdown, financial.. 303, 307, 316, 317, 321, 322, 323, 325, 329, 330, 331
member banks of Federal Reserve System ... 137, 139, 141, 142
Merrill Lynch 314
microeconomics 26
minimum wage laws 193, 194, 228, 233
mixed economies........... 24, 26
monetarism,...................... 153
monetary policy.... 68, 88, 104, 136, 137, 138, 140, 143, 148, 149, 151, 153
money as a measure of value, ... 132
money as a medium of exchange 131, 132, 133, 135
money as a standard of deferred payment. 132
money as a *store of value*. . 132
money in circulation. 143, 144, 352
money supply ... 133, 141, 143, 144, 145, 147, 148, 149, 152, 153, 303, 344
money, definition of.......... 130
money, functions of... 130, 131
monopolistic competition. 192, 201, 202, 276, 283, 284
monopoly 192, 207
Moody's 320
Morgan Stanley 314

N

national debt 117, 120, 122, 128, 129, 302, 325, 326
national defense 23, 41, 43, 87, 166
National Labor Relations Act 216, 219
National Labor Relations Board (NLRB) 219
natural resources 20, 21, 22, 30, 70, 293, 294, 295, 298, 299, 308, 309, 310, 311
New York Times 119
Newsweek 136
Nixon, President Richard . 106, 107
nonprice competition 198, 200, 201
Norris-LaGuardia Anti-Injunction Act 216, 219

O

oligopoly... 192, 198, 199, 201, 206, 207, 208, 276, 283, 284, 353
open-market operations 149, 151
opportunity cost 13, 14, 18, 19, 27, 28, 29, 285

P

paper money 132, 133, 134, 143, 144
partnerships 183
personal income 114, 189
picketing 233
planned economies 25
preferred stock 185
price ceilings 255, 257, 258
price floors 255, 258, 259
price system 37, 38, 39, 106
prime rate 151
private enterprise 41

private sector 26
production costs ... 45, 98, 168, 196, 200, 211, 266, 267, 284, 285, 286
production possibilities curve 16
production possibilities frontier, ... 16
productivity, labor 71
profit 277, 280, 283
profit-maximizing level of output 266, 278, 281
Progress and Poverty 300
progressive tax 51
prolabor legislation ... 218, 219
proportional tax 51
proprietorships 180
proxy 186, 355
public goods 305
public utilities 42, 184
pure competition 192, 193, 194, 195, 201, 276, 277, 283, 284

Q

quantity demanded ... 106, 238, 240, 241, 242, 243, 247, 249, 258
quantity supplied 106, 239, 241, 242, 243, 247, 249, 257, 259

R

Reagan, President Ronald 113, 114, 117, 119, 122
recession of 1981-82 .... 48, 49, 83, 85, 115, 117, 159

regressive tax 51
regulating prices 42
Reich, Robert B 327
required reserves 142, 146, 147, 155, 156, 157, 346,

356
reserve requirement .. 145, 146,
147, 148, 150, 356
resource markets 295
revenue 275, 276, 277
right-to-work laws 222
Robinson-Patman Act 204
Rockefeller, John D. 203

S

savings accounts 144
scarcity 12, 17, 27, 28, 29
seasonal unemployment 80, 84,
88, 91
seniority rights ... 223, 233, 356
Sherman Antitrust Act 203, 204
short run 285
shortages ... 25, 39, 91, 97, 106,
107, 193, 251, 255, 257
silver. 122, 131, 132, 133, 134,
237, 240, 315
Smith, Adam 34
Social Security 99, 142, 356
Standard and Poor's 320
standard of living 61, 62, 70,
99, 160, 161
Standard Oil Trust 203
stocks, . 66, 181, 185, 186, 187,
188
stockholders 185, 186, 187,
188, 189, 206, 303, 342,
344, 357
Stockman, David 115
strike 233
structural unemployment 82,
83, 86, 90, 91
subprime mortgage crisis ... 316
supply ... 8, 113, 237, 239, 240,
242, 243, 246, 247, 248,
249, 250, 252, 253, 255,
256, 259
supply and demand 69, 77,
170, 193, 194, 227, 237,

239, 240, 241, 242, 247,
250, 251, 255, 256, 257,
258
supply, changes in 250, 251
supply, elasticity of 260
supply-side economics . 7, 119,
127, 128, 129, 357
surpluses 39, 91, 120, 124,
125, 126, 251, 255, 259,
262

T

Taft-Hartley Act 219, 220, 221
tariff 165, 174, 176, 357
tax cut 116, 118, 120, 325,
357
taxes 51, 66
tight-money policy ... 149, 151,
153
trade deficits 171
trade surpluses 171
traditional economies 24
U.S. Treasury Department. 314
underemployment 6, 84, 85,
92, 94
unemployed 22, 62, 64, 65, 69,
74, 76, 77, 78, 79, 80, 82,
83, 84, 85, 86, 89, 90, 91,
92, 94, 103, 111, 123, 124,
323, 326, 328, 62, 65, 76,
77, 78,
unemployment, costs of 85
unemployment, frictional 80
unemployment, measuring 6
unemployment, seasonal 84
unemployment, structural 82
union security arrangements
.... 218, 221
union shop 221, 233
unions 211, 217, 222, 223
unlimited liability 181, 184
utilities 43, 185

V

variable costs..... 266, 268, 269
Vietnam War............ 112, 116
Volker, Paul...................... 136

W

wage-price controls 106
wage-push inflation 98
wages.... 34, 98, 105, 106, 167,

193, 194, 210, 211, 212,
214, 215, 218, 222, 223,
227, 228, 229, 238, 284
Wagner Act 219
Wall Street meltdown 313, 315
Wealth of Nations.......... 34, 35
World War II. 48, 85, 106, 116

Y

yellow-dog contracts . 216, 219

About the Author

Allen W. Smith has devoted much of his adult life to battling economic illiteracy and promoting economic education. He taught economics to college students for 30 years before retiring as Professor of Economics at Eastern Illinois University in 1998 to become a full-time writer. Over the years, Smith has written numerous books in his effort to help readers understand economics and government economic policy. *Understanding Inflation and Unemployment*, Smith's first book, became an alternate selection of Fortune Book Club when it was published in 1976. His high school textbook, *Understanding Economics*, published by Random House in 1986, was used in more than 600 schools in 48 states.

For the past decade, Smith has focused his research and writing on government finance and Social Security. He published *The Alleged Budget Surplus, Social Security, and Voodoo Economics* in 2000, and *The Looting of Social Security: How the Government is Draining America's Retirement Account* in 2004. In 2009, Smith published *THE BIG LIE: How Our Government Hoodwinked the Public, Emptied the Social Security Trust Fund, and caused The Great Economic Collapse*. Smith's latest book, released in December 2010, is *The Looting of Social Security: New Release of the book "they" didn't want you to read.*

Smith has appeared on CNN, CNNfn, CNBC, and more than 200 radio talk shows. He holds a B.S. in Education degree from Ball State University and M.A. and Ph.D. degrees in economics from Indiana University.